On Durban's Docks

Rochester Studies in African History and the Diaspora

Toyin Falola, Series Editor
The Jacob and Frances Sanger Mossiker Chair in the
Humanities and University Distinguished Teaching Professor
University of Texas at Austin

Recent Titles

Guardians of the Tradition:
Historians and Historical Writing in Ethiopia and Eritrea
James De Lorenzi

Ira Aldridge: The Last Years, 1855–1867
Bernth Lindfors

Population, Tradition, and Environmental Control in Colonial Kenya
Martin S. Shanguhyia

Humor, Silence, and Civil Society in Nigeria
Ebenezer Obadare

Nation as Grand Narrative: The Nigerian Press and the Politics of Meaning
Wale Adebanwi

The Rise and Demise of Slavery and the Slave Trade in the Atlantic World
Edited by Philip Misevich and Kristin Mann

The Power of the Oath: Mau Mau Nationalism in Kenya, 1952–1960
Mickie Mwanzia Koster

Cotton and Race across the Atlantic: Britain, Africa, and America, 1900–1920
Jonathan E. Robins

Islam, Power, and Dependency in the Gambia River Basin:
The Politics of Land Control, 1790–1940
Assan Sarr

Living Salvation in the East African Revival in Uganda
Jason Bruner

A complete list of titles in the Rochester Studies in African History and the Diaspora series may be found on our website, www.urpress.com.

Dear Suraj & Milena,

The genesis of this book is intricately connected to me being part of your family, as I started the research around the same time that I became part of it. I hope you enjoy it.

Love,

Ralph

On Durban's Docks

Zulu Workers, Rural Households, Global Labor

Ralph Callebert

University of Rochester Press

First published 2017

University of Rochester Press
668 Mt. Hope Avenue, Rochester, NY 14620, USA
www.urpress.com
and Boydell & Brewer Limited
PO Box 9, Woodbridge, Suffolk IP12 3DF, UK
www.boydellandbrewer.com

ISBN-13: 978-1-58046-907-4
ISSN: 1092-5228

Library of Congress Cataloging-in-Publication Data

Names: Callebert, Ralph, 1982– author.
Title: On Durban's docks : Zulu workers, rural households, global labor / Ralph Callebert.
Other titles: Rochester studies in African history and the diaspora ; v. 76.
Description: Rochester : University of Rochester Press, 2017. | Series: Rochester studies in African history and the diaspora ; v. 76 | Includes bibliographical references and index.
Identifiers: LCCN 2017031777 | ISBN 9781580469074 (hardcover : alk. paper)
Subjects: LCSH: Stevedores—South Africa—Durban—Economic conditions—20th century. | Stevedores—South Africa—Durban—Social conditions—20th century. | Labor—South Africa—Durban—History—20th century. | Zulu (African people)—Economic conditions—20th century. | Zulu (African people)—Social conditions—20th century. | Rural-urban relations—South Africa—Durban. | Durban (South Africa)—Economic conditions—20th century. | Durban (South Africa)—Social conditions—20th century.
Classification: LCC HD8039.L82 S573 2017 | DDC 337.7613875440968—dc23 LC record available at https://lccn.loc.gov/2017031777

This publication is printed on acid-free paper.
Printed in the United States of America.

To Raji Singh Soni,
and to Greta Cauwelier and Mark Callebert

Contents

List of Maps

Acknowledgments

As I was finalizing the manuscript for this book, I realized that one apparently simple question lies at the heart of it: What is labor? The shortest answer that I can give to that question is that labor is human activity. Labor is what people do; what they do to survive, reproduce, flourish and thrive, and to entertain themselves. Work is therefore an essentially social phenomenon. The work we do can never occur outside its broader social context. During the 2012 US presidential campaign, Barack Obama was criticized for suggesting that the success of entrepreneurs always depends on both social and physical infrastructure that these successful business leaders did not build themselves: education, bridges, roads, fire services. Of course, he was right. Not only is our current society built on many generations of accumulated "dead labor," to use Karl Marx's phrasing, but going about our daily life is equally impossible without the work of countless living people nearby and far away.

The labor of manufacturing workers is impossible without the work of people on farms, in mines, on plantations, and in other factories. It is also impossible without the domestic labor at home, the labor in the commercial and transport sectors, public works, or the work of people in the informal sector who provide cheap goods and services to these workers. To the extent that the poor form a reserve army of labor, they too are crucial to global chains of production and capital accumulation, though it can certainly be argued that large sections of the world's population are superfluous to even that function. They are surplus populations. Not only is our work dependent on that of others, dead and alive, it also has social meaning. We do not only work to earn a living and to survive, or to feed and socialize a next generation, we also do so to give meaning to our lives. Work gives us a sense of belonging and of being valued; unfortunately, all too often we believe that only paid work can fulfil this function.

All this is to say that I could never have performed the work of writing this book without the many forms of help I have received from numerous people, inevitably many more than I am able to acknowledge here. This assistance was sometimes material, sometimes intellectual, administrative, social, or emotional. First of all, my research would have been impossible without the help of Sibongo Dlamini and Snegugu Lerato Mchunu as interviewers and interpreters, as well as the generous cooperation of seventy-seven interviewees. I cannot and will not claim that this book somehow represents their "authentic" voices and their lived experiences, but I do hope to have at least presented a meaningful analysis that is worthy of their fascinating life histories. The interviews consistently challenged my own presuppositions and the outcome has been that I now think entirely differently about the question of labor, both in South Africa and globally. Most of our interviewees probably do not see themselves as teachers, but I learned a lot from them.

I wish to thank Marc Epprecht and Bob Shenton at Queen's University in Canada who provided both intellectual and practical guidance for my research. They consistently challenged me to think in new ways about African, South African, and labor history, and to question my own presuppositions; and they have not stopped doing so. Bill Freund has been an important intellectual influence for me and continues to be a great mentor to me. He has been very generous with guidance, encouragement, and feedback throughout the research and writing process, and has even provided me with accommodation in Durban. Yvonne Place, also at Queen's, has been both a reliable guide through administrative procedures and a wonderful person with whom to chat. Neither can I forget a certain Labrador Retriever, Riley, who made our chats all-the-more endearing. Further, I wish to thank Nomusa Mngoma for her kindness and patience while teaching me isiZulu.

I have received indispensable administrative and research support from a variety of people and organizations in South Africa. The School of Politics at UKZN hosted me in Durban for my field research. The staff, archivists, and librarians at the Killie Campbell Africana Library and Campbell Collections at UKZN, the Historical Papers Collection at the University of the Witwatersrand, the Local History Museum in Durban, and the South African National Archives depositories in Durban, Pietermaritzburg, and Pretoria have been very helpful and friendly. I especially owe my gratitude to Mwelela Cele, Nellie Somers, and Rebecca Naidoo. I consider David Moore a mentor as well, and he has also hosted me several times in Johannesburg. David Hemson, who wrote a landmark dissertation on dock labor in Durban has given me valuable advice and put me into contact with Sibongo Dlamini. I further wish to thank Kathleen Diga, Danielle Floersch, Biniam Misgun, and Lorraine Thabisile Nkosi. At South African Container Stevedores in Durban, Wandile Mzamo and Yoga Thinnasagren were very helpful during my research, for which I am grateful. During my field research, I was fortunate enough to befriend Zamani Dlamini. Zamani's tragic death in 2010 recalls for me his passionate life. In memory, therefore, he remains a reader of this book.

Many people have read and commented on all or parts of the manuscript. These include, with my sincere apologies if I forgot anyone, Danna Agmon, Jonathan Crush, Jon Felt, Allison Goebel, Matt Heaton, Mark Hunter, Gary Kynoch, Ian McKay, James Morrison, John Munro, Brett Shadle, Barrington Walker, and Phil Zachernuk. Scott Rutherford deserves to be mentioned separately not only for having read parts of the manuscript but also for helping to refine the title. Sonia Kane and Toyin Falola, as well as the two anonymous reviewers for the University of Rochester Press, also provided invaluable insights and advice for further rewriting and editing. Jennifer Grek Martin prepared the maps included in this book. Financial assistance was provided by the Southern African Research Centre, Queen's University, and the Department of History at Queen's University. An earlier version of chapter 5 was published as "Cleaning the Wharves: Pilferage, Bribery and Social Connections on the Durban Docks in the 1950s," in the *Canadian Journal of African Studies* 46, no. 1 (2012): 23–38; and earlier versions of parts of chapter 6 were published in "Working Class Action and Informal Trade on the Durban Docks, 1930s–1950s," in the *Journal of Southern African Studies* 38, no. 4 (2012): 847–61. I wish to thank Taylor & Francis (www.tandfonline.com) for their kind permission to reprint this material here.

Moreover, several chapters have benefitted from various workshops, seminars, and conference presentations. I wish particularly to thank the organizers, attendees, and those who gave me feedback on my work at the Department of Anthropology and Development Studies at the University of Johannesburg, the History Department at UKZN, the North Eastern Workshop on Southern Africa in Burlington, Vermont, several Canadian Association for African Studies conferences, the Harriet Tubman Institute at York University, the IGK Work and Life Cycle in Global History at the Humboldt University of Berlin, the North American Labor History Conference in Detroit, the African Studies Association conference in San Diego, the Historians' Writing Group at Virginia Tech, and the Carter G. Woodson Institute's African Studies Colloquium Series at the University of Virginia. For their constructive criticism in these and other exchanges, I wish to draw special attention to Franco Barchiesi, Keith Breckenridge, Carolyn Brown, Peter Cole, Bernard Dubbeld, the late Jeff Guy, Jason Hickel,

Alex Lichtenstein, John Edwin Mason, Joseph Miller, Kwame Edwin Otu, and Stephen Rockel.

My deepest gratitude, however, is reserved for my family, particularly my parents and my husband. My parents, Greta Cauwelier and Mark Callebert, have been unwavering in their support for my continued studies and my choices to move to far-away places. Moreover, it was their upbringing that fostered in me the intellectual curiosity that was needed for this project. When thanking their partners in the acknowledgments, authors often mention the love and affection they received, as well as their partner's patience. I am incredibly grateful to Raji Singh Soni, my husband, for these important elements in our relationship. However, Raji has not only been my companion in life for about the same amount of time as I have been working on this research but has equally been my partner, sparring partner, inspiration, and coauthor in our intellectual endeavors. I believe that not only have we been, and continue to be, sources of support, honest criticism, and love and laughter for each other, but also that we have influenced each other's thinking and made each other into better intellectuals. Labor in particular is one of the questions we frequently discuss together. This book would not have been what it is today without his influence on my thinking.

Abbreviations

2/DBN	Commissioner or Durban records
3/DBN	Archives of the Town Clerk, Durban
ARB	Department of Labour
CNC	Chief Native Commissioner
COSATU	Congress of South African Trade Unions
CPSA	Communist Party of South Africa
DAR	Durban Archives Repository
DSLSC	Durban Stevedoring Labour Supply Company
GG	Office of the Governor-General of South Africa
ICU	Industrial and Commercial Workers' Union of Africa
ILWCH	*International Labor and Working-Class History*
JAH	*Journal of African History*
JSAS	*Journal of Southern African Studies*
KCAL	Killie Campbell Africana Library and Campbell Collections at the University of KwaZulu-Natal, Durban
KCAV	Killie Campbell Audio-Video Collection
MNAD	Municipal Native Affairs Department
MVE	Ministry of Transport
NAB	Native Advisory Board
NHD	Natal Harbour Department
NTS	Department of Native Affairs
PAR	Pietermaritzburg Archives Repository
PNAB	Port Natal Native Administration Board

SAB	National Archives Repository, Pretoria
SAIRR	South African Institute of Race Relations
SALB	*South African Labour Bulletin*
SAP	South African Police
SAR&H	South African Railways and Harbours administration
SNA	Secretary of Native Affairs
U.G.	Union Government Document
VWN	Social Welfare and Pensions

Introduction

Dock Workers in South African History

In 1874, African casual workers in Durban protested new regulations that limited their freedom and bargaining power. Many of them would have worked on the docks. Durban is a port city on South Africa's Indian Ocean coast, which would become South Africa's main harbor and a crucial node in the trade and communication networks of the Indian Ocean and the British Empire (see map I.1). When the city refused to annul these regulations, scores withdrew their labor and returned to their rural homesteads.[1] This was the first documented strike by African workers in Durban, and, in the more than 140 years since 1874, dock workers have often taken the lead in labor activism in the city. A long history of repression, declining employment, and technological change has not fully stamped out this tradition of protest and activism, as illustrated by dockers' 2008 refusal to unload weapons destined for Zimbabwe's Mugabe regime. The next year they boycotted an Israeli ship to protest apartheid Israel and the bombing of Gaza in Operation Cast Lead (2008–9).[2]

Dock workers in South Africa's foremost port city have repeatedly proven themselves to be radical and strike prone, as dock workers have often been around the world. They engaged in strikes, refused to work overtime, rioted, and boycotted certain cargoes and ships; they also cut corners, dragged their feet, and refused to live where their employers and the government wanted them to live. In 1972–73, they were among the first to participate in the Durban strikes that, even before the 1976 Soweto uprising, reignited resistance to the apartheid regime after a decade of relatively successful repression—the so-called silent decade that followed the 1960 Sharpeville massacre.

These dock workers called themselves *onyathi*, which means "buffaloes" but is also used to refer to strong, forceful men.[3] This self-designation alluded to their physical strength and the collective nature of their work. In the early 1940s, legendary dock leader Zulu Phungula proudly talked about a "strike called inyathi" and invoked the image of a

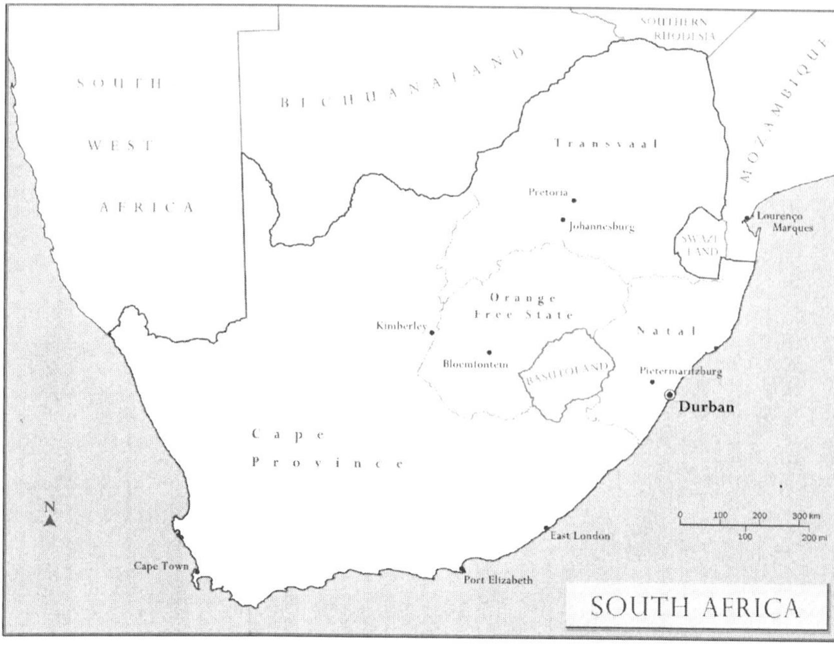

Map I.1. South Africa, c.1950. Map by Jennifer Grek Martin.

steamship to refer to the strength and resolve of the striking workers—labelling them SS *Inyathi*, or Steamship Buffalo.[4] As Africans under apartheid, these workers were banned from unionizing and denied many other political and industrial rights. This lack of formal union organization, however, did not imply passive acceptance of a government-imposed industrial order. In fact, dockers' militancy has been a favorite topic in a long-standing tradition of labor history of Durban. David Hemson in particular stressed a long history of workers' radicalism on the docks. His unpublished PhD dissertation is still one of the most impressive works on Durban's labor history and the most comprehensive account of the city's history of dock labor.[5] Others who have written on this topic have also largely focused on unionization and industrial action.[6]

As was the practice in most ports at that time, Durban's private stevedoring employers and the public South African Railways and Harbours (SAR&H) administration generally employed casual laborers. This type of employment, which was in most harbors only phased out in the 1960s or 1970s, facilitated histories of strikes and radicalism.[7] Dock workers were usually hired per day or for a specific job, rather than on a continuing contract. As the number of laborers seeking a job for the day was often much higher than the numbers required by the employers, periods of unemployment and unpredictable earnings were part of dock workers' lives. Each morning, foremen would hire the laborers they needed for the day from those who presented themselves. This system of casual hiring was unpredictable, often cutthroat, and prone to corruption and favoritism. Irregular job opportunities, brutal working conditions, indifference of employers and officials to these conditions, and the strategic position of these workers in important networks of transport and trade all facilitated their militancy. Moreover, as casual workers they had little to lose, except for one day's pay. The threat of retrenchment had little effect on them.[8]

Workers in the port of Durban did not stand alone in their militancy. Throughout colonial Africa, transport workers have a notable record of industrial action. Port and railway workers occupied strategic positions in the infrastructure of trade and empire; they were acutely aware of this fact not least because they felt a strong presence of the colonial state in their workplace. Transport workers also constituted a sizable and often spatially concentrated workforce with a significant proportion of skilled workers. In the aftermath of the Second World War, a wave of general strikes mostly led by transport workers swept through the continent.[9] These workers played an important role in the nationalist movements of the postwar period, and it is therefore not surprising that they have attracted ample scholarly attention.[10]

Dock workers made international trade possible and therefore helped to produce the process that would later, somewhat problematically, become known as globalization. Nevertheless, the lives of Durban's dock workers in the 1950s did not reflect the cosmopolitanism of the world of global shipping. As African workers under apartheid, they were denied access to the fruits of the international trade they serviced, while segregation and linguistic differences limited their engagement with seamen coming through the city. Most importantly, however, these mostly isiZulu-speaking dock workers generally retained a very strong rural orientation, both economically and socially. Their homes were in the rural areas, which also was where they mostly socialized; they subscribed to rural social ethics and cultural norms, and they invariably strove to retire from urban labor as soon as possible to return permanently to their rural homes. This rural orientation was more than the outcome of apartheid-era influx controls. Durban's dock workers tended to visit their rural homes more frequently, and they retired to the rural areas more quickly, more successfully, and at a higher rate than most other African workers. Not only did their lives contrast sharply with the cosmopolitanism of the shipping sector; their employment in this global industry was also what enabled them to have strongly locally oriented lives. They made clever use of the opportunities dock labor offered, which allowed many of these workers to build and expand their rural homestead at a time when this became increasingly difficult for most African workers. While it is tempting to gaze outward into the ocean from a major port city, as many excellent studies do, this book will mostly follow the workers in the opposite direction, into the rural areas surrounding Durban.

South African Labor History

Reflecting the significant role that organized labor and workers' protests played in decolonization, much of the literature on African labor focuses on working-class organization and consciousness.[11] The same is true for South Africa, which is often seen as more "modern" and more Western than the rest of the continent. Even in South Africa, however, most African workers do not form an unambiguous urban proletariat along the lines of a Western model. The livelihoods of workers' households often rely extensively on informal and rural income, a tendency recognized in much of the scholarship on the rest of the continent. Yet, in South Africa a sense of *exceptionalism* has often kept us from acknowledging such livelihoods.

Hemson wrote about strikes, organization and unionization, and proletarian consciousness. His interest in workers strongly reflected his political commitment, as was the case for many South African intellectuals in the 1970s and 1980s. As a student activist engaged in the Wages Commission and a union organizer, he was mostly concerned with class.[12] In his writings, Durban's dock workers had a strong proletarian consciousness; they were radical, but repressed, and willing to engage in forceful working-class action.

Hemson and other leftist scholars did not only react to the political context in which they were writing—they were of course writing under apartheid and several, including Hemson,[13] lived in exile—they also took issue with an older tradition of liberal and Weberian scholarship that prioritized race and status over class. Many liberal scholars considered the racial oppression of apartheid an irrational anachronism that the color-blind logic of capitalism would eventually dissolve. For Marxists, on the contrary, racism and discrimination were integral to a capitalist system of exploitation, rather than anathema to it. Debating the history and nature of apartheid and segregation thus also amounted to debating the future of South Africa. If race was central to oppression, a future progressive project would have to bring deracialization. If capitalism was the cause, however, only a more radical socialist project could bring an end to injustice.[14] Politics, as much as intellectual factors, determined the dominance of Marxist scholarship over liberal and Weberian approaches. Opposition to apartheid came largely from the African National Congress (ANC), the Communist Party, and independent trade unions, while liberal opposition remained weak.[15] Many scholars within this radical tradition were also involved in the Communist Party.

One of the most influential figures in this tradition was Harold Wolpe. In his seminal 1972 article, which was influenced by an earlier paper by Martin Legassick, he reacted against liberal scholarship that accepted race as the fundamental unit of analysis and that presented the South African state as an instrument of racial dominance but as more or less neutral in terms of class relations.[16] He also challenged the concept of a dual economy, the idea that in "less developed" societies two economic systems coexist, one modern and one traditional. For Wolpe, the South African state was anything but neutral in regard to class relations, as it coerced workers and guaranteed capitalist social relations. Moreover, the supposedly traditional economy was not separate from the modern sector. Rather, the traditional economy subsidized wages in the modern economy through a so-called Reserve subsidy. The capitalist mode of production externalized the cost of the reproduction of labor to the noncapitalist subsistence economy: "When the migrant-labourer has access to means of subsistence, outside the capitalist sector, as he does in South Africa, then the relationship between wages and the cost of reproduction of labour-power is changed. That is to say, capital is able to pay the worker *below* the cost of his reproduction." By assuming the independence of the traditional and modern economies, he argues, the dual economy thesis could not analyze how "capitalism enters into, lives off and transforms the rural African economy."[17] Racist laws, he contends, upheld this rural subsidy and masked the capitalist nature of the state.

In countering the dual economy thesis, radical scholars opposed the portrayal of migrant workers as men of two worlds. This characterization posited that African migrants, who formed the core of South Africa's cheap labor force, were essentially rural people who traveled between two different worlds. They were deeply invested in the rural economy, and continued to be so, and were generally not interested in urban life. Wage labor only supplemented their rural incomes from agriculture and pastoralism. Consequently, their interests did not lie in urban labor, and they could not form a real working class with a proletarian consciousness.[18] For these "strangers" in the white city, urban life was considered dangerous. Attracted by higher wages, they could lose their morality, money, and even family as they lost themselves in corrupting urban pleasures. This account justified low wages, which merely supplemented rural earnings, and the continued existence of segregation and an institutionalized migrant labor system; the latter, of course, was seen as protecting Africans from city life. Challenging this account thus took on political significance. Leftist academics turned their attention to African workers and argued that they did form a real working class that suffered from class oppression. Hemson emphasized the working-class actions of Durban's dock workers, stressing the proletarian nature of their consciousness and the radicalism of their leader, Zulu Phungula. He argued that these workers fought to "force open the possibility of becoming part of thc urban proletariat."[19] They opted for a working-class solution to their poverty and rallied for better wages rather than more Reserve land or agricultural assistance.

This Marxist tradition in southern African history made important contributions to our understanding of African labor and South African society. Scholars asserted that we should see African workers as actual workers and not as "strangers" in the modern economy; they challenged the idea of a dual economy and studied the relationship between apartheid and capitalism; they did not take labor migration for granted but asked how African migrant labor was produced and reproduced. Many of their contributions, including their challenge to the dual economy model and the concept of a Reserve subsidy, are now commonplace. Nevertheless, as I argue elsewhere, the dual economy thesis has survived in different guises.[20]

However, this radical tradition also became subject to substantial criticism.[21] I will focus briefly on three astute points of criticism. First, some Marxist scholars overstated the differences between their work and the older liberal and Weberian scholarship. While changing the focus from race to class, they did not usually dispute that race was an important fault line in South African history; similarly, previous work did not necessarily deny the salience of class analysis. Second, in their quest to find proletarians and to ascertain that African migrants had a working-class consciousness, these authors at times failed to consider other identities. Indeed, for some radical scholars racial, ethnic, or gender identities were little more than false consciousness. Third, some of the structural Marxist scholarship displayed functionalist and teleological tendencies. The existence of apartheid was often read backward to present it as the inevitable outcome of South Africa's history. In Wolpe's account, the function Reserves fulfilled, rather than specific historic events and struggles, explained their existence. Christopher Saunders explains that "though the reserves did eventually come to subsidise capital, they had not come into existence for that purpose: in the early twentieth century many capitalists had seen them as a problem, not a solution, for they locked up labour away from the mines. Their extent was determined in part by the nature of African resistance to white penetration in the nineteenth century. The Wolpe-Legassick argument was ahistorical inasmuch as it suggested a functional relationship had always existed, when in fact that relationship was the product of a particular set of circumstances."[22]

In the 1980s, historians started to pay more attention to aspects of people's consciousness that were not reducible to class or race. The best work did so without dispensing with class analysis. Belinda Bozzoli rendered gender more visible in southern African historiography, criticizing structuralist scholars for reducing women to their function of reproducing cheap labor. Both William Beinart and Peter Delius argued convincingly that rural cultural and social attachments continued to shape African identities.[23] Dunbar Moodie and Patrick Harries, in two classic works published in 1994, concluded that such rural affections were expressions of a struggle against proletarianization (that is, the process by which a population progressively loses access to its own means of production, foremost land, and becomes dependent on wage labor). Holding on to their rural world was a factor in the struggle against becoming part of an uprooted working class.[24] Also in the early 1990s, Keletso Atkins wrote about African workers in nineteenth-century Durban and emphasized Zulu cultural ideas as a source of agency and resistance. Workers fought their oppression, but resistance did not necessarily take the form of trade unions and strikes. Domestic workers formed kitchen associations, convening in their employers' kitchens to sing and talk about employers and working conditions; workers insisted on casual labor, which afforded more agency in the context of labor shortages; most of all, they were fiercely independent.[25]

South African historiography continued to revolve around questions of white domination and the resulting African and black resistance, even if meanings of domination and resistance changed along the way. Since scholarship on class and labor was entangled with the struggle against apartheid, the 1990s did bring change. Few major books on labor history have appeared since 1994, and those that were published generally focused on organizational questions and on relatively recent history.[26] Two decades later, however, it has become increasingly clear that the unilinear transition from rural and traditional migrant workers to a modern and stable urban working class, which both Marxist and liberal scholars expected to happen,[27] did not take place in South or southern Africa.

Affirming class or race over culture, gender, or everyday struggles often resulted in a metanarrative of modernization, a modernist teleology in which labor migration was only a transitory stage artificially perpetuated by white minority regimes. Nevertheless, throughout the subcontinent the livelihoods of many workers' households continue to draw on more than wages alone. In Zambia and Zimbabwe, urban dwellers faced with economic crises rekindle rural connections, reinforcing their claims to rural resources, and make up lost income in the informal sector.[28] In South Africa, the informal sector is increasingly important to families' survival as well, and rural kin continue to play a crucial role in raising children and caring for the sick. The resulting multifaceted livelihoods are nothing new to scholars of other parts of the continent, but a southern African exceptionalism, based on a long political tradition of affirming African workers as modern and urban proletarians, has often kept us from sufficiently valuing the importance of these more complex livelihood strategies.[29]

Livelihood Strategies and Households

The undeniable significance of rural and other identities should not conceal the fact that Durban's dock workers did show evidence of a strong working-class consciousness. They organized as workers and frequently engaged in forceful industrial action. However, this was not a pure and uncomplicated working-class consciousness, and radical scholars did not always pay sufficient attention to the more ambiguous elements of these workers' identity and militancy. When dock workers not only participated in the 1949 anti-Indian pogrom but also took the lead, for example, Hemson attributed this to a displacement of frustrated working-class action after a failed attempt to organize a general strike.[30] Eager to affirm African workers' status as modern proletarians, South African historians often understated the uneven and contradictory nature of the process of proletarianization.[31] In many ways,

Durban's dock workers were not archetypal proletarians with a straightforward working-class consciousness. The combination of continued investments in and attachment to a rural economy, frequent involvement in small-scale trade, and regular experiences of racial discrimination resulted in political ideas and practices that are not reducible to a proletarian class consciousness.

Neither the rural economy nor urban wage labor accounted for the full livelihoods of these workers' households. Reserve agriculture, pastoral activities, wage labor, and small-scale trade all contributed to the households' survival; none of these activities alone could sustain these households. Moreover, kinship and other social relationships too were crucial resources. Studying their livelihood strategies can give us insight into dock workers' consciousness and political actions. In a classic study of social mobility and class formation among the Yoruba peasantry, Sara Berry notes that "to the extent that collective action in the pursuit of socioeconomic advance springs from the conditions of production itself, we may expect farmers' political strategies to resemble their strategies of accumulation and social mobility."[32] Allison Goebel similarly argues that to understand protests by the South African poor, we need to comprehend the internal dynamics of their households and their livelihood strategies.[33] If we accept that there is a link between people's livelihoods and their political consciousness and activism, as I do, without assuming that this would explain everything, we need to grasp how households combined their different economic activities and how members made decisions regarding these livelihoods. Such an understanding allows us to grasp workers' militancy and consciousness within the context of both their broader economic lives and the internal dynamics of their households.

I use the concept of livelihoods to refer to the mix of economic and social strategies used both by members individually and by households collectively for the household and its members to survive, reproduce, and if possible improve their socioeconomic position.[34] In other words, livelihood refers to how people and households survive or thrive. Sarah Mosoetsa studied poor households in KwaZulu-Natal (the province in which Durban is located, formerly known as Natal) and found fractured and conflict-ridden households with complex strategies that go well beyond securing waged employment.[35] Wiseman Chijere Chirwa looks specifically at how the rural economy and wage labor combined in the livelihoods of Malawian migrant workers. He considers how these workers put their wages to work in the rural economy.[36] This approach directs our attention to creative responses from the periphery to economic domination and institutionalized labor migrancy. While the penetration of market forces, dispossession, environmental degradation, or even physical coercion often forced Africans into labor migration, especially in the twentieth century, migrants were never entirely devoid of agency. Individuals and households could and did make strategic decisions about migration, about taking a specific job, or about the use of their wages, even if their options were severely limited. Hence, my emphasis is on livelihood *strategies*.[37]

Livelihood strategies allow us to study labor migrancy beyond a narrow emphasis on wage labor, which accounts only for part of the survival of dock workers' households. Moreover, within debates about southern African labor, there is a tradition of considering the rural and the urban sharply dichotomous; radical authors often stressed urban modernity and working-class militancy while conservatives emphasized essentialized cultural difference and rural traditionalism.[38] However, the livelihoods discussed in this book bridge that divide. Studying how households combined rural and urban activities can shed light on how the rural and the urban economies interacted in the lives of dock workers and their families. These workers earned wages, but wages were not the households' only or even main source of income. Most families had access to other resources, such as land and cattle, and many households were involved in small-scale trade.

A focus on the household can thus help us overcome the dichotomy not only between the rural and the urban but also between formal wage labor and the informal economy. South African labor history has tended to overlook the extent to which workers' households also depend on informal income. A restricted focus on wage labor marginalizes the labor of those who do not engage in supposedly typical wage labor, based on the Western experience, and reduces the experience of those who do to their formal employment. Even global labor history, which strives to broaden labor history beyond the study of "free" wage labor in the West, tends to study primarily commodified forms of labor and workers linked to world markets.[39] The literature on the informal economy, however, discusses this sector as more or less separate from formal wage labor and generally lacks a historical perspective. Moreover, the informal economy in South Africa is often considered as largely a post-apartheid phenomenon.[40] In this book I strive, like Jeanne Marie Penvenne in her study of female workers in Mozambique's cashew industry, to "see connectivity and overcome artificial divisions" between the homestead, formal, and informal economies.[41]

To study these household strategies also involves looking at internal household dynamics. We need to consider individual decisions and activities within the context of the household. Different members have different sources of income, which they redistribute within the household or withhold along gendered and generational lines. Changing livelihoods can thus influence the composition and internal dynamics of the household, and family dynamics in turn shape livelihood strategies. The study of the household can thus offer some insight into the close links between migratory labor and the gendered and generational struggles in the rural areas.

However, standard theories of the household fail us here. Following Jane Guyer, I will argue that the neoclassical model of the profit-maximizing household as a single decision-making unit, the concept of a traditional Zulu *umuzi*, or homestead, and the Chayanovian model of the noncapitalist peasant household all fail to capture adequately the formation and reproduction of these households.[42] A more flexible and multinodal characterization of the household, inspired by Amartya Sen's concept of cooperative conflict, will be used instead.[43] Households are sites of intrahousehold bargaining and cooperative conflict; individuals' bargaining powers determine access to the fruits of this cooperation. The households discussed in this book were reproduced in three geographically separate spheres of material, social, and cultural production and consumption, none of which could provide for the survival and reproduction of the household on its own. These spheres were thus dependent on each other but also separate, as physical distance afforded individual household members some autonomy.

This is not to say economic considerations and struggles within the household can explain everything. Indeed, one cannot reduce questions of gender and culture to economic strategies. At the same time, neither can we separate these questions from economic factors. Derived from the Greek οἰκονόμος, meaning "household management," the etymology of the word "economy" captures its intimate connection with the household. Mark Hunter skillfully links the HIV/AIDS crisis in KwaZulu-Natal to changing gender relationships and household compositions resulting from transformations in the region's political economy, thus "illuminat[ing] the deep connection between political economy and *intimacy*."[44]

While we cannot reduce the cultural and the economic to each other, we should also not dissociate them. In *Marginal Gains*, Guyer contends that economic transactions in Atlantic West Africa cannot be seen either as purely capitalist market transactions devoid of cultural meaning or as expressions of local cultural traditions in isolation from world markets.[45] Similarly, in her study of vernacular capitalists in late colonial India, Ritu Birla argues that while the colonial state hoped to create local capitalists "with rational consciousness and a will effected through contract," the reality was that "other value systems . . . sustained the exchange and production relations of the colonial economy."[46] There was no "rational" market logic that could be isolated from culture. As Karl Polanyi points out: the economy is always embedded in social relations.[47] Correspondingly, dock workers in Durban did not have to be *either* unambiguous proletarians *or* migrants bound by culture and tradition who are unable to recognize their class interests as workers.

However, a focus on livelihoods comes with both advantages and risks. It can bring attention to the complexity of workers' lives and help us avoid a modernist teleology of proletarianization, yet much of the livelihoods literature also paints an overly optimistic picture of people's lives. An emphasis on strategy can portray decisions out of necessity as examples of creativity and empowerment. It may be questionable to write about strategizing and managing assets when households are struggling for bare survival. The focus on internal decision making can also downplay structural causes of inequality and the broader socioeconomic and political context of these decisions. Indeed, these shortcomings likely explain the popularity of this framework among aid donors looking for ways to mitigate the impact of decades of structural adjustment and economic decline without challenging macroeconomic policies or making redistributive demands.[48] Moreover, the livelihoods approach often fails to disaggregate the household. As a result, conflict within the household and the unequal distribution of resources among its members are frequently underestimated.[49] To avoid these pitfalls, first, I will discuss the socioeconomic and political context of Durban and rural Natal in which these livelihoods took shape. Second, I will pay close attention to the internal dynamics of the household.

In this book, I survey and interpret these livelihoods using archival and secondary sources, newspaper articles, and seventy-seven oral histories. I focus on the 1950s because decasualization (that is, the replacement of casual workers by permanent workers) and the introduction of monopoly hiring after the 1959 strikes dramatically changed the labor regime in the port. To extend this account into the 1960s and beyond would require a second book. Moreover, it was exceedingly difficult to find interviewees who started before 1950. Most interviews were conducted in 2009 by Sibongo Dlamini, a former dock worker and union activist, and in 2014 by Snegugu Lerato Mchunu, who was at that time a graduate student at the University of KwaZulu-Natal. Dlamini mainly interviewed African migrant dock workers who started work in Durban between 1939 and 1959, while Mchunu mostly talked with the women (wives, sisters, daughters) in dock workers' households. Almost all interviews were conducted in isiZulu (and in a few instances in isiXhosa) at the homes of the interviewees. The assistance of Sibongo Dlamini and Snegugu Lerato Mchunu has been vital to this research, especially as Dlamini not only conducted interviews but, as a former union organizer, also had the connections needed to find these interviewees.

Of course, the use of oral histories raises questions about accuracy and reliability. Memory is not a factual and unbiased recollection of the past but is composed as a collective act in a certain social, cultural, economic, and political context. Interviewees may present, consciously or not, an account that retrospectively makes sense of their lives.[50] The interviewers and researchers too have their biases. However, just like Luise White's informants in Nairobi, the interviewees for this research were quick to correct my assumptions, and their answers challenged the notion that informants tell you what they think you want to hear. Indeed, there may be some truth to White's assertion that "oral history has been turned into a higher art than perhaps it needs to be."[51] My goal is not to recover "authentic voices" in these interviews but rather to interpret these interviews as texts alongside others.[52]

Interviewees may indeed have tried to make coherent sense of their lives with the benefit of hindsight and may have brought today's biases into that process, as we have in conducting and interpreting these interviews. However, there does not seem to be much reason to distrust the often largely factual answers that were given to our usually rather straightforward questions. For example, interviewees' emphasis on commercial activities may reflect to some extent our present-day neoliberal love affair with entrepreneurs, but it is also true that these workers did start small businesses. Moreover, recurring patterns in these life stories as well as archival and other evidence corroborating their accounts, confirmed in my eyes the general reliability of these interviews. Ultimately, oral sources can be as reliable or untrustworthy as other sources, and reading these accounts against the grain and against other texts is part of our critical methodology as historians, regardless of whether we use oral or written sources.

The Argument

There is plentiful evidence for the working-class consciousness of Durban's dock workers, as they have taken action for better pay and better working conditions numerous times. However, I argue that their consciousness was also more ambiguous. While these workers did organize to defend their interests as wage earners, they also had other concerns and engaged in actions that fit less easily into the image of radical proletarians. In particular, dock workers and their leaders displayed an idiosyncratic mix of concern for workers' issues and defenses of the rights and interests of African petty traders; it is the study of livelihoods and the household that will allow us to understand this seeming contradiction.

The life histories of our interviewees shed some light on this seemingly contradictory mix. These workers were not only wage laborers. In fact, only for a minority of dockers' households were wages the sole, or even main, source of cash income. The rural economy played an important role in sustaining consumption levels and reproducing the household. While some recent work on Durban and South Africa has turned toward the Indian Ocean, this book looks in the opposite direction: to the rural areas and urban townships where dock workers, their households, and urban women lived their lives.[53] Not only did the produce from the land and the milk from livestock lower the need for cash for consumption; women also sold some of the produce. Many dock workers invested some of their wages in agricultural production, and, significantly, more than half engaged in some form of small-scale commercial enterprise: they sold *dagga* in the city, cigarettes and sweets on the docks, and food pilfered from the ships at home or in the townships. Pilferage was often crucial to these livelihoods, as was the casual labor regime that allowed workers the flexibility needed to combine these activities with waged employment. Moreover, not only men engaged in these businesses. Wives in the Reserves and township women, with whom these dock workers may or may not have had romantic or sexual relationships, also sold pilfered cargo and other goods.

Dock workers' households were thus reproduced in three geographically separate spheres of production and consumption: on the docks, in the Reserves, and in the townships. None of these spheres could survive without the other, and none could reproduce the household on its own. The rural *umuzi* could not subsist without the proceeds of urban wage labor, and the artificially low wages for African workers could not sustain a family without continued reliance on the rural economy. Similarly, township women selling pilfered goods contributed to the reproduction of dock workers' households, but their share of the profits also kept their own households afloat. These three spheres did not exist in isolation from each other. Dockers' households straddled the divide between formal wage labor and (what would later become known as) the informal economy, as well as the rural/urban divide. Moreover, dock workers were comparatively mobile and moved between the city and their rural homes more often than, for example, miners. This mobility, though still strictly limited and policed under apartheid laws, facilitated informal trade, as dockers could bring home merchandise more frequently.[54]

These households were neither traditional rural *imizi* with absent members remitting wages nor working-class households forced by racial laws to inhabit rural reserves. These were multinodal households with members in different locations contributing to the reproduction of the household and in which different members had diverging interests. Husbands, wives, mothers, sons, brothers, and daughters had different priorities, while sharing the goal of guaranteeing the reproduction of the household. Individual members cooperated but also contested access to resources. Many men were anxious about their authority as household heads while they were away in the city. By investing their wages in cattle, they both staked a claim in rural patriarchy and kept resources out of the reach of women. Women, however, were often de facto household heads in the absence of their husbands, brothers, or fathers and used this limited independence to maintain control over the household's resources and to prioritize household consumption. Studying the household and its internal struggles therefore allows us to query the reproduction of and challenges to rural patriarchy and its gendered relations; it makes possible a *political economy of gender*.

However, these diverse livelihoods were constantly under threat. Land degradation and overpopulation increasingly strained Reserve agriculture and pastoralism. After the 1959 decasualization of dock labor, many opportunities to combine wage labor with small-scale trade disappeared. Moreover, apartheid authorities were generally not sympathetic toward informal African businesses and made running these progressively more difficult.[55] One could contend that this argument supports the claims of authors like Dambisa Moyo or Hernando de Soto, who argue that overextended governments crush people's inherent entrepreneurial spirit.[56] Indeed, these workers and their families used entrepreneurial strategies in the face of attempts by the state to root out independent income earning opportunities for Africans. Whether this means that these workers possessed an entrepreneurial essence that was waiting to be liberated is less clear. Few showed any intent to become part of a petty bourgeoisie. They rather used these strategies to escape dependence on urban wage labor, and many stopped investing in their businesses once they no longer needed to earn wages. They preferred to invest in cattle and dependents. This was not irrational, as colonial reformers would have it but followed a socioeconomic logic that was not a universal market logic. I explore this argument in more detail in the conclusion.

Furthermore, these entrepreneurial activities were dependent on wage labor. If these laborers had not worked on the docks, they may never have become entrepreneurs. The opportunities to pilfer and the flexibility of *togt* labor made these strategies possible. Their entrepreneurial activities were not merely an expression of an innate commercial instinct but rather a creative way to use the advantages their job offered to become independent from wage labor. Consequently, their interests as laborers and as small-scale entrepreneurs cannot be divorced from each other. Adequate wages, workplace control, flexible hours, and decent working conditions would help them not only as workers but also in the running of their business. The issues informal African traders faced also concerned them, as many considered trade to be their path to early retirement from urban wage labor. There was for these workers no contradiction between defending the interests of laborers and those of African traders.[57]

This book is the result of an Africanist writing back, as it were, to dominant approaches to labor history. In the study of labor, we often make assumptions about what labor is, based on Western experiences of proletarianization and wage labor. Both southern African and global labor history largely continue to focus on wage laborers or at least on workers whose toil feeds into global markets—forced laborers, slaves, cash croppers, and the (mostly) women who reproduce such commodified labor. These forms of labor, however, are far from universal in much of the Global South, where Western-derived accounts of proletarian labor have limited purchase.

Dock workers in South Africa should fit the model of labor as connected to global markets; they should be more recognizably commodified than most African workers. Dock workers are often considered prime examples of proletarian radicals linked to global networks of trade and militancy, and South African workers tend to be more fully proletarianized than workers elsewhere on the continent. Yet, as I argue in this book, even Durban's dock workers poorly suit this conception of labor. Many workers (i.e., all people who work rather than those engaged in wage or recognizably commodified labor) in Africa and the Global South thus either remain invisible or are seen only as reproducing cheap wage labor. Even for those who do have waged employment, this focus narrows their experiences to their formal employment. I thus argue for a broadening of our understanding of labor, to include not just informal and reproductive labor but also redistributive and other forms of labor that are less easily recognized as commodified—for example, gift economies. I do so not only because these forms of labor reproduce or subsidize wage labor but because they are integral to people's lives and livelihoods.

The absence of an unambiguous working class and the limited purchase of the "normative" social relationship of capitalism, wage labor, does not mean that 1950s rural Natal somehow stood outside global capitalism. Indeed, what we observe in this book are what Dipesh Chakrabarty calls "The Two Histories of Capital," which is the title of the second chapter of *Provincializing Europe*.[58] The exploitation of labor can take many different forms under capitalism. Even if the social relations of industrial capitalism in the West are rare in many parts of the African continent, African social relations are still shaped by and part of global processes of capitalist accumulation, directly or indirectly.

The Structure of the Book

Chapter 1 introduces the context of Durban in the first half of the twentieth century, its port, and dock labor. The second part of the chapter discusses the active role of dock workers in Durban's political scene. Here, I present dock workers as working-class radicals, but not only concerned with workers' issues. I develop this theme of a more complicated political consciousness throughout the rest of the book and then pick it up again explicitly in chapter 6. Chapter 2 is in many ways the descriptive core of this book, as it gives an overview of the livelihood strategies of the interviewed dock workers and their households. I identify two ideal-typical paths: some laborers focused on working as many shifts as possible on the docks, maximizing their wages, and spending as little money as possible in the city; others took a more entrepreneurial path, pilfering and building small businesses on the side to maximize their earnings and quicken their return to rural life. Many of these activities constitute what would become known as the informal economy, a concept that is often used as shorthand for a complex set of activities and relations. In this chapter and in this book, I will look at the relations and activities that shape this informal economy. The next three chapters in the book expand on specific aspects of these strategies but can be read as stand-alone chapters as well.

Chapter 3 discusses the working and living conditions in the city and on the docks, as well as the links between the workers' urban labor and their rural livelihoods. This is where I discuss the conceptualization of the household in more detail. I continue to focus on the household in the fourth chapter, which uses a political-economic lens to study gender and generational relations at workers' rural homes. It explores the reproduction of rural patriarchy and gendered expectations, and their contestation, within the household. The picture that emerges is one of both cooperation and conflict, or what Sen calls "cooperative conflict." In chapter 5, I look at the common practices of pilferage and bribery on the docks and argue that these crimes, which workers did not recognize as such, were not merely reactive and opportunistic acts, as they are often labeled in the literature on resistance to proletarianization. These were part of conscious strategies to combine dock labor with small-scale enterprise, as pilferage and bribery made these businesses possible.

In chapter 6, I turn to a more traditional subject for labor historians, industrial action, and I note that dock workers did not organize only around workers' issues. The apparent contradiction between fighting for workers' rights and standing up for the interests of petty traders, combined with strong anti-Indian sentiments, makes more sense when we appreciate that many dock workers were engaged in both formal wage labor and informal enterprise. Dock labor enabled their commercial business, and their interests as wage laborers could thus not be divorced from those of informal entrepreneurs. Moreover, we cannot dismiss their nationalism and anti-Indian sentiments as false consciousness or ignore them in favor of more radical forms of activism and consciousness. Following Gillian Hart, who rightly criticizes much of the literature on South Africa's postapartheid trajectory for not paying enough attention to nationalism as a driver in the country's recent history, this chapter strives toward taking nationalism seriously as a force.[59] In the conclusion, I explore in more detail the implications of the argument developed in this book for the study of labor and for labor history. Building on the work of Karl Polanyi, I argue that common understandings of labor and of universal "rational" economic behavior, as expressed in the figure of the *homo economicus*, have limited purchase in the lives of dock workers in 1950s Durban. This is where I develop my argument for expanding our concept of labor.

In a short epilogue, finally, I reflect on the changes that took place in the harbor and in South Africa in and after 1959. Decasualization and the unrelenting assault of the apartheid state on independent African economic activities made many of the strategies discussed in this book impossible or unsustainable, which highlights the vulnerability of these strategies. Moreover, I argue that the history of the informal economy after 1959 should caution us against romanticized accounts of informal traders pulling themselves up by their bootstraps.

1

Dock Workers and the City, 1910s to 1950s

Durban is known as eThekwini, "at the bay," to isiZulu speakers. This name reflects the centrality of the harbor to the city's social and economic life. As one of the few accessible natural harbors between Port Elizabeth and Maputo (formerly Lourenço Marques), Durban became South Africa's principal port city and a lynchpin of the regional economy. The city's fortunes have therefore historically been linked to shipping. Accordingly, newspapers, authorities, and local elites have often shown great interest in the development and operation of the port.[1] Dock labor particularly worried them. Dock workers were among the city's biggest concentrations of African workers and are unsurprisingly central to its labor history. As casual laborers, they were a major preoccupation for authorities who were perpetually concerned with control over African populations. This chapter sets the scene for the rest of this book. It situates dock laborers within the history and political economy of the province and the region, and within the labor market and political scene of Durban.

Migrant Labor

Like many African laborers in southern Africa, Durban's dockers were migrant workers. The system of oscillating labor migration meant that workers retained their rural homesteads and migrated to the cities or mines as single males, leaving their families behind sometimes for a year at a time. Authorities and mine owners, southern Africa's most influential employers, often actively promoted this migrant labor system or even had a hand in establishing and organizing it.[2] Scholars have extensively debated the origins of migrant labor. Liberals stressed the attractions of the city: the excitement of urban life, modern luxuries and conveniences, and higher wages. Jan Smuts, who was twice prime minister of South Africa, exemplifies this bright lights theory in his 1936 foreword to Monica Hunter's *Reaction to Conquest*: "Johannesburg, with its glittering prizes (on native standards) in wages, the fantastic excitements of its large vivid life, its opportunities of larger more adventurous experience, the prestige of familiarity with the great unknown which attaches to those who have returned from employment there—Johannesburg has become a sort of Mecca of the native, and quite the biggest factor of change to the native all over Southern Africa. It has profoundly disturbed the ancient immemorial life of Africa."[3]

In this interpretation, migration was a positive choice to take advantage of the opportunities the city and the modern economy offered. In the 1960s and 1970s, neo-Marxist scholars refuted the assumption of free choice and emphasized coercion. They argued that migration was not an active choice but the result of political, demographic, economic, and ecological pressures, in short, the result of creeping but incomplete proletarianization. Here, migration was not an opportunity to be taken but was caused by rural impoverishment.[4] Moreover, as labor migration tended to take the youngest and strongest men, and to a lesser extent women, away from the rural areas, it also became a cause of further impoverishment of the rural economy. This emphasis on coercion and pressures too has been challenged, mainly because it leaves little room for African agency and ignores the ways in which local developments influenced the growth of southern African capitalism and its migrant labor system. Both liberal and neo-Marxist scholars regarded precolonial African societies as static and largely disregarded African initiative.[5]

A next generation of historians combined recognition of the compulsion and negative effects of labor migration with sensitivity to African agency.[6] Indeed, the migrant labor system relied significantly on compulsion and ultimately had mostly negative effects on the sending areas, but it was not just an external imposition. The internal dynamics of African societies made migration possible. African communities were, with regional and temporal variations, largely self-sufficient throughout much of the nineteenth century and had little need to sell their labor. Labor was thus often scarce and expensive, a fact deplored by white settlers, mine owners, and officials. However, colonization and environmental factors did effect change. The decline of hunting and raiding opportunities in the nineteenth century meant that the labor of young men was underutilized. Some of that labor was absorbed into agriculture, which was traditionally the female sphere. Men ploughed, but their labor was not needed throughout the year. There was thus a surplus of young male labor rooted in a gendered and generational division of labor. Therefore, young men could leave home for an extended time without undermining agricultural production.[7] Labor migration also depended on African societies' capacity to subordinate women's labor. Maintaining partial rural self-sufficiency, and thus resisting complete proletarianization, depended on female domestic and agricultural labor. To preserve the system of migrant labor, women had to be kept from leaving the homestead.[8]

Early migration brought new opportunities for young men, as the deep rural impoverishment that would characterize the twentieth century had yet to materialize. For young men, a few years of wage labor could still be sufficient to establish themselves as *abanumzane* (homestead heads, sing. *umnumzane*). In the early years of oscillating migration, the per capita output of African agriculture grew in many areas, and when homestead production increasingly came under pressure labor migrancy initially sustained it. African peasantries seized the opportunities new markets provided and invested their wages to increase production and commercialize agriculture.[9] Moreover, wages mitigated the unpredictability of agriculture and helped homesteads to restock after recurring rinderpest epidemics in the 1890s.[10]

New opportunities also allowed young men and women to challenge the social order. Some young women defied patriarchal norms and built new lives for themselves in the cities and mission stations, and young men's independent incomes changed the practice of *ukulobola*, or marriage through the payment of cattle as bridewealth (*ilobolo*). They could buy their own cattle and were thus no longer dependent on their fathers, many of whom struggled to provide *ilobolo* cattle after the decimation of their herds. This newfound independence undermined the authority of male elders and fueled generational and gendered conflicts in rural households. As colonial authorities grew concerned about the perceived flood of young Africans into the cities and the loss of patriarchal discipline, an alliance of colonial and African patriarchs tried to shore up the position of male elders. They codified a one-sided interpretation of customary law, which ossified, distorted, and narrowed these customs.[11]

While early labor migration was characterized by both opportunities and crises, opportunities progressively disappeared in the late nineteenth and early twentieth centuries. A combination of government interventions designed to increase labor supplies, stratification resulting from commercialization, and natural calamities turned the tide. Thus, the entry of Africans into the labor market was increasingly based on socioeconomic and political compulsion. Though it is impossible to put a firm date on this gradual and cumulative process, it seems that by the first decade of the twentieth century labor migration had become less a source of agency and a positive choice than the result of rural impoverishment.[12] The discovery of minerals in the interior, primarily diamonds in Kimberley in 1867 and gold in the Witwatersrand in 1886, had spurred these changes. Mining created a large new demand for cheap African labor, and the building of a railway to the Witwatersrand goldfields transformed agriculture in Natal and shipping in Durban. Mobilizing a large African labor force became a priority for colonial officials throughout southern Africa.

Authorities thus implemented measures to "encourage" Africans to take up wage labor, including taxation and land dispossession. These measures were designed to break African self-sufficiency, increase their cash and consumption needs, and enforce a discipline of hunger. Blanket dispossession, however, was not the norm in these so-called native policies. As much as increasing the labor supply was a priority, most white South Africans would not accept wholesale African migration to the cities and could not envision a South Africa where Africans and whites could mix freely. They wanted a cheap and subservient labor force whose movements were strictly controlled in the name of social order, not a disorderly and dangerous African proletariat. This tension preserved the system of migration of supposedly single male laborers who were paid "bachelor" wages. While many of these workers were married and had families to support, employers and authorities held fast to the myth of single men migrating to earn *ilobolo*. This relieved employers from having to pay wages sufficient to sustain a family and justified measures to keep Africans from settling in the cities. The unpaid labor of women in the Reserves thus subsidized male wages; this is the so-called Reserve subsidy.

In 1897, London allowed Natal to annex Zululand, which had been carved up into weak and dependent chiefdoms after the Anglo-Zulu War of 1879 and had formally become a British colony in 1887. Land north of the uThukela River (see map 1.1), the historical border between Natal and Zululand, was soon alienated for white settler agriculture. The opening up in 1904 of Zululand to white farmers replicated Natal's Reserve system, confining African homesteads to small pockets of land.[13] Moreover, these Reserves were often located in malarial valleys or in areas poorly suited to agriculture and starved of transport infrastructure.[14] The Anglo-Boer War (1899–1902) accelerated African proletarianization. The war caused destruction, disease, and rising grain prices. The latter brought riches to the few but deprivation for many. As such, the war entrenched rural differentiation. While an increased demand for labor offered temporary solace for those displaced, this demand disappeared quickly after the war ended. Moreover, the war brought four South African colonies under British rule and ultimately resulted in their unification as the Union of South Africa in 1910. The establishment of the Union rendered government control over African labor more effective; this increased control over African populations found its clearest expression in the infamous Natives Land Act of 1913.

However, African self-sufficiency was not only broken through political means. The commercialization of agriculture made people more dependent on markets and thus susceptible to commercial exploitation and market fluctuations. The last decade of the nineteenth century also brought frequent droughts, plagues, and epidemics. Nevertheless, natural disasters and fickle markets cannot be isolated from their political context.[15] Land dispossession and taxation made African societies more dependent on trade and destroyed much of their ability to deal with adversity. Tax obligations were inflexible and the Reserve policy limited people's mobility, which had long been an important mechanism to cope with environmental vagaries.[16]

By the early twentieth century most Reserves produced less than half of their food requirements and less than a third of total income requirements. There were regional differences, however: Zululand and Pondoland, the areas just north and south of what was historically Natal, were among the most nearly sufficient areas in the country; Natal south of the uThukela was the least sufficient, covering less than a quarter of its food requirements.[17] However, overall measures of productivity do not take into account socioeconomic differentiation; the reality was already bleak for most commoners in Zululand as well. Throughout the first half of the twentieth century, Reserve agriculture in Natal showed both signs of resilience and decline. Official statistics, which are not always reliable, showed no overall decline in output, but because of population growth this would still have resulted in shrinking per capita yields.[18] A more dramatic and unambiguous rural decline set in after 1955 when urban influx controls compounded overcrowding. A square mile of South African Reserve land had to feed 50 people in 1918, 60 in 1955, and 110 in 1969.[19]

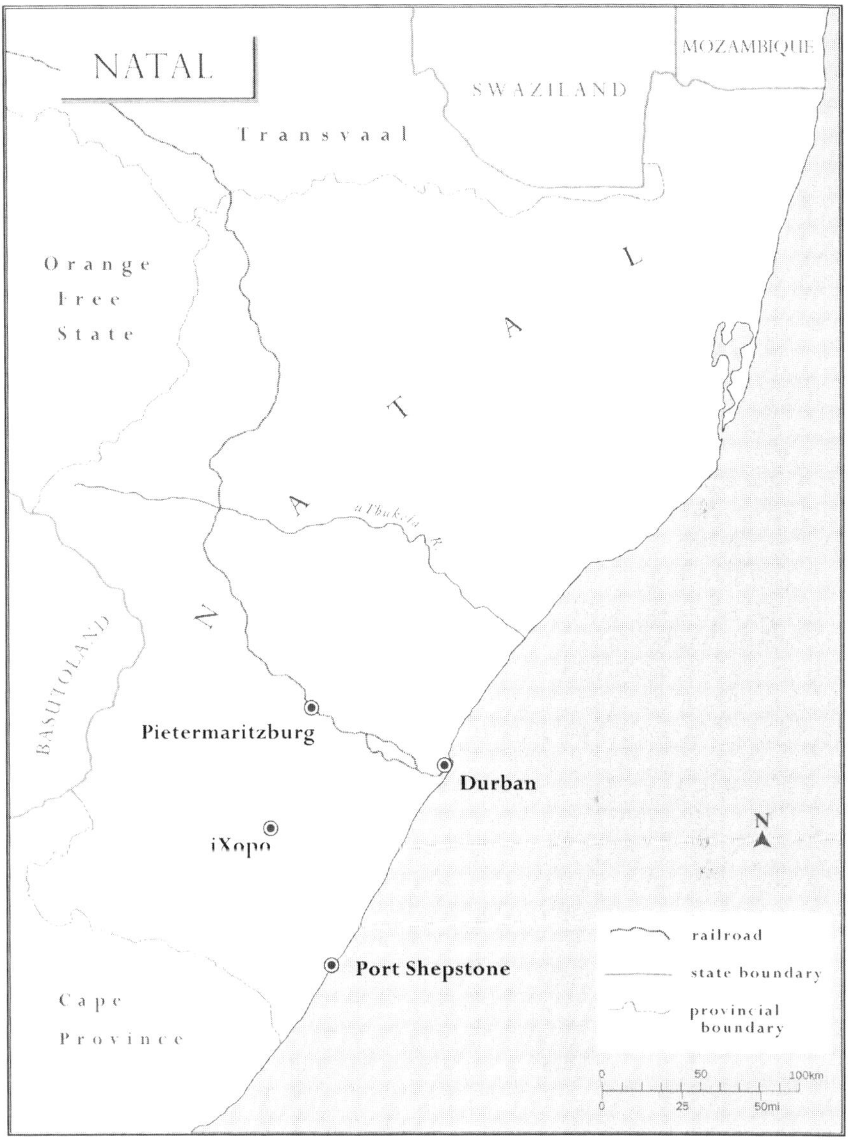

Map 1.1. Natal, c.1950. Map by Jennifer Grek Martin.

Nevertheless, while African societies were being undermined, both socially and economically, they were also being preserved. Most white South Africans did not want large urban African populations and feared the lack of discipline that would result from the decline of rural patriarchy. The disintegration of rural African societies would cause unwelcome social problems and disorder, and could expose the weaknesses of colonial power. A preservationist ethic thus permeated the thinking of colonial officials, as it did elsewhere in British Africa.[20] While this preservationist reflex had to be balanced against the demands for labor, the survival and manipulation of African social and political structures also provided a convenient solution to pressing issues of governance in the context of limited resources. The reliance on patriarchal political hierarchies for ruling African populations was mutually beneficial to African patriarchs anxious to shore up their authority and colonial officials concerned about African urbanization and control. This "accommodation of patriarchs" central to indirect rule was not without tensions; it was as much the outcome of a "makeshift settlement" and continuing African resistance as of conscious colonial design.[21]

The Port and Its Workers

Many Africans from rural Natal, including Zululand, sought wage labor in Durban. For most, the port city was closer than the Rand (short for Witwatersrand), allowing them to visit home more often. Wages in the city were also higher than on white farms. Many found employment on the docks, mostly at the Point, the northern promontory enclosing the harbor (see map 1.2). It was the location of some of the first port facilities and the most important site of shipping activities throughout the period under discussion. After the completion of the railway to the Rand and the dredging of the harbor entrance,[22] shipping grew sharply if unevenly throughout the first six decades of the twentieth century.[23] By 1910, Durban handled almost 40 percent of the country's imports by volume and more than three-quarters of its exports.[24] Durban also became an important coaling stop. Bunkering mostly took place on the Bluff, the southern headland enclosing the bay. The Point remained the main center for general cargo activities until the 1970s, when Durban's first container terminal was built. The most important, labor-intensive, and skilled sector in the harbor was the handling of break-bulk cargo, which is cargo that is neither containerized nor bulk and thus needs to be loaded and unloaded piece by piece, bag by bag, drum by drum, crate by crate.

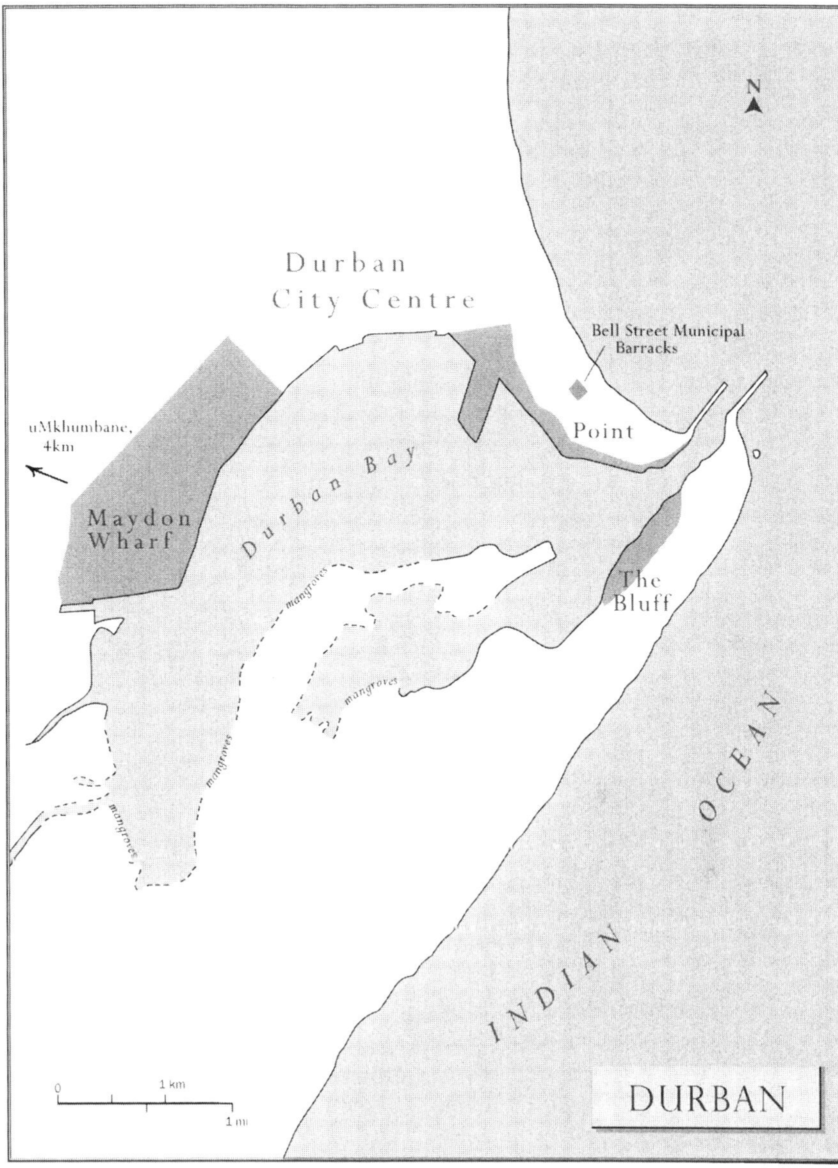

Map 1.2. Durban harbor, c.1950. Shaded areas indicate harbor infrastructure. Map by Jennifer Grek Martin.

Before the introduction of containers, African migrant laborers did most of the work by hand. There were two main groups of dock workers. Stevedores worked in the holds, stacking or unloading cargo, and shore workers handled the cargo wharf-side. In Durban, shore workers were also known as railway workers, as the SAR&H employed them. Stevedoring generally required more skill, was more dangerous, and earned higher wages.[25] Coalers were a third group of workers; they were among the lowest-paid laborers in the port. Bunkering was carried out exclusively by hand until 1907, after which mechanical coaling appliances took over. Smaller amounts of coal, however, continued to be bunkered by hand into the 1950s. Gangs of ten to fifteen would carry heavy baskets over narrow and often unprotected gangways. Bunkering a ship could easily take twenty-four hours of continuous work.[26]

Dock workers were among the largest groups of workers in the city and were pivotal to the smooth operation of the harbor. Dock labor was therefore central to what was known as Durban's labor question: How to increase the supply of cheap and disciplined African labor? The vast majority of these workers were casual, or *togt*, laborers. While the share of *togt* labor was declining, the majority of dockers were still casual workers by 1959. By the 1950s, Zulu workers had come to monopolize the sector, but this had not always been the case. Workers from southern Mozambique were prominent in stevedoring in the 1880s and 1890s, and Durban's small Zanzibari community, which descended from East African Muslim slaves liberated in the late nineteenth century, was also involved in dock work in the early twentieth century.[27]

Togt labor was thus prevalent, but it was also controversial and had been since the nineteenth century. Casual dock workers were notoriously difficult to discipline and often earned much more than did contract laborers. Officials and newspaper commentators believed that *togt* drove up wages and discouraged stable employment; they considered it to be the crux of the city's labor problems. Casual workers refusing to commit to long-term contracts were deemed to be lazy and idle.[28] Apart from a labor problem, *togt* was also considered a moral and social issue, as expressed in a report from the colony's Native Affairs Commission: "It is a class of labour which is under very little or loose control, a circumstance which is detrimental to morality and social order among a people to whom restraint in a form more powerful than public opinion or conscientious scruples is still necessary."[29]

However, *togt* served a purpose for both workers and harbor employers. Labor needs followed the unpredictable rhythm of shipping, and casual labor offered firms the flexibility they needed. Organized labor has frequently denounced casual work for offloading the insecurities of the maritime sector onto the laborers, but Durban's employers stressed that dock workers preferred *togt* and would not accept weekly or monthly contracts.[30] This was at least partly true, and several interviewees had been offered and had refused permanent employment. For workers, casual labor offered higher wages than did most other jobs and an opportunity to escape many of the punitive measures of South Africa's pass and labor laws. For example, casual workers could leave a job with poor working conditions or low pay after one day. Monthly workers, in contrast, were limited in their ability to look for new work by the requirement to have your previous employer sign your pass.[31]

Despite these advantages, dock labor was also backbreaking and dangerous. Accidents were frequent occurrences, and mechanization at the beginning of the twentieth century was limited to cranes. All cargo had to be loaded onto and unloaded from nets attached to these cranes or winches by hand. Subsequent innovations did not substantially change the nature of dock labor until containerization eliminated much of the manual labor in the 1970s. Thus, when in the latter half of the 1950s the port handled about eight million tons of cargo per year, this was mostly lifted, carried, and stacked by hand by a few thousand African workers.[32]

Togt dock laborers presented themselves for hiring each morning. The absence of long-term contracts and the nature of the workplace, which was difficult to supervise, created a double challenge for employers: securing reliable access to labor and disciplining it. In Durban, as elsewhere, shippers relied on intermediaries to navigate these issues. These African intermediaries supervised and hired gangs from those workers who presented themselves. Companies bought not only labor through these gang leaders but also its administration and supervision. Consequently, employers knew very little about their workers. These gang leaders, known in Durban as *izinduna* (sing. *induna*), were quintessentially ambiguous figures: at the same time laborer, labor contractor, and supervisor. Workers needed them for employment; management needed them for access to labor, supervision, and workplace discipline.[33]

Apart from getting the job done, the role of *izinduna* was not strictly defined.[34] The *induna* gave the worker access to a job, and the worker helped the gang reach its quota. A relationship of mutual dependence could thus develop between workers and their immediate supervisors, replete with patronage, favoritism, bribery, and victimization. To get the job done and retain his position, the intermediary had to control and discipline the workers; but to hold on to his power over the workers, he had to represent their grievances and protect them from excessive exploitation.[35] In the port of Durban, where employers and workers did not speak the same language, *izinduna* were also interpreters, and their position took on the characteristics of traditional Zulu hierarchies. Supposedly, they were an urban-industrial extension of the rural *izinduna*, the middle tier of the Zulu political hierarchy, but the relationship between workers and supervisors was a new one forged in the realm of urban labor.

The partially imagined authoritarianism of Zulu political structures, stripped of its nuances and negotiability, facilitated the use of African foremen in the interest of discipline. This does not mean that workers were not pleased to have Africans as their immediate supervisors. For workers it was often easier to create a relationship of interdependence with other Africans; claims to tradition or common ancestry could result in preferential hiring, protection, and access to pilferage opportunities. Indeed, workers often expressed their relationship with the foremen in the language of kinship. However, the relation between *izinduna* and workers was certainly not without conflict and some *izinduna* were seen as mere "boss boys"—that is, creations of the employer.

The relative agency and independence of *togt* workers, compared to other African laborers, concerned employers and authorities. By outsourcing hiring and workplace supervision to intermediaries, employers gave up much of their control over the workforce while *togt* workers had nothing to lose in a labor conflict but one day of pay. Moreover, employers were often in fierce competition for the best stevedoring labor, and the system of daily hiring allowed workers to use this strong bargaining position on a daily basis. As a result, *togt* workers earned wages significantly above the average for African workers. However, employers maintained a labor pool in excess of their usual needs by rotating hiring, thus creating downward pressure on wages. Many dockers were hired just frequently enough not to be too discouraged and to stay in dock employment. This surplus could also serve to deter strikes.[36]

Many *togt* laborers worked for private stevedoring companies and, despite official reservations, the parastatal SAR&H also employed casual workers. In fact, the railways employed about half of all *togt* workers at the Point and established first claim on their labor by housing them. Several stevedoring companies similarly had their own compounds, which created some stability in the work patterns of many casual workers. Through free housing, employers exerted control over a group

Table 1.1. Examples of monthly earnings by *togt* stevedores, June 1954

Badge#	Shifts	Employer	Rate per Shift	Pay
A10	20 days	African Associated	10s 3d	£10 5s 0d
	6 days	Others	10s 3d	£3 1s 6d
	1 Sunday	Not specified	15s	15s 0d
	8 nights, 5–9 p.m.	Not specified	4s 6d	£1 16s 0d
			Total:	£15 17s 6d
A45	14 days	African Associated	10s 3d	£7 3s 6d
	12 days	Others	10s 3d	£6 3s 0d
	2 Sundays	Not specified	15s	£1 10s 0d
	6 nights, 5–9 p.m.	Not specified	4s 6d	£1 7s 0d
			Total:	£16 3s 6d
A68	8 days	African Associated	10s 3d	£4 2s 0d
	18 days	Others	10s 3d	£9 4s 6d
	1 Sunday	Not specified	15s	15s 0d
	4 nights, 5–9 p.m.	Not specified	4s 6d	18s 0d
			Total:	£14 19s 6d

Note: £1 is 20s, and 1s is 12d.
Source: SAB, ARB, vol. 3315, file 1196/5/2, part 1, undated and untitled document.

that was notoriously difficult to discipline. Workers living in these compounds were required to offer their labor first to the company that houses them. Only if their regular employer did not need them could they seek employment elsewhere.[37] In practice, many casual dock workers usually worked for the same employer. Table 1.1 illustrates this pattern with sample earnings of *togt* stevedores at African Associated Agency and Stevedoring. For the workers in this sample, casual dock labor was not occasional employment but a full-time occupation without the security of a permanent job and with higher wages. Their free accommodation was dependent on offering their labor every day, a condition employers and authorities exploited several times in the 1950s to put pressure on strikers.[38]

Most dock workers lived near the Point and thus very close to the white residential and commercial areas of the inner city and the beachfront. Moreover, *togt* workers did not necessarily work every day and all day; they could have a considerable amount of (often involuntary) free time. This presence of Africans without apparent purpose, that is, not currently working for white employers, invoked fears of crime and disease among white Durbanites, as well as complaints about drunkenness, prostitution, and indecency. An outbreak of the plague in an interracial informal settlement at the Point in 1902 and the presence of *amalaita* youth gangs engaged in petty crimes and street fights further fueled these fears.[39] Most activities by Africans other than working, eating, and sleeping came to be construed as unwanted behavior. This absolutist perception of authority banked on the notion that young African men, separated from the authority of their elders, needed to be reined in.[40] Durban's labor question and the problem of the relative independence of *togt* workers thus came to be understood as a police problem. A language of order, control, and segregation justified the interventions that made Durban's, and South Africa's, labor markets highly coercive.

The first attempts to increase control over casual workers in the city date back to 1874, when the city's first registration scheme established the principle that Africans were welcome in town only as laborers. This made racial segregation integral to labor policy. The law was designed to limit African workers' freedom and introduced passes as well as fines, prison sentences, and exile for pass law violations. The 1902 Togt Law restricted access to the city even further, as arriving African workers were given just five days to find employment. Bargaining over wages also became illegal. The law compelled *togt* laborers to sleep in municipal or employer-provided compounds, and it set fixed daily wage rates. Such laws created a multitude of offenses resulting in thousands of arrests each year, as laborers continued to resist and ignore these rules.[41] Africans' urban presence was in effect criminalized, except within very narrowly circumscribed conditions. The 1925 Economic and Wage Commission acknowledged that these measures undermined laborers' bargaining power but considered them fair for an African population supposedly shielded from exploitation by their access to Reserve land.[42]

The limited success of the badges *togt* laborers had to wear "on some conspicuous part of [their] person"[43] illustrate the extent to which some of these measures were disregarded. These badges were proof of their registration as casual laborers, for which they had to pay a fee, but soon fell into disuse. Employers regularly hired workers without a badge, which broadened the labor pool and thus put pressure on wages. Moreover, workers passed their badges on to others, who could wear them without being registered.[44] In the late 1950s, the harbor remained one of the few places where Africans without passes could find work.[45] While these regulations were habitually ignored and contraventions inconsistently prosecuted, pass laws could also be used to exert pressure on strikers. Striking *togt* laborers could not be prosecuted for breach of contract, but the bylaws stipulated that they could not refuse work at certain rates. Both their residence in the compounds and in town thus depended on accepting work.

These measures gave rise to a full-fledged bureaucracy for their enforcement in the form of the Municipal Native Affairs Department (MNAD). The cost of this machinery of control and oppression was born by African workers themselves, as Durban's town council did not consider it appropriate to let whites pay for "services" rendered to Africans. Under what became known as the Durban System of native administration, which was copied by municipalities throughout southern Africa, the city monopolized the brewing and sale of low-alcohol sorghum beer, or *utshwala*, and outlawed the consumption of other alcoholic beverages by Africans. It sold this beer in municipal beer halls, and the proceeds, together with *togt* registration fees, funded the MNAD and the municipal *togt* compound on Bell Street.[46] The establishment of the Durban System also constituted an offensive against female brewers, whose income and urban residence facilitated the emergence of African urban households and communities outside the controls of the compounds.

The government's control over the African population, however, remained tenuous, and many Africans continued to carve out an independent existence. Much of the first half of the twentieth century was characterized by a drawn-out struggle to force workers into compounds, as it was more feasible to discipline a work force that lived in one easily policed place. Moreover, cheap housing lessened cash needs and reduced upward pressures on wages.[47] In 1902, however, only one in seven *togt* workers lived in such compounds.[48] Many lived in the servants' quarters of white households or on the streets, or they lived in periurban informal settlements where Indians, Africans, and poor whites slept, ate, and drank together.[49] Authorities considered these spaces dens of vice but were mostly unable to clear them.

By midcentury many dock workers lived in the compounds of one of the stevedoring employers or the SAR&H; others lived in the Bell

Street municipal barracks at the Point (see map 1.2). However, many also continued to live in servants' quarters or moved to townships outside the city; the first African townships were built from the 1930s onward to cope with the pace of urbanization.[50] Living on the outskirts of town added long commutes to already long workdays and meant having to leave even earlier to present for hiring at 6:30 a.m. Moreover, casual laborers risked making this long trip without finding employment, in which case they would hang around the Point hoping that more jobs would become available during the day. Police and white inhabitants deplored this practice, which they considered loitering and a nuisance.[51]

Others slept on the verandas of dockside sheds or in downtown parks. They slept on the ground, and the verandas or trees offered little protection against heavy summer rainstorms. On cold winter nights there was little to shield them from the wind, and there were no sanitary provisions, except for public lavatories. Police considered those who slept outside vagrants and delinquents, and police harassment was common.[52] To protect themselves against robbers, veranda dwellers kept each other company; they cooked together on small paraffin stoves and smoked *dagga*. They helped each other find work and taught each other to pilfer.[53] These conditions were nevertheless attractive enough for many to opt to live there rather than to submit to the disciplines of overcrowded and filthy compounds.

During the 1930s and 1940s, growing numbers moved into informal settlements on the outskirts of town.[54] Cato Manor, known to Africans as uMkhumbane, was the most important of these and was forcibly cleared in the 1950s, as it was too close to white residential areas for apartheid mores. However, before its demolition uMkhumbane developed as one of the main centers of African cultural life, enterprise, and politics. Iain Edwards quotes Brutus Mthethwe, a dock worker: "It was the African city, uMkhumbane. It was not Thekwini, it was ours."[55] As uMkhumbane initially fell beyond city limits, Africans there were not subject to constant police harassment and bylaw restrictions, while still being at easy commuting distance from the city and its industrial areas. Even after Durban's borders were expanded in 1932, with the express intention of exerting control over uMkhumbane's inhabitants, the settlement remained an important hub for independent African cultural and economic activities. Its *shebeens* were the center of much of Durban's working-class culture, as thousands of workers flocked into the area on weekends. Like Brutus Mthethwe, many dock workers would thus have been familiar with the settlement, even if most did not live there.

Urban Control and Politics

Despite frequent oppression of African working-class action, Durban's dock workers have a long-standing reputation of being particularly strike prone and radical. They were instrumental in both the 1929 and 1949 unrests, and were on the frontlines of Durban's 1972–73 strikes, which was one of the first major episodes of popular resistance after the Sharpeville massacre.[56] Dockers were also the first significant constituency of the Industrial and Commercial Workers' Union of Africa (ICU), enthusiastically joined the pass burning campaign organized by the Communist Party of South Africa (CPSA), and were on the forefront of the wave of nonwhite labor activism in the early 1940s. Dock workers were central to Durban's urban politics; authorities' attempts to bring African workers under stricter control were therefore largely focused on *togt* dock workers. These workers were among the most radical in the city; they were not just looking for incremental gains, but much of their activism struck at the core of South Africa's cheap labor system. Nevertheless, they did not only fight for their interests as wage laborers. They also challenged racial discrimination, stood up for the rights of aspiring African traders, and subscribed to a segregationist ethic of economic nationalism. Many of these ideas are generally considered more characteristic of a petty-bourgeois consciousness than a working-class one.

Trying to contain this militancy was the job of Durban's native affairs bureaucracy, which in the first decades of the twentieth century coalesced into what David Hemson calls a "sophisticated programme of paternalistic social control"[57] and increasingly constrained African urban lives. Subsequent MNAD managers interpreted their mandate to include helping employers deal with labor shortages and suppressing labor unrests. In June 1918, a deputation of *togt* workers approached the MNAD, their only access to local government, with a request for higher wages. Manager J. S. Marwick believed these demands to be preposterous and instead organized a meeting with employers to coordinate their response. Convinced that these laborers could not have organized independently, an act that requires more agency and intelligence than he attributed to Africans, he looked for agitators. He blamed John Langalibalele Dube, a prominent *kholwa*[58] politician and newspaper editor, despite Dube's explicit discomfort with working-class action.[59] The department could also be counted on to recruit strike breakers and to remind workers of the legally binding nature of their one-sided, nonnegotiated contracts.[60] With the government acting as strike breaker and labor broker, employers could remain silent about their own labor policies and disguise them in neutral terms as being in line with national laws and local bylaws.

In the immediate aftermath of the First World War, however, African militancy in Durban lagged behind the rest of the country. This changed in the 1920s when the ICU started organizing in Natal. After a difficult start, which led National Secretary Clements Kadalie to lament that Zulu people "seemed so tame and ready to submit to anything the official European suggested,"[61] the provincial branch quickly grew into the union's biggest under A. W. G. Champion. The ICU, as much a political movement as a trade union, was only the second prominent African political organization to emerge in the province after Dube's Natal Native Congress (NNC).[62] The NNC mostly represented a small propertied *kholwa* elite. Radicals within the ICU leadership derided NNC politicians as *ama-respectable*, or "respectable people," hinting at their concerns about respectability and status over workers' issues. Much of the ICU leadership, however, equally eschewed language of class and industrial action, preferring a discourse of incipient Zulu nationalism, respectability, and Garveyite self-help. Nevertheless, the ICU did take up workers' grievances, even if it was hardly a typical trade union.[63]

The union captured the imagination of Durban's laboring poor and of hard-up rural tenants being forced off their land. A focus on mass meetings, petitioning authorities, and frequently successful legal challenges to farm evictions and oppressive legislation accounted for its large membership. Dock workers formed its first important constituency, but it was in rural Natal that it built a mass base. The 1924 electoral victory of the Pact Coalition of nationalists and the whites-only Labour Party bolstered the ICU's appeal to rural tenants and an aspiring black middle class. Commercializing white farmers found it easier to expel African tenants under the new government, and avenues for advancement for middle-class Africans were progressively closed off. This stunted middle class came to make up the leadership of the ICU and transformed it from a trade union into a popular movement fighting evictions and racial discrimination.[64] In the countryside, the union grew through young migrants who learned about it in Durban and became self-proclaimed organizers upon their return. They infused the ICU's message with their own millenarian discourse of a new order. They articulated the resentment of rural Africans, voiced militant demands for the return of African land, invoked symbols of Zulu nationalism, and challenged evictions with some success. The very name of the union, pronounced "I see you," became a symbol of empowerment, letting farmers, employers, and officials know that their abuses would no longer go unnoticed and unchallenged.

However, as evictions relentlessly continued and landlords "sniffed out" ICU members, the union's preference for litigation did little to guarantee lasting organization and proved more expensive than it could afford. After reaching eighty-eight thousand members in 1927, the union had all but disappeared by the end of the decade, but it did not go down without one last fight. In the late 1920s the ICU *yase* Natal, which seceded under Champion's leadership from the national organization, recruited female beer brewers to bolster its financial position. These brewers opposed the municipal beer monopoly and were concerned about plans to open a beer hall at the edge of town. These plans demonstrated the city's commitment to extending control over the periurban areas where brewers eked out an independent existence. Their opposition coincided with the resentment of dock workers who regarded beer halls as symbols of their oppression.[65] The interests of these two groups coalesced in the 1929 boycott of municipal beer halls. The boycott started in the Bell Street barracks, where a *togt* worker advocated boycotting an Indian store across the street. The owner of this store allegedly was behind a clampdown on workers brewing *mahewu* (fermented porridge) in the compound. The Indian trader considered these *mahewu* brewers competition. When the worker advocating this boycott was stripped of his registration badge, workers extended the boycott to the Point beer hall and joined the Anti-Kaffir Beer Manufacturing League.[66]

The threat to the livelihoods of periurban brewers and traders in the compounds, resentment about dependency on municipal beer halls for leisurely drinking and socializing, and frustration about the arbitrary powers of compound managers combined into a common focus on beer halls as a central institution of subordination.[67] The ICU and Champion picked up on these grievances and helped to organize the boycott, which erupted in riots in June. Women took the boycott to other parts of the province. For them, beer monopolies were not only competition but also drained the migrant wages on which homesteads depended.[68] Riots and the boycott of a crucial instrument of urban control represented a challenge to the legitimacy of white authorities and their capacity to rule. The government grew concerned about this open defiance, which was compounded by a refusal to pay taxes. Dock workers were at the center of this resistance and authorities responded in November with a massive early morning raid on several Point compounds, arresting more than six hundred tax defaulters.[69]

Still convinced that African laborers could not have legitimate grievances or organize independently, Marwick found a new scapegoat. By 1929, Dube was no longer considered a dangerous radical but was rather part of the chorus denouncing the ICU *yase* Natal and labeling Champion a dangerous man who preached contempt for white authority. Marwick believed Champion to be in league with communists and criminals, manufacturing grievances with the goal of disturbing peaceful race relations.[70] Both Champion and Dube, however, were remarkably moderate to be considered dangerous radicals. By the mid-1920s, the conservative NNC had fallen back on its small following of the propertied *kholwa* elite. The position of the lower-middle-class ICU leadership, consisting largely of skilled or white-collar workers and small-scale entrepreneurs, was more ambiguous and had the potential to inspire alliances both with African workers and with elites. This middle-class leadership aspired to elite status and respectability but was vulnerable at the hands of a government intent on eliminating competition for white entrepreneurs and skilled workers. They were thus increasingly pushed into an alliance with and into the ranks of the African working class.[71]

Populist language, successful court cases, and passionate appeals to ethnic solidarity, skillfully invoking an illustrious Zulu past, guaranteed the ICU support among the laboring poor, but the leadership frequently had a different agenda. The union often addressed the concerns of African traders more effectively than those of workers; and, even when the union adopted workers' issues, these issues generally did not address the relationships among labor, capital, and the state.[72] The ICU lodged complaints about rents and trading hours for entrepreneurs or about the quality of compound accommodation and the cost of *togt* badges. Rather than industrial action, the union advocated Garveyite economic separatism, stressing self-help, self-improvement, and cooperative societies.[73]

In the context of rapidly disappearing opportunities for the educated middle class and for chronically undercapitalized African entrepreneurs, these groups turned to economic nationalism, urging Africans to bring their business to them rather than to Europeans or Indians. They also increasingly came to rely on the ICU for income. The union provided them with salaried positions, and its All-African Cooperative Society offered an opportunity to put their entrepreneurial skills to use. Champion in particular used the union to promote his business ventures and accessed union funds to finance these.[74] The beer halls, which symbolized the marginalization of African enterprise, were thus suitable targets for the ICU leadership, yet dock workers initiated the boycott. This boycott not only channeled resentment over the beer monopoly but was also a reaction to the stifling of petty traders in the compounds, as workers equally begrudged the lack of opportunity for African entrepreneurs. This resentment was directed not only at the state but also at direct competitors, such as the Indian trader targeted for a boycott in 1929.[75] These grievances translated into support for economic segregation and calls for an "Africa for the Africans."[76]

While the leadership shied away from radical action and advised against strikes, workers appropriated the discourse of the ICU, just as farm tenants had done before them. By 1929, the union had to step up the rhetoric in order not to be outpaced by the rank and file. Dock workers took the initiative, organized the boycott, and marched on the city. The middle-class leadership followed behind the workers, yet the limited reforms in the aftermath of the riots were meant to appease this leadership, for example, by establishing a Native Advisory Board (NAB). This board was conceived of as buffer between workers and the authorities, a response to a situation where shared experiences of racial oppression facilitated cross-class alliances.[77] Co-opted into the NAB, the ICU leadership rescinded its support for the boycott, which continued as it started, spontaneously carried by the workers. After dropping its support, the ICU lost much of its influence.

Several scholars have pinned the blame for the ICU's demise on the petty-bourgeois origins of its leadership.[78] However, the socioeconomic distance between the leadership and the rank and file was generally small. The African lower middle class was under constant threat of being pushed into the ranks of unskilled laborers. Moreover, they shared experiences of racial oppression and at least some dock workers shared the leadership's concern for the interest of African traders. Culturally, there was often more distance. Many ICU leaders were Christians and subscribed to an ideal of status and respectability; Champion, for example, was a teetotaler. The rank and file subsidized these middle-class tastes, as dues were not only used to fund the leadership's business ventures but also to run the African Workers' Club, which despite its name did not attract laborers but rather the aspiring middle class.[79]

By 1930, the ideological rift between the union's leadership and its membership had become exposed. The CPSA and its local leader, Johannes Nkosi, filled the void. The party's African membership grew spectacularly in the early 1930s following the adoption of its new South African Native Republic strategy. This strategy had been advanced by the Comintern and prioritized a democratic anticolonial revolution as the first step to a classless society. As with the beer boycott, the state rather than employers was the main target of their activism. This time the focus was on the pass system.[80] Durban's workers were keenly aware of the political nature of their exploitation. Beer halls and pass books were part of the system of racial oppression and exploitation. The beer boycott thus evolved into a pass burning campaign in 1930, in which Africans burned the passes they were required to carry. It was a dangerous strategy that exposed participants to prosecution, but the CPSA believed its support to be strong enough. "'You cannot imprison millions,' they said," Edward Roux recalls in his *Time Longer Than Rope*.[81] The pass burning event on December 16, Dingaan's Day, drew a large turnout, despite the ICU's denunciation. Dock workers in particular responded in great numbers. Police shot at the protestors and killed four people, including Nkosi.[82] Roux tried to keep the party's momentum going but was arrested and deported from Durban.

The protested pass system was part of a range of measures designed to curb African freedom of movement and maintain an entirely rural contract labor force. African workers, however, refused to conform to official fantasies. Large groups of laborers, especially dock workers, continued to work on a casual basis, and a lively informal economy mushroomed. There were still possibilities to earn a livelihood outside of contract labor, and a social and cultural life that was suppressed in the compounds flourished at the edge of town, where one could find African family life, *shebeens*, *dagga*, prostitutes, and more.[83] Especially women bore the brunt of measures to eliminate these opportunities, as their mere presence symbolized the emergence of an African urban proletariat and their earnings enabled urban family life. These uncontrolled spaces survived multiple attempts to clear them, yet one should not romanticize the lives of the urban poor. Many Africans did manage to build relatively independent livelihoods, but they did so in the context of a repressive society and enduring poverty.

One of the main hubs of African life, culture, and politics throughout the 1940s and 1950s was uMkhumbane. It had been a center of Indian market gardening, but, as African migration increased, especially during the Second World War, Indian landlords took to renting out makeshift shacks. Indians were shopkeepers, bus operators, and landlords in uMkhumbane.[84] For African entrepreneurs too it was a haven beyond the grasp of a bureaucracy bent on restricting independent African business. They ran shops and *shebeens*, produced artisanal crafts, and sold *dagga*; they even sold forged and stolen passes. Authorities considered this a place where "undesirable natives" flocked to and where they engaged in activities that "to them are remunerative but are in many cases undesirable from every social and moral point of view."[85]

In the late 1940s, an urban millenarian populism known as New Africa originated in uMkhumbane. Some of the characteristics of this discourse of a New Africa, which uMkhumbane came to symbolize, were an emphasis on the dignity of ordinary Africans, faith in the power of education, and a belief in an alternative and distinctly African society. This struggle for a manifestly African society incorporated economic nationalism and a vibrant cooperative movement that exhorted Africans to spend their money with African entrepreneurs and to avoid commercial exploitation by white and Indian shopkeepers. Indeed, African nationalism was not just the preserve of the middle class but was equally carried by workers.[86] However, by 1950 most cooperatives had become little more than profit-driven enterprises without an interest in transforming society.[87]

More forceful industrial activism emerged on the docks under the leadership of Zulu Phungula, a militant *togt* stevedore from a farm near iXopo (see map 1.1). Hemson attributes to him a central role in his account. He considers Phungula to be "free of the politics of ambiguous deference characteristic of the petty bourgeoisie" and to have a proletarian outlook despite being a rural migrant.[88] In the context of wartime inflation and high workloads, Phungula became a particularly militant leader who was still remembered by workers interviewed in the 1980s and in 2009.[89] Moreover, his demands were as radical as his actions. In May 1941, he and two other *togt* stevedores asked for their daily wage to be doubled, directly challenging Durban's cheap labor system.[90] Employers denied responsibility in this matter and referred to African wages as a legal matter for which only the government has authority.[91]

The government unsurprisingly granted only minimal increases and declared stevedoring a controlled industry under war regulations, yet dock workers were not easily intimidated and went on strike. When the native commissioner threatened to send the strikers home, Phungula asserted their urban status: "The Government must show us where to go because our homes are here in Durban."[92] He recognized the link between low African wages and institutionalized migratory labor. While most dock workers were migrants and had strong attachments to their rural homes, he would not let this serve as an excuse to depress wages. The government predictably repressed the strikes, used African troops to replace strikers, and arrested Phungula. Two years later, after another conflict with the authorities, he was banished from Durban for five years.[93]

Phungula returned in 1948 and continued his organizing. He wrote a report on the economic conditions of Natal's African workers as president of the newly founded and short-lived Dock Workers' Union. The report argued that Africans could no longer live off the land and had become dependent on wage labor. Workers thus brought their wives and children to the city, where they lived in poverty. This destitution, he claimed, appealing to white fears, breeds crime: "The wife brews (isiqata) with the mind to supplement wages and still there is not enough. It is not true that natives like isiqata [a strong home-brewed alcoholic beverage]. Women by doing so are trying to help their husbands. They all left their homes with the idea of helping each other. Here you are, the children burgle, they pick-pocket because they are starving and naked on account of the government and the employers."[94] In this report, Phungula did not call for more and better land or for agricultural assistance; rather, he called for better wages for urban African workers and proposed a general strike to achieve this. At a mass meeting open to all African workers in the city, his call was defeated by a more gradualist approach of petitioning the government.

For Hemson, there was a direct link between this defeat and the anti-Indian pogrom of January 1949: "The strategy of a general strike having been defeated, the African workers turned toward more nationalistic forms of action. Instead of class action the African workers turned against Indian people."[95] This violence, in which dock workers once again played a leading role, and its late but bloody suppression left 142 dead and more than one thousand wounded. White newspapers portrayed this as an unprovoked outburst of violence by a savage African mob.[96] However, this pogrom was neither simply the doing of a savage mob nor a surrogate for repressed working-class action. Starting as a spontaneous reaction to an act of violence by an Indian merchant, not an unusual occurrence, and emboldened by police inaction, which seemed to indicate that Indians were licensed scapegoats, spontaneous violence turned into organized attacks emerging from the compounds and beer halls.[97] The initial attacks mostly targeted traders in the Grey Street commercial area, but when the violence turned to the fringes of town poor Indians also became the victims of what amounted to an effort to evict the Indian population. Not only were shops looted, but young girls were raped and houses and shacks were burned down. Yet, many Africans also protected their Indian neighbors, landlords, or employers, sometimes at the expense of their own lives.

There is no easy explanation as to why a significant group of Africans turned on Durban's Indian population and what follows is at best an incomplete interpretation. It is also not clear how widespread African participation in this violence was, as there are no reliable estimates. While many Africans were appalled by the violence, they often expressed sympathy for the motives.[98] Indeed, tensions between Indians and Africans were nothing new in Durban, especially in the context of rapid urbanization in the 1940s that increasingly put Indians and Africans in a landlord-tenant or storekeeper-customer relation.[99] These relations were frequently experienced as exploitative; the 1940s thus brought calls for more opportunities for African entrepreneurs and for Africans to withdraw their patronage from Indian traders. However, these relationships were not only or purely exploitative; Indian housing and services made African urban life beyond the controls of municipal and employer-run compounds possible. Antipathy against Indian traders, landlords, and bus operators was nevertheless rife, and the complaints were well known: overcharging, exploitative rents, and arrogance.[100] The latter grievance suggests that apart from unequal commercial relationships, the differential legal and social positions of both groups also inspired resentment.

African aspiring entrepreneurs often found their ambitions frustrated by better capitalized Indian competitors with easier access to credit, licenses, and suppliers. Moreover, by 1949 the influx of wages that fueled the informal redistributive economy in places like uMkhumbane dried up. Real wages declined, and entry into the city became more difficult. This resulted in fewer opportunities for African traders, as fewer workers had less money to spend.[101] When the violence subsided, the African cooperative movement organized a boycott of Indian traders, which received the support of the ANC's Natal branch against the wishes of the national organization. Many African entrepreneurs took advantage of the commercial void left by the killed or expelled Indian traders and landlords.

It thus seems that economic nationalism was a significant motivation for this pogrom, but the question remains why dock workers were at the center of it. They were not in direct competition for jobs or business with Indians, and, as many lived in the compounds at the Point, they would have had limited interactions with Indian landlords and bus operators. However, many visited informal settlements like uMkhumbane regularly and were aware of African traders' grievances. Many dock workers also had commercial aspirations themselves and were equally frustrated by the limited opportunities for African entrepreneurship. Phungula espoused an economic nationalism similar to that of New Africa and tried at least twice to establish cooperative ventures.

He and other dock leaders were regularly as concerned about the rights of African petty entrepreneurs as about those of workers.[102]

After the pogrom, many Africans felt a sense of victory; they had usurped an Indian area. However, their victory was pyrrhic and short lived. The challenge to the established order that this violence represented put the questions of informal settlements and unlicensed businesses on top of the official agenda. Despite considerable indecisiveness and infighting among different levels of government, uMkhumbane was cleared of its inhabitants within a decade. The opportunities for African entrepreneurs disappeared with the settlement, as government-built townships were designed to be more easily policed. Informal settlements had concerned authorities even before the pogrom. In 1947, the Broome Commission concluded that the city's housing problem was linked to the problem of casual labor. A more stable labor force would mean less continuous flux of workers and make it easier to accommodate laborers in official housing. This would also help to control and discipline the work force.[103] This concern with labor stabilization was inspired by the 1930s discovery of urban African poverty in liberal scholarship, with poverty datum surveys and scholarship exploring the links among poverty, social unrest, and "moral collapse."[104]

The least stable of all laborers were *togt* dock workers, who by 1950 were the only substantial group of casual laborers remaining. Some attempts at decasualizing dock labor had been made in the 1930s, but by the 1950s employers grew increasingly concerned about the lack of control over their labor force and its comparatively high wages. Moreover, the apartheid government expressed its displeasure at the presence of thousands of comparatively independent African workers in the city.[105] While employers and officials continued to discuss the future of dock labor, two labor disruptions in early 1959 galvanized opinions to bring an end to casual labor. In February and March, stevedores twice refused to work overtime.[106] In response, employers agreed among themselves to no longer compete for daily labor but rather to establish a hiring monopoly for a newly established Durban Stevedoring Labour Supply Company (DSLSC). The DSLSC would in turn supply labor to the stevedoring companies. Workers were now hired by the week and received a weekly allowance; they received extra pay for the days that they actually worked. They became part of a labor pool.

Consequently, workers lost their relative freedom as *togt* workers and the bargaining power that came from daily competition for their labor, yet there were mixed reactions to these changes. On the one hand, some welcomed it, as "there were days when we did not work because there was no work for us, although our wish was that we should work daily."[107] Many appreciated the security permanent labor offered and talked about a permanent job as an opportunity for those who were strong and willing to commit to hard work.[108] On the other hand, workers continued to resist attempts at decasualization throughout the 1950s.[109] They defended the freedom and higher wages of casual employment and opposed employers' attempts to increase control over hiring and the workplace.

Exerting control over migrant African dock workers, who were difficult to discipline but pivotal to the city's economy, was a major preoccupation for authorities and employers in Durban. Dock workers in turn regularly took a leading role in urban politics. The picture that emerges is one of dock workers as radicals willing to challenge the system of cheap African labor at the core of South Africa's political economy. However, their political and socioeconomic consciousness was not a straightforwardly working-class one. They were equally concerned with the rights of informal African traders as they were with workers' issues, and they espoused an economic nationalism that fueled the anti-Indian violence of January 1949. As I will further argue in chapter 6, this more complicated political consciousness can be best understood when we look at their broader livelihoods.

2

One Head of Cattle Named Salt, Another Named Beans

Livelihood Strategies in the 1950s

Mtukatshelwa Phewa came to Durban to work on the docks after his parents died in 1957. His aunt took him under her wing and brought him to the city; she asked a dock worker she knew to show him where to present for hiring. He was taken on the same day, and it did not take him long to figure out that dock labor offered opportunities to earn some money on the side. He pilfered spilled cargoes, especially rice, sugar, beans, maize, and samp, and took them back to his aunt's shack in uMkhumbane. Generally, he would carry it in bags on his shoulder, but when there was too much he would take a taxi. His aunt sold these pilfered goods from her shack, and later they built an extension to serve as a spaza shop. She also sold matches, paraffin, and other basic consumption items. Such African-run businesses, however, were illegal, and they bribed police officers to prevent being shut down and arrested. The success of this shop allowed him to marry and to establish an *umuzi* for himself and his aunt near Izingolweni in the early 1960s. Nevertheless, he continued to work, and pilfer, on the docks. His wife and aunt established a new shop at their rural home, and he asked Mdu Jama, a colleague who owned a *bakkie*, to transport the pilfered goods. Because he wanted the freedom to work on those ships that carried the goods their store needed, he refused to become a permanent worker. Instead, he made sure to keep the *izinduna* happy by buying them beer and meat, so that they would hire him on the ships on which he wanted to work. He retired from urban wage labor in 1983 at the age of fifty, after he had put his children through school. He and his wife still run the store and own four taxis.

The intersections between rural identity and urban wage labor have been an important topic in southern African history since the 1980s. However, a third thread in the lives of at least some African workers has not received the same attention, namely that of small-scale informal entrepreneurialism dependent on their waged labor. The livelihoods of dock workers' households relied mostly on three forms of income: urban wage labor, rural agriculture and pastoralism, and small-scale entrepreneurialism. It is by studying these livelihoods that we can begin to understand the peculiar mix of working-class radicalism and petty-bourgeois concerns about trading rights and economic segregation noted in the previous chapter. This chapter discusses the livelihood strategies of these dock workers and their households, and identifies different trends and strategies. As such, it is the descriptive core of this book. The three upcoming chapters will discuss in more detail specific aspects of these strategies, though they can be read as stand-alone chapters as well.

Wage labor represented only part of the livelihoods of Durban's dock workers, and their strategies were not based only on individual decisions. The choices they made and the interests they defended should thus be seen in the context of households in which they were not the only ones earning income, consuming, and making decisions. Moreover, households are not devoid of conflict, and members did not perfectly coordinate their decisions. As men were often away in the city and communication was difficult, close coordination was impossible. These livelihood strategies are thus not necessarily perfectly coherent or without contradictions. However, the members of dock workers' households purposefully combined different sources of income. Such strategizing directs our attention to creative responses to economic and political domination under apartheid and the migrant labor regime. Though labor migration was a consequence of colonization and proletarianization, it was also a decision about which people thought and strategized. Workers did make their own choices, but only in the context of socioeconomic duress and severely restricted options. In Marx's famous words: "Man makes his own history, but he does not make it out of the whole cloth; he does not make it out of conditions chosen by himself."[1] The same, of course, goes for women.

Some Commonalities

In many ways the livelihood strategies of most dock workers were very similar. For example, none of the interviewees ever seriously considered settling in town; all presently live in the rural areas of KwaZulu-Natal and the Eastern Cape. For Doda Nxele, "it was only money that brought [him] there [to Durban]." Many interviewees even had a certain disdain for those who chose an urban future and settled in the city. Some considered them stupid; others thought that they were lured by city women. Moreover, "people laugh at you when you stay permanently in the city," Vela Mtolo explained: "They call you *umbhunguka*."[2] Indeed, there was moral sanction against permanently moving to the city, especially if this meant that one abandoned one's rural family and stopped sending remittances. Only a few dock workers did not dismiss an urban future out of hand. Lihlo Budu was not interested in moving to the city himself, but he did invest in a house for his children. They would be able to use it when they came to Durban for schooling. Rather than a home, a house in the city was an asset for your kin, a source of rent income, or the basis for a small business.[3] Dumile Ndlovu, on the contrary, kept the option of an urban future open for some time, as the area he was from was torn apart by faction fights. When he found a new home near Port Shepstone (see map 1.1), however, living in Durban was no longer on the cards. The cost of living in the city and the necessity of paying rent, even after retirement, played a major role in making urban life so unattractive.

While one had to pay rent in the city, almost all interviewees had access to some land in the Reserves or, as tenants, on white-owned farms. This facilitated their strong rural orientation. Their plots were often rather small but were nevertheless very important. After all, without land one cannot establish an *umuzi*, which is "where you build your home and raise your children."[4] This attachment to rural life is a common theme in the historiography of southern Africa. William Beinart and Peter Delius both offer valuable insights into the importance of rural life in migrants' consciousness.[5] Dunbar Moodie argues that this rural attachment "implied resistance to proletarianization."[6] Of course, these authors responded to a radical tradition that often prioritized class over other sources of consciousness.

While these dock workers displayed a strong rural orientation, we should not ignore their urban strategies. Indeed, their eventual goal was to return to the Reserves, but this did not keep them from engaging extensively with the urban economy and from using urban commercial and working-class strategies to achieve this goal. Few dock workers avoided Durban's social life, confined themselves to the compounds, or interacted almost exclusively with people from their home area (*abakhaya*). Such behavior, isolating migrants from their urban environment, was known as "incapsulation" and was often enforced by the *abakhaya*. Philip and Iona Mayer famously discuss this incapsulation, which limited the risk of workers absconding from their rural kin, among African workers in East London (see map I.1), but it was rare among Durban's dock workers.[7] Their means to achieve their rural goals were at least partly urban. A strong rural identity did not exclude urban enterprise or elements of working-class consciousness.

Beinart reminds us that "an interpretation of migrancy based on the memories of old men who have long settled back into rural life is bound to overstress the importance of rural links."[8] It is possible that dock workers' urban lives were more important than they acknowledge today, as a necessary phase on the road to their rural retirement. Indeed, while their life histories confirmed their commitment to a return to their rural homes, most workers actively took advantage of the opportunities offered by the urban economy during an extended period of their lives.

Most workers also had remarkably similar early life trajectories. They came to Durban in their late teens or early twenties, and their stated motivations for doing so fell into three broad categories. First, many were forced to leave the rural areas because of crises in their homesteads. *Imizi* were destroyed by faction fights, homesteads were stricken by witchcraft, and several workers came to the city after they lost one or both of their parents. In Thoko Mlaba's case, the death of her husband, a dock worker who died on the job, brought her to Durban. In an act of racial paternalism, her husband's employer hired her as a cleaner at his old wage. However, these crises were usually only the proverbial last straw, as rural poverty was widespread. The crisis was the trigger, but poverty was the deeper cause. Second, going to the city to work was also something people came to expect of young men: "When a boy turns eighteen, he must go to work."[9] It was part of becoming a man, evidence of one's masculinity; it was what allowed young men to pay *ilobolo* and to get married. After they married, they still had to work to establish their own *umuzi* and to become independent from their patriarch. Only then could they become patriarchs themselves. However, by the 1950s it was no longer possible for most young men to earn wages for a few years, marry, establish themselves as *abanumzane*, and then retire from urban wage labor.

Third, workers mentioned specific goals as their reason to come to Durban. Many interviewees came to earn money for buying cattle, for establishing or improving their *umuzi*, or for enclosing and irrigating their land. Such specific objectives were part of broader strategies to make their homesteads into viable economic units. Therefore, one could mistake these dockers for target workers who only engaged in wage labor as long as was necessary to achieve these specific goals. However, their work histories did not fit that picture. Most were not merely dependent on wages for buying cattle or improving their *umuzi* but also for daily consumption and survival. Wage labor had become a lifelong reality for most African workers. The myths of African migrants as target workers and of wage labor as just a phase in their lives nevertheless remained central to white employers' and officials' understandings of African labor. They thus argued that higher wages would not result in an increased labor supply, as they did not believe that African workers depended on wages. Instead, they assumed that Africans would simply reach their targets, for example buying cattle for *ilobolo*, more quickly and leave the city earlier, in effect reducing the labor supply.[10] These were convenient myths that justified low African wages.

What workers' different stated motivations have in common is socioeconomic stress. Ultimately, persistent rural poverty was the main reason for migration. South African Reserves generally did not produce enough to feed their populations, and the situation in rural Natal south of the uThukela River (see map 1.1) was particularly dire. Necessity therefore explains why they came to Durban to find a job, but they often ended up on the docks because of their connections. The vast majority of interviewees had contacts on the docks before they came to Durban. Dock labor was a job people landed by having connections: uncles, brothers, cousins, or *abakhaya* made arrangements for new workers to be hired. Recruitment through kinship and *abakhaya* networks was facilitated by the fact that hiring *togt* laborers was the responsibility of the *induna* and thus an informal affair. Being on good terms with *izinduna* thus increased your kin's chances of finding employment, as did bribery and coming from the same area. This state of affairs was in sharp contrast with hiring practices after 1959 when organized recruitment in the rural areas, often in cooperation with traditional authorities, became an important strategy to increase control over the dock labor force.[11]

Since their employment was usually arranged in advance, dock labor was their first urban job for most interviewees. Only one started with the traditional first job for young African men, poorly paid domestic service. Once they started working on the docks, their job stability was remarkable. In the 1950s, an African worker in Durban remained in one job on average between eleven and eighteen months, depending on the sector,[12] but for most interviewees dock labor was their first and only urban job. Though there were significant differences, the average length of employment on the docks was twenty-five years, which also highlights many workers' continuing dependence on wages. Dock labor was thus more than a phase in life. The fact that dock workers earned relatively good money partially explains this unusual loyalty to their job. African Associated Agency and Stevedoring, one of Durban's major stevedoring firms, estimated in 1954 that the average *togt* stevedore earned about £15 per month.[13] When shipping was good and there were plentiful opportunities to work overtime and extra shifts, one could earn as much as £6 per week in the late 1950s.[14] Very few African workers in Durban earned comparable wages.

Nevertheless, their loyalty to one job does not imply that they had no grievances. Only one interviewee had a son who ended up working in the port. Moreover, his son was only a dock worker for a short time. While most owed their jobs to kin and *abakhaya*, they did not want their own sons to work on the docks, as they considered the work too dangerous and strenuous. They wanted their children to go to school and get better jobs; dock work was acceptable for them, as they were uneducated, but they believed that, as Cacile Khozana put it, "no one in [their] family should do such a hard job after having been to school." While dock workers mostly looked back with pride on their working lives, on their time as *onyathi*, they did not romanticize this experience and wanted their children to be more socially mobile than they themselves. In a changing world where Reserve agriculture was increasingly unable to feed homesteads, tenants were being evicted from white-owned farms, and people grew progressively more dependent on exploitative unskilled labor, education was seen as the key to social mobility.[15] Most interviewees thus prided themselves on having paid for at least some schooling for their children.

Having access to land was important for establishing an *umuzi*, but this land was also where one could raise cattle. Almost all interviewees had access to some land and attached great importance to it; most also invested part of their wages in livestock, especially cattle. Cattle were central to their attempts to reconstruct a peasant world, a traditional idyll based on pastoralism, peasant agriculture, and the traditional Zulu *umuzi*. Khethekwakhe Zondo "just wanted to carry on with the old ways by having enough cattle for ploughing and agriculture." However, Zondo worked on the docks for fifty years. "Carry[ing] on with the old ways" was possible only through continued reliance on wage labor. This pastoralist idyll was no longer sustainable, as the material base of the traditional *umuzi* had been undermined.

Of course, this romanticized picture of traditional Zulu society was also one of rural patriarchy in which male workers could claim customary authority. The rural homestead was the place where they had authority and could become respected men. In urban South Africa, African men had very little power and were subject to racial paternalism, but it was the frequently denigrating experience of urban wage labor that allowed them to marry, build their *umuzi*, and claim their position near the top of the rural patriarchal hierarchy. In the city they were "boys," at home they were "men."[16]

Wage labor enabled workers to buy cattle for *ilobolo*. Traditionally, their fathers would have paid for bridewealth, yet having access to resources and cattle of one's own gave young men some independence. Combined with the inability of many patriarchs of impoverished homesteads to provide *ilobolo*, this youthful autonomy caused tensions and conflict within many *imizi*.[17] A Pondo elder quoted by Monica Hunter expressed these generational tensions: "Formerly an *umzi* was under the thumb of the father, now it is under the thumb of the son. Things are bad now."[18] Nevertheless, patriarchs had an ace up their sleeve. As migrant labor became entrenched, the price of bridewealth tended to inflate. This allowed elders to lay claim to a portion of migrants' wages. In effect, *ilobolo* payments constituted a redistribution of resources toward the elder generation.[19] Mothers and grandmothers too frequently insisted on high bridewealth payments. They were often the ones with effective control over the homestead and its resources when the men were away, and they would not accept their daughters and themselves being devalued by low *ilobolo*.[20]

Cattle were thus more than commodities to be bought, sold, or eaten. They played an important social role in African societies across the subcontinent. The value of livestock cannot be reduced to a monetary value and decisions about cattle could thus seem irrational according to a formal market logic. For example, people would often not sell their cattle when prices were high or when herds exceeded the land's grazing capacity. Colonial officials and anthropologists pathologized such decisions as symptoms of a cattle complex, an obsession with cattle as source of status rather than as an economic resource.[21] The fact that cattle has a more than economic value does not mean that livestock was not valued as a productive asset as well. They were a source of milk, hides, meat, and more, and even though selling cattle was frowned upon, there was a market, and money could be made from breeding livestock.

At least ten interviewees successfully built up their herds as a form of self-reproducing capital to carry them through their rural retirement.[22]

For some the breeding and selling of cattle became a business in itself, and some had herds as big as eighty or even one hundred head. Mzwakhe Sosibo withdrew from wage labor in 1975, and in 2009 he still lived off the herd he had built up. Mpho Jaca retired after his two daughters were married, and the *ilobolo* he received brought his herd up to sufficient size.[23] Of course, these workers also had limited alternative options to invest their wages, as they were barred from owning land in the Reserves and assets in town.

Cattle were expensive, however, and African laborers' low wages made it difficult to amass the money they needed to buy cattle.[24] Therefore, many workers participated in *stokvels*, a type of rotating credit association (RCA). These RCAs are voluntary associations in which members regularly contribute to a communal fund; the fund is given alternatingly to one of the participants until all have received the money. Such associations were and still are common in South Africa and around the world.[25] In the most basic type of *stokvel*, two people who have a close relationship and trust each other agree to contribute at regular intervals, say once a month, a certain amount of money to a fund. Alternately, one of them gets the money, thus creating a "lean month, fat month" pattern in their finances. In alternate months, these contributors are then able to afford expenses they would not be able to afford otherwise. This association can be expanded by incorporating other trusted people. *Stokvels* can grow up to ten or fifteen members, but usually not more. Trust tends to disappear in larger groups, putting them at greater risk of disintegration.[26]

These RCAs allow people to save in the face of immediate pressures to spend their limited cash on daily consumption needs. As one participant explained to Hilda Kuper and Selma Kaplan: "The contribution is not much and I would spend it in any case on nothing. This way I put it away until it is my turn to be on and then I can really buy something with it."[27] RCAs thus enable larger purchases. At least thirty-four interviewees participated in *stokvels* and used the money to buy cattle or for other expenses they could otherwise not afford. The social character of these associations enforced a saving discipline. There was pressure from the other participants to make your weekly or monthly contribution that was absent when saving at the post office or a bank. *Stokvels* also were a source of solidarity and reciprocity, as they molded and reinforced relationships of trust. Establishing a social support system could thus be an important reason to join an RCA as well.[28]

Workers wanted to hold on to their land so that they would have a place to graze their cattle, and RCAs could help them buy this cattle.

Yet households did not use their Reserve land only for grazing. While the livestock economy persisted better than Reserve agriculture in mid-century Natal, people continued to work the land. Women and children planted and reaped crops, even if yields were often low. Several dock workers' wives, mothers, sisters, or aunts sold some of their produce, others bartered, but many did not grow enough to do either. Those who sold their produce used the cash to pay for other consumption needs or to invest in seeds, fertilizers, and barbed wire to fence their land. Independent from their fathers or husbands, this source of income provided these women with limited financial autonomy. The most important reason for planting, however, remained direct consumption. Even if the returns on their labor were low, the significance of continued peasant agriculture should not be underestimated. For Dumile Ndlovu, it was "important because my wife was not a lazy woman. By committing herself to garden labor, we could spend less and sell some vegetables from the garden." By refusing to give up on the poor and insufficient Reserve lands, women fought complete dependence on their husbands' insecure and generally inadequate wages. These crops seldom covered much of households' consumption needs, but interviewees insisted that at least they helped lower cash needs. Dock workers' wages were thus indeed subsidized by Reserve production, as Wolpe famously argues.

While most workers left decisions regarding the use of their land to the women in their households—though some insisted that "no women could make decisions"[29]—they often stressed their own role in investment. Investing in their land required cash, the use of which was generally considered a male prerogative. Even today, investments are still often seen as a male domain.[30] By far the most common investment was enclosing the land with fences or barbed wire to keep livestock from damaging the crops. The second–most common investment in agriculture was acquiring a generator and hoses to water the land. Some of those generators were stolen from the wharves. Cash was also used to buy fertilizers and seeds.

Different Strategies

Durban's dock workers were committed to a return to the land. How and when they could retire from urban wage labor, however, differed and was largely dependent on their livelihood strategies. Two distinct strategies emerged from the interviews. Some maximized their earnings by picking up extra night and weekend shifts, and minimized their expenses in the city in order to send home as much money as possible. Others opted for a more commercial-entrepreneurial route to maximize their return on urban wage labor. In fact, a majority of interviewees had some small commercial business on the side, which allowed them to augment their earnings. Sometimes these small businesses even became their main source of income.

The first strategy relied on the comparatively good money that could be made when the port was busy and one was willing to double up on shifts. This was especially true during the 1950s when the tonnage handled in Durban grew by 50 percent in one decade.[31] In 1958, the Natal Employers' Association called stevedoring labor "incomparably the highest paid labour of its type in Durban."[32] Interviewees confirmed that dock wages were comparatively high and that there usually were opportunities to pick up extra shifts. Thus, many dock workers doubled up on their shifts to earn as much as possible.[33] Of course, one could always slack off during the day shift to have enough energy left for overtime.[34] Not only did several workers not feel that they needed other sources of income; some also had limited confidence in their entrepreneurial skills. Bongeka Faku said that he "just worked" because he was not educated, and for Lihlo Budu entrepreneurialism was "for educated people." For others, dock labor was just too demanding to combine with other forms of work.

Workers usually combined this strategy of working double shifts with efforts to minimize their expenditures. Permanent workers could typically stay in the company compounds where food and accommodation were free; *togt* workers were not guaranteed places in these compounds but could rent space in the municipal Bell Street barracks. Workers who stayed in company compounds could keep their expenditures on consumption in the city to a minimum: "If I was given 'two bob' [2s], that 'two bob' would last me till the end of next year. I wouldn't have bought anything with it."[35] Budget surveys reveal the difference living in a compound made, as rent and food were invariably the largest items in urban African household budgets.[36] Nevertheless, some workers did not want to live in these compounds, which were generally crowded and uncomfortable, and others could not live there, because they were not permanent workers or because there were no beds available. Half of the interviewees did not live in the compounds for at least some of their time on the docks, and more than a third never did. These workers had to find other ways to live in Durban without spending too much of their hard-earned cash.

One worker lived in a company compound even though he did not have permission to do so. Phumla Nyathikazi started as a permanent worker but decided to work on a casual basis after six months. As he had been allowed to live in the company compound before, he had befriended the security guards, who let him sneak in. A much more common strategy was to live off pilfered food from the docks. Bags and crates of food regularly broke during loading and unloading, and there was always loose food strewn around the holds and wharves. Taking some of that spillage was not considered theft by either workers or employers. Popular and convenient items to pilfer were flour, samp, beans, sugar, tinned fish, salt, and rice. I discuss pilferage in more detail in chapter 5. Sleeping on the verandas of dockside sheds and in parks could also help workers save some money. Police were aware of this longstanding practice and did little to put an end to it, though some harassment did occur.[37]

Minimizing expenditure was of course not a strategy used only by those working as many shifts as possible. Dock workers who had a business on the side wanted to keep their costs down as well and used similar strategies. A majority of interviewees engaged in some sort of commercial venture aside from their dock labor. The easiest and most common sector in which to branch out was small-scale retailing. A small number of these workers ended up as successful entrepreneurs with substantial businesses, but they all started off by selling a limited array of consumption goods. They engaged in three main categories of retailing: selling *dagga* in town and on the docks; selling cigarettes, matches, sweets, and fruit on the docks; and selling pilfered goods at home or in the townships.

The selling of cigarettes, sweets, and the like, in the city was the most accessible and least risky of these ventures. Thoko Mlaba started peddling these items shortly after she arrived on the docks. She heard people asking for these and decided to invest some of her wages. She sold her merchandise in the township, on her way to work, and on the job. The limited investment required made this a very popular strategy to supplement wages. Workers spent some of their wages on buying these goods in bulk and then resold them in smaller quantities that poorly paid workers could afford, making a small profit in the process. This sort of penny capitalism also existed on the gold fields.[38] The ease of entry, however, made it a highly competitive sector, and profits were significantly smaller than in rural commerce.

Food, cigarettes, and sweets were not the only items in high demand. Ship crews used to ask workers for *dagga*, which was sold to them by about a dozen interviewees. They also sold *dagga* in the hostels and compounds. Like beer brewers, *dagga* sellers did not look upon their business as a crime.[39] Moreover, they often had *izinduna* and supervisors among their customers. As such, selling *dagga* was not only a source of income but also provided them with valuable contacts that enabled other businesses and ensured access to jobs. Foremen and *izinduna* who were also satisfied customers engaged in preferential hiring, promoted workers who gave them access to good *dagga*, or looked the other way when these workers looted cargoes. One dock worker paid bus drivers with marijuana to transport pilfered goods to his wife, who sold these at their rural home.

For others, pilferage became a mainstay of their livelihoods. The most active pilferers were often *togt* laborers. Phumla Nyathikazi even quit his permanent position after six months to become a casual worker: "In those six months, I had started to steal the cargo and had found ways of making money. There were no good chances for this if you worked permanently. If a ship with nice things is at a certain berth you can't go and work on it, but if you're a casual worker, you present yourself for hiring at the company that deals with that ship." Being a *togt* worker gave dock workers the freedom to choose not only on which ship to work but also when to work. This allowed the flexibility to take a day off to spend time on other businesses. Some also declined a place in the compounds to evade the tighter policing that would complicate their (often illegal) businesses. The advantage of a permanent job, however, was that it offered a degree of stability in the uncertain world of petty entrepreneurialism and shipping.[40] All the interviewees who did not have side businesses were permanent workers, and few workers remained casual against their wishes. In the 1950s, laborers who were interested and were strong enough could usually find a permanent position within days.[41]

Selling goods could take much time out of one's day, and several workers mentioned that, between dock work and selling, they did not have much time to socialize. Moreover, the best time to sell small consumer items was when people were on the job and thus when the seller should also be working. Several dockers therefore entered into commercial partnerships with township women, with whom they may or may not have had emotional and sexual relationships. These women offered their labor and time, selling goods in the townships or on the docks during the day, and dock workers offered access to pilfered goods to sell and to a client base of their colleagues, *izinduna*, and white supervisors. The interviews provided several successful examples of such collaboration. These women were not strictly speaking part of dock workers' households, but they did contribute to the survival and reproduction of these households. However, two men took their commercial partners as their second wives, and another one gave her R400 when he retired from the city in 1976.[42] Mtukatshelwa Phewa, mentioned at the beginning of this chapter, teamed up with his aunt instead.

Selling pilfered goods did not take place only in Durban. The harbor was these workers' source of commercial opportunities, but invariably their eventual goal was to retire to their rural homes. To do this, they had to become independent from wage labor, and dock workers considered small-scale commercial enterprise to be their ticket out of wage dependence. Of course, a successful return to the rural home did not imply the restauration of a long-lost precapitalist peasant idyll. Their independence from wage labor was only achieved within a colonial capitalist order and by becoming small-scale entrepreneurs. These workers adapted to economic changes and used them to their own advantage, rather than solely resisting them.[43]

With the intention to eventually return there, a number of dock workers diversified their enterprises into the rural areas. Their businesses were in the end only the means to a rural goal. Establishing a rural business had two major advantages: it provided a ready source of income in their home area for when they retired from urban labor, and they could operate in the less competitive rural environment. Stores in rural areas were scarce, and people often had to make long journeys into town to buy what they needed. Profitable rural businesses, most commonly tea rooms and stores, enabled a number of interviewees to retire from dock work early. Wives, mothers, and other women in these households played a big role in these successes, just like township women did for urban businesses. Women sold fowl and produce from the land and the pilfered goods their husbands sent home. As these stores expanded, some workers bought goods in the city to sell at home, rather than just relying on pilferage. Such businesses also offered women some independence, as absent men had little insight into the day-to-day running of these operations. However, the success of these businesses was ultimately dependent on male employment on the docks.

All interviewees wanted to go back home and leave urban wage labor, but two clearly different strategies to reach that goal emerged. One strategy consisted of keeping one's head down and doubling up on shifts while minimizing their expenditures on everyday consumption.

This is in line with much of the literature on labor migration in southern Africa. The other strategy was more entrepreneurial than most of this literature allows for. Dock work offered something for both groups: good wages and the opportunity to frequently engage in overtime and weekend work, on the one hand, and commercial opportunities enabled by pilferage and the flexibility of *togt*, on the other. The former strategy, however, did not preclude a one-off deal. One interviewee received a number of guns from a white supervisor and sold them, and another received occasional shares of pilfered goods from supervisors and *izinduna*. Neither, however, pilfered habitually or built a business on selling pilfered goods.

The commercial strategy was not only more popular among the interviewed dock workers but also enabled them to become independent from wage labor more quickly. There was a clear correlation between having a business and retiring from the city early. Almost all interviewees who did not engage in commercial activities worked on the docks their whole adult life and retired in their old age. The majority of workers with a side business, however, retired from wage labor within fifteen years. Such short careers in urban wage labor were very unusual for Africans in the 1950s. By then, wage labor was no longer just a phase in life that enabled young men to marry and to establish their *imizi*; it had become a lifelong reality.[44]

Entrepreneurial Strategies

Dock workers' livelihoods were often more complex than a discussion of wage labor and the rural economy alone can express. The idea of a normative *umuzi* with one or more male members who are absent and remit wages does not capture the more complex relationships between migrants and their rural homesteads, between enterprising township women and dock workers, or between women in the rural areas and in the townships. Neither is the dock worker's household a working-class household forced by apartheid authorities to live in the Reserves, which over time developed into little more than rural slums.

Low wages and limited socioeconomic security or mobility persuaded some African workers to rely on their entrepreneurial skills to find other sources of income. In the absence of any form of social security, a little bad luck could suddenly change people's cash needs, their earning potential, and thus their livelihoods. When they got ill, workers had to become creative. When Madela Cebekulu could not work for a month, he explained, "I sent home for fowls and sold them in Durban. I used money that was over from my wages. I had eight lots of fowls but I did not know how much I made out of them. Sometimes there were fourteen to twenty fowls in a crate. I sometimes got £2.0.0. for a crate of fowls."[45] Since many of these additional sources of income were insecure and irregular, however, workers generally appreciated waged employment as a source of stability and regularity.

Historians of migrant labor in South Africa have often paid scant attention to these small-scale entrepreneurs. While Patrick Harries and Dunbar Moodie both acknowledge the presence of petty accumulators in mine compounds, they do not expand on this phenomenon.[46] In different contexts, African entrepreneurs have received more attention. Philip Bonner and Noor Nieftagodien note the sheer number of commercial and other businesses in Alexandra in the 1940s and explain how urban property ownership and entrepreneurialism were rooted in prior rural livelihoods. In an interesting reversal of the livelihoods studied here, these propertied commercial elites had their origins among the prosperous sharecroppers and better-off labor tenants expelled from white farms. They liquidated their rural assets and used their practical skills to invest in urban property and businesses.[47] Kas Maine, the sharecropper who is the subject of Charles van Onselen's *The Seed Is Mine*, was also as much an entrepreneur as a farm worker.

Iain Edwards writes about uMkhumbane (see chapter 1) as "an entrepreneur's paradise."[48] The petty traders in uMkhumbane may have had more in common with dock workers extending into trade than the better-capitalized property owners of Alexandra. They were often "not fully employed or unemployed" and were constantly on the lookout to supplement their incomes with new business ventures.[49] Other historians writing about African entrepreneurs have focused on female beer brewers.[50] Further studies of African small-scale trade have been largely confined to the literature on the informal economy, which tends to deal with a much later period. Moreover, these writings frequently discuss the informal economy in isolation from formal wage labor.[51] Little has been written on entrepreneurialism in the lives of migrant laborers.

The intersections between wage labor and small-scale business, however, have been discussed much more extensively in other parts of the continent. As was the case with Yoruba cocoa farmers in Nigeria, Frafra migrants in Accra, and porters in pre- and early colonial East Africa, commercial ventures were the most common side business for Durban's dock workers.[52] The three most popular commercial businesses were the selling of *dagga*, hawking cigarettes and other small consumption items, and selling pilfered food at home or in the townships, but there were some less common ventures as well. Some sold the chili peppers and peanuts their wives grew, and others raised chickens. There were some money lenders, and several dock workers sold stolen guns. It is no coincidence that the interviewees who sold guns all came from areas plagued by faction fights. They mostly sold these guns to their *abakhaya* for protection. Mdu Jama used his wages to repair his father's *bakkie*, and, as one of the few Africans with a car in his area, he earned good money providing transport. He supplemented these earnings by working weekends on the docks and selling bovine heads in the city. In later decades, some workers also invested in taxis. Renting out rooms, a popular strategy among both Indians and Africans with some capital in uMkhumbane,[53] was not common among dock workers. There were few dock workers who had a shack or house in Durban.

One of Keith Hart's Frafra informants in Accra talked about his time as an entrepreneur as "a time when he was free."[54] Our interviewees expressed very similar feelings about wage dependence. They experienced retiring to the land and becoming independent from their urban job as a liberation. The businesses that made this possible signified freedom from hard physical labor, poor working conditions, compound regulations, and municipal bylaws; these enabled an escape from an urban environment they did not enjoy and from abusive *izindunа* and supervisors. Being able to choose when and where to work, and not to work on a permanent basis, was also seen as a form of freedom. Mdu Jama and Mtukatshelwa Phewa, who cooperated in their business ventures, contemplated working as permanent laborers but agreed that the strict regulations that came with a contract and with living in a compound would limit their freedom and their ability to accumulate independently. They thus decided to remain casual workers.

Living in a compound, however, did not have to impede the running of a business. In fact, compounds were lively hubs of both legal and illegal African trade. Close to the Bell Street *togt* barracks was one of the Municipal Native Eating Houses where licensed African caterers and traders could rent stalls. Apart from twenty-four caterers and ten butchers, there were also eleven general traders and four grocers.[55] Only Africans were allowed to trade in these eating houses, as authorities enforced commercial segregation. An exception was made after the First World War but was quickly rescinded following protests from African stall holders. The Native Affairs and Police Committee was "of the opinion that the principle of allowing a European to trade in the

Native institutions is a wrong one."[56] In protesting the presence of a white competitor, the stall holders subscribed to this segregationist discourse and displayed an economic nationalism that would also characterize the New Africa movement in the 1940s: "This is a Native and not a whitemans [*sic*] market."[57]

Africans were running businesses in company compounds as well. They tended to work together in groups of three, so that one of them could go home without having to close their shop and risk losing their customer base. Compounds were opportune places to sell goods, as customers had limited alternatives.[58] Though such businesses were generally in contravention of compound regulations, they were frequently tolerated. Such tolerance was part of the moral economy of the compound, and occasional attempts to crack down on commercial activities were met with moral outrage from workers and traders alike. Some *izinduna* did not only tolerate these activities but also engaged in brewing and trading themselves. As such, they could make a profit and at the same time control the extent of the beer trade.[59]

In its constant struggle to control African workers and to prevent the emergence of alternatives to wage labor, the Durban municipality limited the legal scope of African trade.[60] Few licenses were awarded to Africans, and curbing unlicensed trade was a major preoccupation for authorities. The Victoria-Grey Street area, uMkhumbane, and the Point were the main centers of this illegal trade,[61] which many Africans did not consider illegitimate.[62] While attempts to limit African trade have at times been interpreted as ploys to limit competition for white entrepreneurs,[63] there were few if any white traders to protect in uMkhumbane or in African townships. The MNAD's own justification was that informal trade constituted "unfair competition" for licensed traders and that "overtrading" had to be prevented. Authorities favored a small orderly group of traders with "high standards" over chaotic markets with many minor traders in fierce competition.[64] These preferences reflected a general interest in control and order, as well as concerns about the informal income generating opportunities that facilitated African urban family life and allowed a degree of independence from wage labor. Such measures were also strongly gendered. Women were more likely to be involved in trade, especially beer brewing, but less likely to receive licenses. The mere presence of African women in the city, which was evidence of emergent urban family life, challenged the very core of the migrant labor system, which was built on the fiction that single men migrated on their own to remit wages to households that otherwise continued to reside in the rural areas.[65]

Commercial activities were thus central to the livelihoods of many dock workers. While there were some who doubled up on shifts and sent home as much of their wages as possible, the majority diversified their strategies. Those who had a business often did not have just one. The complex and multiple livelihoods highlighted by the sustainable livelihoods literature are thus nothing new. Doda Nxele sold *dagga* in the city and pilfered goods for his wife to sell in Msinga; later they opened a tea room. Sicelo Mbokazi's wife ran a tea room and a chicken farm at home, and he sold cigarettes and matches at work. These enterprises were never disconnected from their rural livelihoods. Zitha Xaba had one head of cattle named Salt and another named Beans, after the goods he pilfered and sold. These names symbolized the link between his commercial activities and the rural economy. Even investing in cattle, which is often seen as evidence of a conservative rural outlook, did not exclude commercial strategies. The rearing and selling of cattle itself could be a profitable business.

While the literature on southern African labor has been rather quiet on workers combining waged employment and small-scale enterprise, this is not the case in other parts of the continent.[66] The strategies of these dock workers were remarkably similar to those of civil servants in Kenya who "straddled" employment and private enterprise, to which Michael Cowen and Kabiru Kanyanjui have drawn our attention. These "straddlers" also used the resources that their wage labor offered, in this case comparatively good wages, to invest in small businesses and in agriculture.[67] Access to cargo and the flexibility of *togt* labor made dock work especially suitable for such strategies. These employee-entrepreneurs often diversified their activities because colonial restrictions kept them from achieving significant social mobility or security through wage labor or business alone.[68] Transport workers elsewhere on the continent have moved into business as well. Porters and drivers, for example, frequently became entrepreneurs.[69]

Chirwa argues that Malawian migrant workers investing in commercial fishing contributed to rural economic development.[70] It seems unlikely, however, that dock workers' side businesses had a similar developmental potential. These were mostly investments in the sphere of circulation rather than in production. These rural stores typically sold goods that were sourced from the city, and such commercial activities lacked a substantial economic multiplier effect. Legassick even argues that rural African traders used the uncompetitive and segregated rural context to commercially exploit other rural Africans.[71] It is thus not surprising that African traders often supported commercial segregation, a phenomenon I discuss in more detail in chapter 6. However, Legassick's assessment may be too harsh, as the socioeconomic difference between the rural African petty bourgeoisie and others was often small, just like between the lower-middle-class ICU leadership and African workers. Shula Marks and Richard Rathbone point out that these were frequently "the same people at different but often closely juxtaposed periods of their lives."[72]

This small-scale African trade would become known as the informal economy in later decades and has since attracted significant scholarly attention,[73] yet scholars of South Africa only picked up on this literature comparatively recently.[74] While this literature often treats the informal sector as a recent phenomenon and as one more or less separate from formal wage labor, small-scale commercial activity was already common among Durban's dock workers in the 1950s and should not be seen as somehow disconnected from their jobs on the docks. The literature on the informal economy thus fails to capture the complex livelihoods of these workers, as does much of the historiography on South African labor, which often ignores the petty accumulator side of their lives. Moreover, while there are certainly important similarities between small-scale trade then and now, there are also key differences. Much of the informal trade that takes place today is survivalist in nature.[75] However, dock workers in the 1950s, before the advent of mass unemployment, traded from a comparative position of strength: they had jobs and were paid better than most other African workers, and they often did not trade to survive but rather to accumulate enough capital to retire from urban wage labor. The literature on straddling may thus offer a more appropriate point of comparison than that on the informal economy.

Conclusion

These laborers were not only dock workers. For many, waged employment in the city was just one element in their more complex livelihoods. Thus, while they took pride in their hard and collective labor on the docks, being *onyathi* did not determine their identity. They were also traders, husbands, and rural men. Their economic activities were not fixed and did not determine their identity. Though their lives could certainly be tough and their options were constrained, they came closer than most of us to being able, as Marx and Engels envisioned, "to do one thing today and another tomorrow, to hunt in the morning, fish in the afternoon, rear cattle in the evening, criticise after dinner, just as I have a mind, without ever becoming hunter, fisherman, herdsman or critic."[76]

It was, however, dock labor that enabled other parts of their livelihoods. The relatively high wages, access to cargoes, and the flexibility to work extra shifts or to spend time on a side business afforded dock workers a certain agency. Their employment enabled them to choose between different livelihood strategies, and a good number of workers managed to withdraw their labor relatively quickly and to become independent from wage income. It is important, however, not to romanticize this agency. The context for these livelihoods is a period of rural impoverishment that reduced the options available to African migrants and made alternatives to wage labor more precarious. Not only were rural conditions changing; the urban labor market underwent a transformation as well. Both Maynard Swanson and Keletso Atkins attribute the strong bargaining position of laborers in Durban largely to the *togt* system.[77] Authorities and employers struggled for a century to eliminate this form of labor, or at least to curb its comparatively privileged position in the labor market. They finally managed to eliminate *togt* labor after the 1959 strikes by establishing a labor pool based on monopoly hiring.

While the abolition of *togt* certainly offered some advantages for workers, most importantly by mitigating the insecurity of casual labor, it also closed off many opportunities that enabled these different strategies. Monopoly hiring decreased workers' bargaining power, and stricter controls over their movements, activities, and use of time limited the flexibility that dock work offered to engage in other enterprises. From the 1970s onward containerization also reduced the opportunities to pilfer. The petty accumulator strategy thus became less feasible for dock workers. These changes painfully illustrate the precariousness of the strategies discussed in this chapter.

The livelihoods of dock workers' households revolved around three spheres of production and consumption: the rural Reserves or white commercial farms where the women raised families, grew crops, sold pilfered foods and produce, and where cattle was raised; the docks where men earned wages and pilfered cargoes; and the compounds and townships where both dock workers and urban women ran small businesses. Of course, township women were not always part of this picture. Wolpe and Legassick both argue, with good reason, that the rural sphere subsidized urban labor; others have also argued that the informal economy today subsidizes cheap labor as much as the Reserve economy once did.[78] Some scholars are therefore uncomfortable with the emphasis on agency and the management of household assets in much of the literature on the informal economy and livelihoods—a focus that too easily creates the perception that the poor are pulling themselves up by their bootstraps.[79]

The argument of a Reserve subsidy is valuable insofar as it is true that these laborers could be paid less than the cost of the reproduction of their labor because their households continued to stave off complete proletarianization. However, the lives of these dock workers suggest a more complex relationship among the three nodes of their households. While commercial enterprise, Reserve agriculture, and pastoralism did indeed make it possible for laborers to survive on otherwise insufficient wages, this was not a one-directional subsidy. Dock labor also subsidized the rural homestead, as well as some female-headed households in the townships.[80] Moreover, dock labor made these commercial activities possible. To the extent that workers managed to leave the labor market as a result of these strategies, they cannot be seen as mere victims of a system of "articulation of modes of production"[81] in which the noncapitalist economy is preserved so that it could subsidize migrant wages. The withdrawal of labor was a common form of resistance to forced proletarianization and poor working conditions throughout the continent.[82] Such withdrawals added to the regular labor shortages that dock employers experienced and thus constituted an upward pressure on wages as well. These strategies can be read both as a form of informal resistance and as a subsidy to wages, as even those who managed to leave the labor market early subsidized their own wages while they worked on the docks. These workers went through a phase of intense self-exploitation before they could retire to the rural areas.

In this chapter, I started to explain the idiosyncratic mix of working-class action and mobilization in support of the interests of small-scale African traders. It should not be surprising that the political strategies of Durban's dock workers reflected the fact that petty entrepreneurialism played an important role in their livelihoods. Nevertheless, this does not make them into an African petty bourgeoisie. For most, their businesses represented only part of their livelihoods, and their interests as workers were equally important to them.

3

Work and Life between the City and the Countryside

Velile Goba started working on the docks at a more mature age than did most dock workers. He was twenty-nine when he first came to Durban in 1954. His father's *umuzi* in uMzimkhulu was largely self-sufficient, and there was thus no urgent need for him to supplement the homestead's income. However, he wanted to have his own money and be independent from his father. His uncle asked an *induna* to hire him as a stevedore. He was also offered the option of working as a domestic laborer in the house of one of the white supervisors on the docks, but he preferred the much better-paid dock work. He lived and ate in the compound and could thus save most of his wages. Moreover, his mother and his wife grew chili peppers at home, and he sold these on the docks. Later on, he also started selling cigarettes after his customers asked for them, but he never expanded his trade into the rural areas.

Saving most of his wages and earning some money on the side eventually allowed Velile Goba to pay *ilobolo* and to establish his own *umuzi*. His wife continued to grow some produce on their land but not enough for the household to live off. Nevertheless, he always remained committed to returning to his rural homestead. He had no interest in city women and did not extensively socialize in Durban, not even with his *abakhaya*. All his time was taken up by either working on the ships or hawking his goods. He did manage to go home every few weeks, and he socialized there: he went to parties, drank beer, ate meat, and danced. He continued to work on the docks for more than thirty-five years until 1990, when he was sixty-five. He did not want his sons to follow in his footsteps, as dock work was too grueling and too dangerous, and many *izinduna* used abusive language. He therefore made sure that they could go to school and land a better job.

As Velile Goba asserted, dock labor was and, despite many improvements in workplace safety, remains arduous and unsafe. Common experiences of exploitation and (both physical and socioeconomic) insecurity, as well as the use of work gangs, engendered among workers a sense of solidarity rooted in the workplace. Nevertheless, it would be too simple to conclude that this resulted in an uncomplicated working-class consciousness. There were intricate links between the rural and the urban livelihoods of Velile Goba and many other dock workers. Their wage labor on the docks was only part of their lives and livelihoods, and racial discrimination and repression in the city shaped their identities as well. This chapter discusses their living and working conditions in the city as well as the connections between their urban labor and rural livelihoods.

Working Conditions

Being a dock worker was not an easy job, as this short excerpt from Tina Sideris illustrates:

> There are lots of things pressing down on the workers at the docks. The work is heavy and very dangerous. The pay is low. Foreman [*sic*] swear at workers and treat them badly. And after a long day's work the men can't go home to rest.
>
> Their families live far away in the countryside. So the workers go back to the compounds. The compounds are not like home. The beds are hard. There are no children playing. There are no women. And the food is bad.
>
> But the dockworkers don't just sit and feel sorry for themselves. They are brave fighters. They have fought many times for the things all workers want—more money, shorter hours and a little bit of freedom.[1]

Among the many issues workers faced were the dangers of working on the docks; injuries were indeed a common occurrence, and "sometimes people died. It is so dangerous there."[2] Consequently, many dock workers did not want their sons to follow in their footsteps; dock labor was too hazardous. Zwelinjani Sithole was injured on duty in 1963 and thus forced to retire; Thoko Mlaba's husband was killed on the job. Several leaders of the 1958 and 1959 strikes also died on the job a few years later.[3] The workers interviewed by Sideris were equally aware of the dangers of working on the docks, and one even had the scars to prove it. Falling to his death, however, was what really scared Mr. Delwa: "It was the time when steamships used coal as fuel. . . . Our job was the adding of coal to the ships. We used to run on a plank carrying baskets full of coal. If you didn't know that the plank was rotten and you walked on it, then you fell on the ground and died."[4] In 1958, the prominent trade unionist Moses Mabhida noted that dock work was "constantly endangering the lives of employees."[5]

Not only was dock work dangerous; it was also heavy and arduous: "The vests we wore got old after one week of work because we sweated so much. Everyday we took off our vests. We had to squeeze out the water," Mr. Mkhwanazi explained.[6] Workers loaded and unloaded cargoes by hand and had to cope with temperatures that could easily reach 100°F or more in the hold. However, workers had each other's backs. They would go easy on somebody who was exhausted or in pain, and they looked out for each other's safety, regardless of the origins of the workers.[7] Furthermore, some cargoes, like sulfur or urea, could irritate their skin and eyes, but employers generally did not provide protective clothing or safety glasses. Instead, workers brought a bottle of milk to wash their eyes out. Strains and hernias were common work-related injuries.[8] In the early twentieth century, not even children escaped these harsh conditions, as William Beinart recounts: "Child labourers from the Transkei were used for coal loading in the Durban docks in the early 1920s, running up steep gang planks with baskets of coal. These 'Grimy Imps of the Wharfside,' some 'mere picannins of 12,' were presented as 'grubby but happy' and their employment justified on the grounds of their 'extraordinary agility.'"[9] However, there is no indication that the use of child labor was still prevalent in the 1950s.

The exhausting day of dock laborers started early. They would get up as early as 4:30 a.m. to be ready for hiring, which took place at 6 a.m. at SAR&H and at 6:30 a.m. at most major stevedoring companies.[10] Particularly those workers who did not live at the Point had to wake up early, as they had to take a bus or walk to the harbor. The hiring process was hectic and stressful. Large numbers of workers were trying to grab the attention of the *izinduna*, which often involved pushing and shoving; managing to stand out in this chaos could make the difference between having a job for the day or not. Having a good relationship with the *izinduna* could also take some of the insecurity and stress out of this process.[11] Work generally started at 7 a.m. and continued until noon, when there was a one hour break for lunch. They resumed work at 1 p.m. and worked until 5 p.m. At five, there was a two-hour dinner break before overtime started, which lasted until 11 p.m., six hours or less before they would have to be up again.[12] Within this time, a work gang would have lifted and moved many tons of cargo. Working overtime was in theory voluntary, but when stevedoring laborers boycotted overtime in April 1958 their employers, organized in the Durban Stevedores' Association, tried to evict them from the company compounds.[13] Most dock workers toiled for nine or even up to thirteen hours per day, but some would only work overtime shifts. These workers took advantage of the attractive wage rates for overtime and of the fact that the regulations requiring *togt* registration badges were seldom enforced. They would work their regular job in town during the day and then make their way to the docks in time for night shift hiring. Others only worked weekends and went back home on Monday.

The work rhythm became even more extreme during the Second World War, when a blackout to prevent air raids restricted the use of artificial light after sundown; this, of course, shortened the workday. At the same time the large number of ships berthing in Durban, including many involved in the war effort, made it impossible to abolish overtime. Instead, workers' dinner break was eliminated to make as much use of daylight as possible. Dock workers were thus required to work continuously from 1 to 9 p.m. after having labored for five hours before noon.[14] Moreover, when hungry workers came off the job at 9 p.m., the caterers at the Native Eating House were closed per local bylaws.[15] Rather than granting the workers a break, the bylaws were amended to allow caterers to stay open longer. Work patterns changed in 1959 when around-the-clock operations were introduced in the Durban harbor.

The long hours left little time to rest one's tired and aching body; recuperating from the hard work could thus be difficult. *Togt* laborers could cope with the pace of work by taking a day off to recover whenever necessary. Some workers did not take up offers of permanent employment because they found dock work too demanding to make a full-time commitment.[16] Zulu Phungula told employers and authorities that he seldom worked overtime, because he was already too tired after the regular shift.[17] The phasing out of casual labor in 1959 curbed this freedom to take time off.

Stevedoring work in Durban was performed in a similar fashion as in other ports around the world before containerization.[18] Central to this process was the work gang, which was led by an intermediary—in Durban this was an *induna*. A white supervisor, in turn, was in charge of all the gangs on one ship. Most of the cargo handled in Durban was break-bulk transported in bags, boxes, drums, or as individual items. Gangs of eight to sixteen stevedores would work in the hold, though unloading generally requires fewer workers than loading. The cargo was lifted and put into nets by hand when unloading, or taken from the nets and carefully stacked in the hold when loading. The latter had to happen in such a way that the stacks were stable and the weight distributed evenly. Bad weight distribution or unstable stacking could make the ship roll or even capsize. The skills and experience of stevedores were thus essential to the work process. Hiring unskilled or inexperienced workers could lead to accidents, unsafely stacked goods, damaged cargo, and poor weight distribution.

Two types of stevedores were not part of these work gangs but worked closely with them: the gangway and winch men. The winch men handled the mechanical winches that lifted the nets with cargoes in and out of the hold. If cranes rather than winches were used, these were generally operated by white workers. Gangway men used recognized signals to coordinate the activities of the winch men and the work gangs. They bore significant responsibility: poor timing or bad positioning could result in damaged cargoes or even injuries. The experience of the winch and gangway men were crucial. Despite this obvious value of skills and experience, employers both in Durban and around the world considered stevedores to be unskilled and thus easily replaceable.[19] Moreover, formal training was nonexistent, even for winch and gangway men. Workers learned on the job; the *induna* would show what to do, and others would learn by example.[20]

On the wharves, there were similar gangs of African laborers offloading the nets onto carts, railway carriages, or forklifts, or loading the goods from these onto the nets. These dock workers were employed by the SAR&H. Bulk cargoes, like grain, sugar, coal, or oil, were usually loaded mechanically through the bunkering facilities at the Bluff and the grain elevators at Maydon Wharf, though small amounts of coal were still bunkered manually into the 1950s. When finishing the unloading of bulk cargoes, however, there would always be a remainder that could be removed only by hand.

Common experiences of oppression, irregular and uncertain work opportunities, and brutal working conditions fostered solidarity. Working in gangs also had that effect, although *izinduna* did not hire existing gangs as happened in some ports; rather, they formed new gangs during hiring each morning. The dangers of the job meant that workers had to look out for each other's safety and cooperate. Moreover, wage differences between regular workers and gangway or winch men were small, which allowed these distinct groups of workers to identify more closely with each other. A stevedore in Durban in 1959 earned

14s per day, gangway and winch men took home 16s 6d; even an *induna* took home only 19s.[21] These numbers, however, reflected a recent wage increase for *izinduna* without a similar increase for other workers. This unequal treatment was among the reasons for the 1959 work stoppages.[22] In the relatively egalitarian and solidary context of the work gang, workers did not accept significant differences in pay.

These protests did not mean that the relations between workers and *izinduna* were necessarily antagonistic. At the same time acting as labor brokers, laborers, and supervisors, these intermediaries were both allies for the workers and instruments of social control and discipline in the workplace. They had to be both: they had to exercise their authority over workers to get the job done and thus to maintain their legitimacy in the eyes of the employer, but to do so they also had to gain and retain the trust and respect of the workers. Otherwise, the laborers could retaliate with go-slows or even walk away from the job. As such, *izinduna* would often stand up for the workers or avoid pushing them too harshly. They would also hire people they knew, often relatives and *abakhaya*, which reinforced existing hiring patterns.[23] Hiring relatives and *abakhaya* came with a mutual sense of responsibility and facilitated discipline, though *izinduna* were not shy about using strong language to assert their authority either.[24] Around the world, dock labor was thus often dominated by one group of workers, and Durban was no different.[25] In Durban, isiZulu speakers dominated the sector. Of course, while hiring one's own played an important role in creating such a homogenous workforce, the geographic location of the port did too. In the mid-1950s more than 90 percent of all African dock workers were Zulu, and among stevedores this predominance was even greater.[26]

Izinduna would often allow minor breaches of discipline, such as petty theft, absenteeism, and a certain amount of slacking off. The latter was important for workers to recuperate. They were also frequently engaged in pilferage themselves. That *izinduna* tolerated certain actions came to be expected and was part of a set of mutually accepted but unwritten rules that governed the workplace and the compounds, a moral economy of the docks. When these rules were broken, workers would fiercely defend them. Dock workers started their 1929 beer hall boycott after a conflict over the brewing of *mahewu* in the municipal compound, something that was against compound regulations but generally tolerated and understood by the workers to be acceptable. In 1956, workers at the Consolidated Stevedoring & Forwarding Agency struck when an *induna* disallowed an engagement ceremony that would have brought outsiders into the compound.[27] Workers considered these actions breaches of the moral economy of the compounds, that is, breaches of the mutual expectations among *izinduna*, employers, and laborers.

Though it was a tough job, dock work did have its advantages, and workers took pride in being *onyathi*. Dock workers were paid more than most unschooled African laborers in Durban. However, African wages in Durban, including those for stevedores, were significantly lower than those in other major South African centers of employment. In the early 1930s average African wages were lower only in Pretoria.[28] By the 1940s, Durban's stevedores earned half of those in Cape Town, and while the gap had narrowed by 1959, they still earned about 20 percent less.[29] These low wages were partially the result of the overwhelming migratory nature of Durban's African labor force. There were fewer African families living in Durban than in other cities, and wage labor was thus mostly performed by migrating men. Even domestic labor continued to be the preserve of young African men. The low percentage of permanent urban residence among African workers guaranteed the continued Reserve subsidy of their wages.[30]

The generally migratory nature of Durban's workforce also resulted in a very casual and transitory labor market, one where few African workers stayed in the same job for a long time. Many workers engaged in so-called job hopping.[31] Commissioner Broome, appointed in 1947 "to enquire into the legitimate needs and grievances of the Native population in the City of Durban," considered Durban's entire labor supply to resemble a huge casual market.[32] While *togt* workers often appreciated the flexibility and independence that casual labor offered them, the bargaining power that came from being able to walk away from a job and from daily competition for one's labor was greatly reduced when labor shortages turned into a permanent labor surplus. Disciplining casual labor remained difficult, however, as the sanction of the sack had limited effect. A *togt* laborer had little to lose in a strike or by breaking the rules of the workplace, except for one day's pay. Even when striking dock workers were purportedly replaced by fresh workers untainted by radical ideas, the outsourcing of hiring to African intermediaries meant that employers did not have enough control over this process to ensure that strikers would not just be rehired. It was therefore possible for the casual stevedores interviewed for this book still to be employed on the docks in the 1960s, although they were in theory all replaced in April 1959.[33]

During the 1940s and 1950s, employers and authorities slowly came to realize that casual migrant labor had drawbacks for them as well. It was at this time that they cautiously started to experiment with transforming the port's labor regime. As early as 1937, the mayor of Durban acknowledged that the instability of labor, that is, the frequent changing of jobs, was very inefficient. He pleaded for the establishment of labor bureaus that could place Africans in jobs for which they had already acquired some skills.[34] The Durban Stevedores' Association, South African Conference Lines, and the Natal Employers' Association informed the Native Administration Committee in 1950 that they were willing to establish a labor pool but that the workers were not willing to accept permanent positions.[35] These hesitant openings to the possibility of a stable urbanized working class were in line with similar developments throughout the continent. After the Second World War, both Britain and France explored new approaches to labor and social policy in their African colonies. Their concerns were usually very similar: the inefficiency of migrant labor, strikes, disorder, and the growth of informal settlements.[36]

The lack of socioeconomic differentiation among African workers facilitated solidarity. Some officials believed that a more stratified and stabilized workforce could break up such solidarity. A range of commission reports exemplified this new thinking about African labor and urbanization. The 1947–48 Broome Commission concluded that a more stable labor force was needed to deal with the problems of urban housing and social disorder.[37] Earlier that decade the Smit Committee argued that African urbanization was a reality that could not be undone and that poor and unemployed Africans should be accommodated in the cities rather than sent back to the rural areas. Its report further recommended that African trade unions should be allowed to register and that African workers should be recognized as employees, albeit still with restricted rights, rather than as servants. This represented a significant departure in the official discourse on African labor and urbanization. The report even challenged the idea that the Reserve subsidy justified low African wages; it argued that "the claim that the remuneration of the country dweller should be lower can only be sustained if it is considered equitable that industry should accept what would amount to a subsidy from the employee fortunate enough to possess private resources, a frankly untenable position. There is the further difficulty that were differential wages fixed for townsmen and countrymen, married and single, employers would very naturally favour the 'unspoiled' newcomer from the country."[38]

This openness to policy reforms came at a time of urban crisis caused by a large influx of Africans into the cities during the Second

World War. In 1948, an important change in policy was enacted with the introduction of contribution-based unemployment insurance that, on paper, did not exclude Africans. This was unacceptable to many who refused to relinquish the idea that Africans had free social security in the rural areas in the form of kin and land. Newspapers were bombarded with accounts of Africans supposedly abusing the insurance and inviting dismissal, preferring to live off unemployment benefits rather than working.[39] As tends to be the case with such accounts, most were heavily exaggerated or plainly incorrect. In reality, few Africans could enjoy the benefits of the jobseeker's allowance, and access was further restricted in the next few years.[40]

As the wartime crisis waned, these reforms took a back seat and were eventually dropped from official discourse in South Africa. Elsewhere on the continent, however, labor stabilization, urbanization, and fostering so-called responsible trade unionism were increasingly the guiding policies.[41] Through organizations like the South African Institute of Race Relations, white liberal intellectuals in South Africa continued to advocate for labor stabilization and for improved public services for urban Africans. After the 1948 National Party victory, however, stabilization and orderly urbanization were dropped from official policy discourse. Instead of liberalization, African workers faced further restrictions of urban residency, increasingly draconian pass laws, and forced resettlement in the Reserves under the new apartheid regime. Apartheid policy was characterized by both continuity and change. Many of the National Party's policies were continuations from the preceding segregationist era, yet the hesitant openings to more liberal policies were closed off. It would take several more decades before African trade unions were recognized, influx controls lifted, and social security and welfare extended to African workers.[42]

Even if there was little change in overall labor policies, for Durban's stevedores the labor regime did change dramatically in the late 1950s. This too was in line with changes taking place in ports throughout Africa and the world.[43] Casual labor was replaced by a labor pool in which a rotation system guaranteed the spread of employment opportunities. A hiring monopoly under the DSLSC was established in 1959, eliminating the bargaining power and flexibility of *togt* labor. These changes limited the supply of labor and increased the disciplinary powers of the employer, effectively ending a period of dock worker militancy and heralding a silent decade of successful repression. While a labor pool had certain advantages for African workers—for example, it limited the variability of their earnings—the most notable effects of monopoly hiring were the stifling of militancy and increased control over the labor force. The formation of the DSLSC suited apartheid policies, as the new company increasingly recruited laborers directly from the rural areas. It gradually reduced the share of urban workers in the pool and thus reinforced the migrant labor system.[44]

Living Conditions

Most dock workers lived in one of the company compounds at the Point or in the municipal Bell Street *togt* barracks. These were some of the few places where they could legally stay in town. Those who slept in company compounds were either permanent workers or casual laborers who had to offer their services to that company first; only if the company that housed them did not need their labor could they look for a job elsewhere. *Togt* workers in the Bell Street barracks could offer their labor to any employer. These accommodations were very uncomfortable and even unsafe, which was hardly a new problem. In 1911 Durban's chief constable called the SAR&H compound "by no means attractive" and added that "there are no windows, and the buildings are low and uncomfortable and in summer time the heat is very great and it must be impossible for Natives to rest properly in comfort." The building had received a negative review from the medical officer of health as well.[45]

Accommodation for African workers throughout the city was generally of poor quality, and by the early 1940s the state of the Bell Street *togt* barracks had become a source of official concern. The Smit Committee had been "unfavourably impressed by some of those [housing schemes] seen, notably the Bell Street Compound at Durban, which was over-crowded, dirty, and quite unfit for the purpose for which it was being used."[46] Nevertheless, it took until the end of that decade before the city council started to take these concerns seriously. The acting manager of the MNAD described the condition of these barracks again in 1948: "This accommodation is in a deplorable condition, and unless completely renovated in the immediate future, will cause loss of human life to inmates. It is definitely *not fit for human habitation*."[47] In fact, eighteen of the nineteen buildings at Bell Street had been condemned years earlier.

Yet immediate action was still not taken. Only the following year did officials start to vacate those buildings that were in the worst condition. They no longer admitted new residents, and beds falling vacant in the worst buildings were left unoccupied; unoccupied beds in other buildings were assigned to the residents of the vacated structures. Authorities also took temporary measures to strengthen the remaining buildings.[48] By August 1949, seven years after the Smit report was published, the most dilapidated buildings were closed, but no new barracks had been built to compensate for the lost capacity.[49]

Workers could rent a bed by the month or by the day in these unpleasant dwellings, or their accommodation could be free if it was employer provided. However, many compounds were so overcrowded that even floor space was rented out. The actual beds were nothing more than wooden boards, which workers made a bit more comfortable by sleeping on top of multiple blankets. There could be as many as thirty people in a single room, and in some compounds people had to move sideways between the beds and the walls. With so many people sleeping in these poorly ventilated buildings, the rooms quickly smelled of sweat, and the air turned stale. Getting a good night's sleep was difficult, as there was almost constant noise; those who worked overtime tended to arrive after 11 p.m., and the first workers would get up before 5 a.m. There was thus very little quiet time. Moreover, the bathrooms lacked privacy and were often inadequate for the number of people living there. With so many workers using these facilities, they never remained sanitary for very long.[50] These crowded and confined spaces created an unhealthy living environment for *togt* workers, which was exacerbated by poor air circulation and unhygienic conditions. Such living arrangements undoubtedly contributed to many workers becoming ill.

Life in the compounds was also heavily regulated. While these were not closed compounds, they did serve to police the lives of workers off the job. The "inmates," as officials and employers called the workers living in the compounds, found regulations disallowing visits from women and outsiders especially burdensome. A worker's wife could legally visit him only after he had been in Durban for two years and even then only when there was municipal accommodation for women available, which was seldom the case.[51] Even outside the compounds Africans were constricted by a plethora of regulations, such as curfews, pass laws, the city's brewing monopoly, and more. African workers' leisure time was thus constantly policed, and complaints about police harassment were common.[52] Of course, many of these regulations were also habitually ignored.

Many African workers in Durban cooked for themselves to save some money, but dock workers had limited time to do so when they worked overtime. Therefore, the Native Eating House on Bell Street, which catered mostly to dock laborers, had comparatively more caterers than did the eating houses in other parts of the city. There were also more butchers, which was possibly an indication that workers at the Point, who were usually engaged in demanding physical labor, preferred protein-rich food. Offal in particular was an important part of their diets.[53] Workers staying in company compounds usually received rations, but these meals were not always palatable. Sometimes, they would refuse to eat the free food and spend their own money to buy another meal instead.[54] Indeed, the living conditions of dock workers were often such that, as Zulu Phungula pointed out, "even strangers and soldiers coming from other countries are surprised at the state of affairs when they see how we are starving."[55]

Not all dock workers lived in the compounds, however. Some workers refused to live there, and others could not find a free bed. Several interviewees lived on the verandas of sheds at the Point or in nearby parks, though most of those workers spent only limited time in dock labor. Others lived in informal settlements or in the early townships, where life was not as closely policed as it was, at least in theory, in the compounds.[56] With a significant number of dock workers living with other African and Indian workers in informal settlements and townships, they were not particularly isolated from the rest of the working class. Such supposed isolation has been cited as a cause for the strike-prone nature of dock labor globally but did not seem to play an important role in Durban.[57]

There were of course also advantages to living in the compounds, especially if one received free food. Workers who did not have to spend their own wages on food could save a significant amount of money and could thus send a larger portion of their wages home or invest the money in cattle or a business venture. Others achieved the same goal by living outside and by eating pilfered food. Rent and basic needs in the city were expensive and consumed a significant portion of the migrants' earnings.[58] Moreover, living in a compound could also be a way to shield oneself from the expenses and the corrupting influences of urban life. Such incapsulation served to keep migrants from becoming absconders, people who no longer return home, abandon their homestead, and stop sending remittances. Some workers would actively avoid spending money in the city; they socialized mostly with their *abakhaya* and steered clear of getting involved with urban women who could divert their wages and lure them away from their rural families. Compounds allowed workers to save their money and to avoid getting dragged into an expensive urban lifestyle.[59]

Most dock workers in Durban, however, did not specifically limit their interactions to *abakhaya*, and a number had relationships with urban women. Even if some workers preferred the isolation and savings of living in the compound, almost all still visited the municipal beer halls, townships, and informal settlements. Especially on weekends they would seek out the festive atmosphere of uMkhumbane to drink and dance.[60] The more "respectable" leisure activities that were often organized and encouraged by the MNAD, including going to films and concerts, playing soccer, or *ingoma* dance competitions, were not mentioned by the interviewees.[61] Drinking beer was the most important way to socialize and relax, and it was not unusual for dock workers to drink the low-alcohol *utshwala* between the regular and the overtime shift. Nevertheless, the majority of interviewees also remarked that they preferred rural life over city life.

Workers could legally buy and consume beer only in the municipal beer halls, where it was brewed under municipal monopoly, but they could also go to the outskirts of town where African women brewed it illegally. The livelihoods of urban African women were particularly insecure, as they had limited legal income-earning opportunities and their relationships with men were often unstable. A relationship with an employed man could provide a regular source of income, but few men would consider city women as potential wives. Even if they were in a stable relationship, the income of the male "breadwinner" could be insecure as well and was seldom sufficient to feed a family.[62] Women thus had to find independent sources of income, which often meant brewing and selling beer. This brought them into conflict with the police. For although brewing was a task traditionally performed by women, in the city it was against the law. Brewing was nevertheless the lynchpin of the African informal economy and of urban working-class culture, and it was central to the livelihoods of many urban African women and families.[63] Moreover, having access to a source of income independently from a man afforded these women certain status and freedom.

To manage the insecurities of urban life, women increasingly formed female-linked families structured around grandmothers, sisters, cohabitating women, mothers and daughters, and so on, rather than around a male homestead head. This alternative to normative marriage came about in a context where men found it increasingly difficult to provide *ilobolo* for marriage or to act as providers. Women thus found new sources of domestic support and income.[64] People also relied on the metaphysical to deal with the difficulties and dangers of city life; they visited *izangoma* (diviners, sing. *isangoma*) and *izinyanga* (traditional healers or herbalists, sing. *inyanga*) or joined urban churches.[65]

Land and Labor

Frederick Cooper notes the intricate social and economic connections between the rural and urban lives of dock workers in Mombasa: "What officials called casualism was, for workers, part of a complex web of social relations and culture connecting workplace, urban residence, and farms."[66] Similar observations are appropriate for Durban's dock laborers as well. Indeed, the sharp dichotomy that is sometimes assumed between the city and the countryside, with one representing modernity and the other tradition or backwardness, needs to be qualified. While these workers spent much of their time on the wharves and in the holds of ships, they still considered the rural *imizi* to be their true homes and aspired to return to live there as *abanumzane*. In Durban, they had no power, and their lives were closely policed; they worked hard for very little money and lived in often deplorable circumstances away from their family and kin. It was often difficult for them to create a sense of belonging in the city. In the rural areas, they could feel at home and gain authority and respect by becoming homestead heads. This rural life was more than an idyllic dream, as most dock workers went home relatively often compared to migrants to the Rand. Moreover, their land in the Reserves, which was generally cultivated by their wives or mothers, did contribute to the households' livelihoods, and dock laborers continued to invest their wages in both agriculture and cattle.[67]

Most dock workers went home once every few weeks or at least once every few months. Mzo Mzongo explained that "people who worked in Durban visited usually once a month, those from Jo'burg only once per year." This was possible because Durban was closer for most workers, which was considered a major advantage of working in the port city. Even permanent workers would regularly go home over the weekend, and some casual workers would alternately spend two or three weeks in Durban and two or three weeks at home. The freedom of *togt* labor made this possible. Doda Nxele "was working as a casual worker. Therefore, nothing forced me to be at work all the time." Workers who lived farther away, for example, in the Eastern Cape, tended to visit home less frequently.

When migrants arrived home, they expected their wives to brew them beer: "In our culture, when your wife knows that you are coming, she must make beer. When you come home, your neighbors come by to greet you. Then you bring an *ukhamba* (clay pot) full of beer, share it with them, and socialize together."[68] Though their time at home would often be busy with ploughing and making repairs, the interviewees mostly recalled their socializing. They remembered drinking beer, dancing, visiting friends and kin, and participating in ceremonies for which livestock was sacrificed.

While the men would generally help out with cultivation when they were home, most of the agricultural labor fell on the shoulders of women and youth. Labor was spread thin in agriculture, and yields suffered if ploughing could not be done at the ideal time, weeding was not done systematically, or there were not enough people scaring away the birds. Moreover, some women were reluctant to make decisions about investments without the consent of their absent husbands, which could stifle agricultural innovation. Some men insisted on their prerogative to make decisions in the household, including those regarding agriculture, though most acknowledged that women were the actual cultivators and were allowed to make decisions about the day-to-day running of the household and about agriculture. Some also left their mother in charge of such decisions, which could lead to tensions between wives and their mothers-in-law.[69] Regarding investments for which cash was needed, however, most men insisted that only they could make decisions.

It was through marriage that households gained access to agricultural land in the Reserves. However, when a couple married, the wife would at first move in with her husband and in-laws. Only when they had accumulated sufficient resources and secured access to land could they establish their own homestead and become independent. The communally owned Reserve land was allocated by the *induna*, who is in this context not a gang leader on the docks but the local headman and deputy of the chief. The allocated land would normally consist of a site for the homestead itself, a small plot nearby (*izala*), a small garden for vegetables (*isife*), and a main field (*insimu*). If a homestead had multiple wives, the same plots would be available for each wife. Homesteads also had access to grazing commonage. As Reserves were increasingly overcrowded, however, most *imizi* did not receive enough land to be able to live off.[70] This shortage benefited the *izinduna* in charge of allocation. Well aware that the demand for land exceeded the availability, many demanded bribes in return for allocating a plot or accumulated land themselves to rent out. This newfound importance could also solidify political support in their power struggles with chiefs, as people tended to support those who could give them access to land.[71]

Having multiple fields helped families make it through the year, as people planted different fields at different times. The *izife* (plural of *isife*) were planted in September and yielded the first crops by December, mostly vegetables. These early crops carried the family to the main harvest. The main fields were ploughed and planted in October and November but would yield only in March, or later if they were planted with sorghum. August was the month in which there was the least agricultural work to be done. Throughout the first half of the twentieth century, migration patterns reflected this seasonal pattern. More African migrants offered their labor in the cities during the winter months and especially August, when their labor was not needed on the land, and workers continued to leave urban employment during the ploughing and harvest seasons.[72] Reserve agriculture thus continued to be important enough to leave wage employment for, but by the 1960s this pattern became significantly less pronounced.[73] This is in line with Charles Simkins's observations that the extension of influx controls in the mid-1950s was the real turning point for the productivity of Reserve agriculture.[74]

Despite the declining returns of Reserve agriculture, dock workers thus continued to invest in cultivation. Another important avenue for investment was cattle and other livestock, which was often purchased with the proceeds of *stokvels*, as discussed in chapter 2. There where land shortages were less acute the cattle economy fared better in the first half of the twentieth century than Reserve agriculture did, as it was less labor intensive and thus more suitable for a society where the out-migration of men caused labor shortages.[75] The herding labor it did require was traditionally performed by young boys.

One important reason for young dock workers to invest in cattle was to be able to marry. Marriage was expensive; the cost included not only *ilobolo* but also numerous *izibizo* gifts offered during the negotiations with the bride's family. Yet marriage through *ukulobola* was also an investment in affines and as such in a social support network.[76] The relationship with affines and even kin is ultimately a social rather than a biological one, and the institution of marriage does not involve merely the married couple. The circulation of cattle builds and maintains these relationships. Studying livelihoods is therefore not just a matter of studying how physical and material subsistence is guaranteed; the lineage too needs to be reproduced. The latter could only be done through the exchange of cattle.[77] As such, a head of cattle is worth more than its monetary exchange value or the milk it produces; it is not simply subject to a formal and reductionist market valuation.

Indeed, the aphorism that "money has no calves" not only refers to the fact that cattle is a form of self-reproducing capital but also that cash money cannot be seen or loaned out. The visibility of cattle allowed absent migrants to maintain a presence and a tangible stake in rural society, and the loaning out of cattle to poor rural dwellers, or *ukusisa,* established clientelistic relationships. Money does not serve the same social function as cattle does. By investing in cattle migrants not only staked their claim in rural society but also did their part to reproduce a rural patriarchy in which they, as men, could one day become respected *abanumzane.*

The ultimate goal of building a rural patriarchal homestead was to retire on the land once the homestead was built up and one's sons were old enough to find wage labor themselves. However, the ideal of early retirement, where labor migration was only a stage in the life of a young African man to help him gain economic independence, had mostly become a myth by midcentury.[78] The Reserves could no longer act as a form of social security as they once did, offering subsistence for the elderly, the sick, and the young. Nevertheless, workers kept returning to their land in their old age for at least two reasons, even if that retirement now came much later. Firstly, they had no security in the city and very limited opportunities to acquire property. Thus, they would need a continuing source of cash income to pay rent. Secondly, there was a general antiurban sentiment among many migrants. Such feelings, rooted in a strong attachment to rural life and culture, have been an important theme in much of the literature on South African labor; these sentiments were also in evidence here, even if less starkly so than in some other contexts. These dock workers were not interested in settling in the city, but that did not stop them from enjoying urban social life and using urban resources to achieve their rural goals.

Investing in cattle allowed workers to cling to a crumbling patriarchal homestead and to take their place in a patriarchal society in which they still had power and authority, but that does not mean that such decisions or their intent to return to the countryside were purely the result of instrumental calculation. Such an instrumentalist approach discounts the migrants' own cultural logic. Though rebuilding the rural homesteads that were increasingly unsustainable did affirm their male authority, their will to do so cannot be explained as simply the outcome of coldly calculative considerations of power. Utilitarian motives undoubtedly played a role, but dock workers also held fast to their rural homes because these were part of their lifeworld and moral universe; they believed this rural life was how Zulu people were meant to live—an opinion shared by many Zulu women and youths who did not have power and authority in rural society. To reduce their rural attachments to mere instrumentalism is to assume a liberal individualism that can only obfuscate the ways in which their lifeworlds produced their worldviews.[79]

The Household

The rural and the urban economic and social spheres were closely connected in the lives of Durban's dock workers, just as they were for the laborers in Mombasa's port. Their urban labor cannot be understood in isolation from their rural livelihoods. Not only did their livelihoods combine wage labor and informal enterprise; they also straddled the rural and the urban spheres. Workers desired to become rural homestead heads and to no longer depend on urban wage labor, but this did not mean that they avoided interaction with urban society altogether. Many dock workers took advantage of the opportunities their job in the city offered to devise strategies that would allow them to return to the countryside.

This return to the countryside did not just reunite a rural household from which the dock worker had been missing. The strategies and domestic relations described in this book defy easy identification with the traditional rural Zulu *umuzi*, with the noncapitalist Chayanovian peasant household that balances self-exploitation and drudgery, or with neoclassical models of profit-maximizing households.[80] How then should we think about the household? These households were not just rural homesteads with a missing member, as urban wages and informal businesses were central to their reproduction. Neither were these simply proletarian households forced by law to reside in the countryside and to engage in labor migration, as the rural economy was vital to their economic strategies as well. Even women selling pilfered goods in the townships, but who were not married to or even necessarily in a relationship with dock workers, contributed to the reproduction of these households while having their own households and strategies. These households cannot be pinned down geographically; they did not exist in one place but rather in two or three separate locations. Moreover, they changed over time. These were mutually dependent spheres of consumption and production—the rural homestead, the urban workplace, and the urban township—which together reproduced the household as a whole.

However, these spheres were also separate, as distance and the difficulty of communication granted some autonomy to different members in different locations. Men and women in these different places made decisions regarding wage labor, agriculture, consumption, and commerce both in consultation and on their own initiative. Income was pooled, but also at least partially kept out of the hands of other members, as they struggled for and negotiated over the control of the household's resources and strategies. When men invested their wages in cattle, for example, they also kept these resources out of the hands of women who could not access or sell cattle, even if their decision to do so cannot be reduced to that rationale. In turn, women selling some produce at home would at times neglect to inform their husbands about this in order to maintain exclusive access to these cash resources. At least one dock worker condemned this practice as theft, as he considered all the household's resources to belong to him alone.[81] However, each of these spheres was dependent on the others, and together these reproduced the household as a whole.

It thus seems insufficient to consider the relationship between the rural and the urban as simply one in which the Reserve economy subsidizes urban wage labor, because the links between members in these different locations were more complex. Moreover, neoclassical and other theoretical models of the household often obscure gendered, generational, and other conflicts within the household. Here, the household is seen as a socioeconomic cluster that links and includes these separate but dependent spheres of production, consumption, and reproduction. In the words of Jane Guyer, "Thought of in terms of rights and duties, households are constituted by a series of implicit or explicit contracts, not by total subsumption of the members into a solidary unit whose internal relationships can be taken as given."[82] Indeed, all members of the household do not have identical interests, and internal conflicts and struggles do influence decisions taken both as individuals and collectively. While members have common interests in the reproduction of the household, which is equally a cultural and an economic imperative, they also have their own priorities, including investing in cattle, becoming an *umnumzane*, or immediate household consumption. The household is thus a complex set of relations among individuals who both combine resources and make joint decisions, but who also have their own strategies and resources and may struggle over these with other members.

4

My Children Never Went to Bed Hungry

Gender, Households, and Reproductive Labor

Two Phewa households reside across a little valley from each other near Izingolweni, about twenty-five miles inland from Port Shepstone (see map 1.1) along the N2 highway. One household consists of Banelisiwe, Thembeni, and some of their grandchildren; in the other household Florence and Matha live, also with a few grandchildren. Banelisiwe, Florence, and Matha are the late Nsizwana Phewa's daughters; Banelisiwe from his first wife, Florence and Matha from his second wife. Thembeni is Banelisiwe's sister-in-law; she was married to Nsizwana's eldest son, who has also passed away. Both Nsizwana, who was born in 1909, and Thembeni's husband worked on the Durban docks for many years.

These women remember the 1950s and 1960s as a time when life was easier and better. They worked hard, collecting water and firewood, working on the fields, cooking and cleaning, but they were never short of anything and had little need for money. Now, however, one needs money for everything, they complained, and their grandchildren struggle to find jobs. The two households used to live together in one big homestead, and Nsizwana's two wives regularly cooked together. Their children played together as well. Banelisiwe and Thembeni, who belonged to the house of the senior wife, remember both houses being equal and their mothers getting along well. According to Florence and Matha, however, the senior house was somewhat better off; they did agree that there was little discord between their mothers. The Phewas grew some beans, maize, sweet potatoes, *amadumbe* (taro), and other crops, and raised cattle, goats, and poultry. Nsizwana would come home about every three months but also regularly sent home samp and flour. The little bit of cash they needed was mostly used for clothes. Only Banelisiwe received one year of schooling. She was taught by a white lady from overseas, but people used to think that education was not important for girls. Education, people used to say, would make women "too smart for [their] own good."[1]

Dock labor in Durban and small-scale commercial activities, whether or not supported by pilferage, were crucial to the survival and reproduction of these households. However, women and youth in Izingolweni and other rural locations performed the actual labor of reproduction—that is, the work performed in the private sphere that sustains and reproduces the household: cooking, cleaning, raising children, and so on. Women's role cannot be reduced to this reproductive labor, however; many engaged in entrepreneurial activities, grew produce and livestock to sell, and struggled with other members over the livelihood strategies of their households. This chapter focuses on their work and life "away in the locations," to use a phrase coined by William Beinart and Colin Bundy.[2]

Life and struggles in rural households mostly fall outside the historical record and are therefore difficult to recover through archival research. These struggles took place hidden away in the rural areas and in the private sphere. The literature on labor migration has frequently characterized women and children as merely two-dimensional victims without agency. The role of women was often reduced to their functionality to colonial capitalism, that is, to reproducing cheap wage labor.[3] However, since the 1980s gender has become a much more prominent theme. A number of influential books, including Belinda Bozzoli's *Women of Phokeng* and Cherryl Walker's *Women and Gender in Southern Africa to 1945*, have focused on women and labor migration. More recently, other questions about gender and sexuality have been brought into the limelight, such as masculinity and non-heteronormative identities.[4] Nevertheless, the experiences of women who did not break out of the customary order—though they often did challenge it—and stayed behind in the rural areas remain some of the hardest to recover.[5]

Rural women's lack of overt resistance to patriarchy, remaining loyal to the "traditional" rural household, has at times been interpreted as a sign of innate conservatism. Such judgments, however, betray a lack of sensitivity to these women's socioeconomic context. We can also consider women's defense of the rural homestead as a defense of their access to certain vital resources for her and her family's survival, such as land and the earnings of migrant men. Indeed, women potentially have an interest in protecting their roles as homemakers because the patriarchal homestead can offer security and stability, as it did for the Phewas. That does not mean that they did not contest patriarchal definitions of the homestead and of women's role within it.[6] Gender and generational inequalities are not timeless and unchanging; they are constantly contested and renegotiated. There is, in other words, no timeless and unchanging Zulu patriarchy. My focus here is not on a presumed cultural essentialism or on timeless tradition, but rather on the constant construction and reconstruction of gendered and generational relations.

Within the household women and men, youth and elders, struggled over access to resources by appealing to or challenging generational and gendered expectations, as well as relations of power within the household. These domestic conflicts intensified as wage labor and migration became more entrenched: young men gained access to income independently from their *abanumzane*, women gained a certain rural autonomy as men spent most of their time in the city, and there was always the possibility of young women making their way to the city to gain their independence.[7] Women and youths contested traditional norms by running away, securing access to their own resources, going to court, and engaging in more subtle challenges.[8] Even without openly rebelling, rural women dealt with the challenges of the migrant labor system, rural poverty, and their subordinate position in the patriarchal household. They strategized and made decisions, both independently from men and in dialogue with them. Women thus had their own life strategies and were more than mere pawns in male strategies for socioeconomic advancement and survival. They eked out an income from their own spheres of production, predominantly based in agriculture and petty trade, and defended their access to this income. The independence gained from such income, however, was limited, as women continued to face many legal and customary restrictions, and homesteads remained dependent on men's wages and pilfered goods. Many rural women thus found themselves in what Dunbar Moodie describes as a "male-dependent independence."[9]

Of course, men were also dependent on women to keep their rural homesteads alive, to sell pilfered goods, and for social and sexual enjoyment. And men too engaged in domestic struggles over gendered and generational norms and expectations in order to enhance their position in the homestead. They fought to exert their authority while being absent from the homestead, strove to keep their wages and other household resources from being used by their wives for purposes they did not agree to, and worked to secure their position in their rural communities by building an *umuzi* and investing in cattle. It was their absence from the rural home that both allowed men to build their *imizi* and thus to take their place in a rural patriarchal system as *abanumzane*, and opened up spaces for women to eke out a limited autonomy.

To understand these domestic struggles, we need to look at the composition and internal dynamics of the household, a theme already taken up in chapter 3, and understand the decisions and activities of individuals within this context. Different members have different sources of income, which they redistribute and struggle over along gendered and generational lines. They appeal to or challenge generational and gendered norms, trying to shift or maintain the relations of power within the household. Changing livelihoods, giving different members access to or depriving them of money and other resources, can thus influence the composition of the household and its internal power relations; family dynamics in turn shape livelihoods. Studying these struggles, therefore, allows us to explore the imbricated nature of labor migration, on the one hand, and changing gender and generational relations in the countryside, on the other. In other words, this approach allows for a *political economy of gender*.

A focus on political economy and labor is in itself nothing new to the study of gender in Africa. However, this account is not simply about the reconstruction and bolstering of rural patriarchy, nor is it only about migrant men holding on to male power and controlling women in rural households.[10] Certainly, the preservation of rural patriarchy and men trying to work their way up to being patriarchs are important themes in this chapter, but the relation between migrant labor and gender is also more complicated. Since households are the site where gender relations are reproduced and negotiated, the less than straightforward composition of these households and their multifaceted livelihoods make for a political economy of gender that amounts to more than a reconstruction of patriarchy. Moreover, the relative conservatism of both women and men is partially rooted in their interests in socioeconomic stability for women and in becoming an *umnumzane* for men, but it cannot be explained away by such "objective" interests. In this chapter, I will thus neither adopt a purely culturalist approach to the study of gender nor a vulgar approach to political economy that reduces culture and tradition to mere effects of economic structures. The economic sphere cannot be divorced from the sociocultural sphere, but neither can the latter be considered a simple effect of the former.

Social Reproduction and Women's Agency

Harold Wolpe's argument about the articulation of a noncapitalist and a capitalist mode of production in South Africa has been very influential. In this account, the capitalist economy outsources the cost of the social reproduction of wage labor to the noncapitalist economy in the rural Reserves. Segregation and later apartheid forestalled the demographic collapse of these Reserves that would otherwise likely have resulted from their economic decline. As such, the rural labor of reproduction subsidizes cheap migratory wage labor in the cities and in the mines.[11] Though very useful, this structuralist account reduces the meaning of women's labor and their experiences to their reproductive labor. Moreover, as discussed in the introduction, this approach is ahistorical and functionalist.

Despite these and other significant problems with Wolpe's argument, it remains valuable and influential.[12] Michael Burawoy illustrates how an emphasis on the spatial separation of wage labor and its reproduction can take us beyond individual push-and-pull factors when studying migration; such an emphasis shifts the attention to the cheapness of the reproduction of labor and the powerlessness of the laborer at the place of employment.[13] The concept of a Reserve subsidy remains persuasive, and even those critical of Wolpe's thesis generally acknowledge its importance.[14] Consequently, two important legacies of this structuralist tradition deserve to be taken seriously. First, this literature did not understand migration as merely the result of individual choices but rather studied how the system of labor migration was continuously produced and reproduced. Second, it challenged the concept of a dual economy and forced us to bring the rural economy into discussions of wage labor. One important nexus where the urban and rural economies interact is the migrant laborer's household.

The household does not only reproduce wage labor, however, it also reproduces the lineage. The reproduction of the lineage has its own logic, one that cannot be subsumed under a capitalist market logic and yet cannot be dissociated from the reproduction of wage labor.[15] This at least partially explains why African workers continued to invest their wages in cattle and held fast to their diminishing rural assets; these were required to marry and thus to reproduce the household and the lineage—that is, to reproduce rural patriarchy and its gendered and generational norms. This form of reproduction cannot be understood merely in terms of market logic or simply as reducing the cost of social reproduction. Lineage reproduction has its own noncapitalist economic and social logic that revolves around cattle and wealth in people.[16] Wolpe problematically subsumes this different economic logic under the interests of capital.

This does not mean that households and lineages are not also economic institutions. People gain access to economic resources through kinship and membership of households, and as such their economic role is substantial. As Sara Berry points out, throughout much of sub-Saharan Africa, "rights of access to land, labour and capital were rarely sold for cash or material goods alone."[17] Access to productive resources depends on participation in both social institutions and the market. Households' livelihoods therefore cannot be reduced to market logic, and struggles within the household are always also struggles over access to resources.

Within the patriarchal household and the lineage, women and youths are certainly subordinates, but they are not entirely without agency. Women's struggles, however, largely took place within the often invisible private sphere, that is, within the household. Wolpe could thus portray women as merely reproducing South Africa's low-paid and mostly masculine workforce, as cogs within a capitalist machine. The struggles that took place within the household remained invisible; they were mere quibbles on the sidelines. Leslie Bank notes that the private sphere is often seen as consisting of "spaces where traditional roles are entrenched and re-enacted without innovation and change."[18] However, there can be no clear distinction between the public and the private.[19] Our tendency to consider the public and private spheres as separate can blind us to the political nature of women's struggles.[20] When women move to the city, they challenge the system of segregation that would keep them on the land; when they confront rural patriarchs and assert their autonomy, they also challenge the alliance of African and colonial patriarchs that was central to South Africa's system of indirect rule. Indeed, despite its efforts to separate the public and private spheres in legal terms, the colonial state continuously interfered in African private life.[21]

The Household and Its Conflicts

Though labor migration did lower the cost of labor, it did not originate merely because of the needs of capital. The southern African system of oscillating labor migration also emerged from the internal dynamics of the patriarchal *umuzi*, which Wolpe and others largely neglected. The sexual and generational division of labor in African societies made it possible at first to send young men to the city to work without undermining the homestead economy (see chapter 1). It is beyond the scope of this book to discuss in great detail the symbolic, sociopolitical, and economic structure of the Zulu household and its settlement pattern, the so-called Central Cattle Pattern; others have done this very well already.[22] However, a brief discussion of some of its main principles of organization and reproduction is necessary. As R. W. Connell reminds us, we cannot simply assume to know the households this chapter discusses:

> Conservative ideology speaks of the family as the "foundation of society" and traditional sociology has often seen it as the simplest of institutions, the building-block for more elaborate structures. Far from being the basis of society, the family is one of its most complex products. There is nothing simple about it.[23]

For Friedrich Engels the origins of the patriarchal family, and later the monogamous nuclear family, are intricately bound up with those of private property; in Europe both emerged in conjuncture.[24] However, where throughout most of European history land was the main factor of scarcity, on much of the African continent it was labor rather than land that was in short supply. Consequently, Zulu society, like many other African societies, did not value wealth in things, that is, private property, as much as it valued wealth in people and their labor. Jeff Guy discusses the Zulu socioeconomic structure as an "animate" mode of production and contrasts it with the "profoundly, qualitatively, different" inanimate mode of production colonialism brings: "Pre-conquest African societies were structured around the creation and control of people—*abantu*; they were replaced by societies structured around the creation and control of things—*izinto*."[25] Patriarchy could thus emerge without the development of private property.

Central to the control of people is the control of women and their reproductive capacities, that is, their ability to give birth to and raise the next generation. Claude Meillassoux outlines how lineages reproduced themselves and centers his analysis on certain demographic balances that need to be struck: between productive and unproductive (elderly, young children, infirm) members, and between the whole group and women who can biologically and socially bear children. To maintain these balances individual households and lineages exchanged people; most importantly, they exchanged wives who could perform agricultural and domestic labor, and ensure biological reproduction. The needs of the lineage thus subjected women but not only women. Youths were equally subject to domestic arrangements and customs that guaranteed intergenerational distribution in favor of the elderly. Gender and generational inequality was thus at the core of the African household.[26]

The exchange of bridewealth in the form of cattle structured this circulation of women and the control over their reproductive and productive labor. This *ilobolo* was compensation for the sending household's loss of female labor and reproductive capacity. Marriage through *ukulobola* was neither a straightforward purchase of a wife, as colonial and missionary reformers often believed, nor a private affair between two individuals. It was a protracted process that took place over an extended period, as bridewealth was usually too high to be paid at once. This created a lasting bond between two lineages and a continuing relation of indebtedness toward the elders.[27] As labor migration became expected from young men, elders gained access to the migrants' earnings through *ilobolo*. Young men's increased earning power and mounting demands by both fathers and mothers inflated bridewealth.[28] The continued use of cattle to *ukulobola* was testament to their enduring cultural significance and contributed to their lasting importance as a means of investment. Cattle were needed to marry and to reproduce the lineage. In a society where the ownership and exchange of cattle continued to mediate wealth and access to human and other resources, the exclusion of women from this form of capital entrenched male power. Moreover, women could secure access to land only via their husbands or male elders.

In an agricultural economy, the control of female and juvenile labor was central to the reproduction of the household. Women and children were social and economic assets, access to which was secured through the exchange of cattle. The relation between a father and a child was not necessarily a biological one, as even a genetically unrelated child was an asset. Not the biological father but he who paid *ilobolo* had the legitimate claim to fatherhood. It was thus cattle that allowed men to build their own *umuzi* and to amass their own wealth in people. Some scholars have therefore argued that *ilobolo* may more accurately be considered a child-price than a bride-price.[29] Senior men's control over cattle upheld their position at the top of the patriarchal hierarchy, even as the advent of labor migration did give young men access to their own resources.

Labor within the *umuzi* was thus divided along gendered and generational lines. Women and youths performed most of the productive and reproductive labor. Women performed more labor than men, and young men worked harder than elder men. Older women also worked less and could gain a certain prestige. In particular, they had considerable authority over their daughters-in-law.[30] The domestic labor that fell on the shoulders of women generally took more than six hours per day, and children had to work as well: girls helped their mothers with household chores, and boys herded cattle.[31] Indeed, most female interviewees remembered helping out by collecting water and firewood, cooking, and cleaning; and men recalled herding cattle in their youth. The adult homestead head, by contrast, did traditionally not work much. He did fulfil an important ritual role, however, by performing the rites that connect the living with their ancestors, the *amadlozi* who look out for the family but can cause significant misfortune when neglected or dissatisfied.[32] Even if men were away for most of the year, performing these rituals remained their responsibility regardless of how absent and unreliable they otherwise were.[33] These ceremonies were the only household decisions Dudu Dumakude bothered involving her husband in, as he had a drinking problem and was never around.

This account, of course, offers only a snapshot of the structure of the patriarchal homestead, and rural patriarchy was neither static nor did it remain unchallenged. Rather than portraying Zulu patriarchy as eternal and unchanging, as an essence of Zulu culture, this account is meant to identify the fault lines along which conflicts were likely to emerge. Women and youth may seem devoid of agency, but they did resist—even if this resistance did frequently not take the form of an overt and direct challenge to patriarchy. Short of abandoning the homestead or openly defying the *umnumzane*, most youths and women engaged in some combination of accommodation and resistance. Even in their oppression, they did have a stake in the patriarchal homestead. Young men had the prospect of buying into this hierarchy (with *ilobolo*) and becoming homestead heads themselves. Mothers were often concerned about stability, security, and access to resources for their family, which a sustainable *umuzi* could offer.[34] Young women, on the contrary, worked hard and had little to look forward to except more domestic drudgery. They were the more likely candidates to desert their homesteads, yet young men ran away as well. As the Reserve economy continued to decline, the promise of becoming the head of a viable homestead became increasingly tenuous. Future rewards were growing thin.

These households were not unitary institutions. They were not undivided decision-making units striving to either maximize their profits, as assumed by neoclassical economics, or to maintain consumption with the least amount of drudgery, as in Chayanov's theory of the peasant household. Rather, households are complex networks of social and economic relations among interdependent individuals that are always rife with both conflict and cooperation. Access to social and economic resources both influences the relations within these households and is governed by the internal structure of the household. Hence, my focus on struggle and accommodation.

The Government's Children: Masculinity and the Reproduction of Rural Patriarchy

Although some men did break with the traditional expectations of the rural homestead, most dock workers interviewed were rather conservative and aspired to become respectable *abanumzane*. They wanted to return to their rural homes even if the incapsulation the Mayers wrote about was unusual in Durban and among dock workers (see chapter 2). These men engaged in wage labor to maintain and rebuild their desired rural life that was slipping away under colonial impoverishment. They could do so because of African society's capacity to subordinate the agricultural and domestic labor of women that was needed for the day-to-day survival of the homestead. It was thus their control over the productive and reproductive capacities of women that allowed male workers to stave off complete proletarianization and to take up their position in an, albeit impoverished, rural patriarchy.[35]

These workers were hardly passive victims in a system of labor migration instituted and perpetuated because it subsidized urban African labor. Urban wages equally subsidized the rural economy, which was increasingly dependent on these remittances. Migrant laborers not only ensured high profits for their employers; they also reproduced the gendered and generational relations of a patriarchal society that could no longer subsist without their wages. They did the latter on their own account. They kept alive the patriarchal homestead in which they would one day become homestead heads; achieving this status remained the most valued marker of masculinity. This does not mean that labor migration was the result of crude calculation: the ideological pull of the rural home was strong.[36] Relinquishing their access to rural land was not an option. Nelson Ndaba explained that "my ancestors would leave me if I did that," and Zithulele Chemane that a Zulu man is "nothing without land . . . you cannot make your own home."

Through marriage and the establishment of an *umuzi* male migrants secured their position in rural society. They used their wages to purchase cattle for *ilobolo* and to build the homestead. Building their homestead was about more than providing shelter for their household, it also established workers in their social role as husband, father, and *umnumzane*; by doing so, they gained respect and moral standing as a member of the rural community. During the first half of the twentieth century migrancy thus became an expected step in the process of homestead reproduction. Working in the city became an expectation for young men, interviewees insisted. Urban wage labor was a novel initiation that helped African workers become respected men in the countryside.[37]

As migrants tried to rebuild patriarchal homesteads in the Reserves, new forms of male socialization emerged in the cities. Since the early twentieth century, Durban's *amalaita* gangs of young male domestic servants fulfilled the socializing function rural youth associations once did. These young workers were now adult men with household responsibilities, of which they were reminded by elders, colleagues, and even songs.[38] Labor migration symbolized maturity and independence. Young dock workers no longer wanted to depend on their fathers. Velile Goba "had to go to work and not depend on [his] father's things." Their socialization included warnings against getting involved with city women, as affairs could threaten their commitment to the rural homestead and consume money that could otherwise be remitted. Few interviewees considered urban women viable long-term partners, often calling them *izifebe* (prostitute or adulteress, sing. *isifebe*). These women, they said, were after the workers' money, were too independent, and were sexually too assertive and "naughty." However, some did have affairs in Durban—some short lived, others more enduring. Three interviewees even married women they met in the city and another three had relations that were serious enough that their rural wife and urban partner had the chance to meet.[39]

To buy their way into the patriarchal hierarchy, workers needed access to cattle and other livestock. These were forms of capital that were essential for performing certain ceremonies and fulfilling their social obligations. Although a partial monetization of *ilobolo* was taking place, especially in the cities, most interviewees paid at least part of the bridewealth in cattle. To marry a second or third wife, as several interviewees did, they needed to accumulate more cattle. The size of its herds was an important measure of the wealth, prosperity, and prestige of a homestead. Several interviewees were thus proud that they owned at one point more than eighty or even one hundred head of cattle, though many had just a handful.[40] They could use these cattle to gain dependents and clients, in other words, to increase their wealth in people, not only through marriage but also through *ukusisa*. Prestige, social standing, masculinity, and the reproduction of the household were inextricable from cattle ownership. Almost all interviewed dock workers therefore invested at least part of their wages in livestock. Although many also invested in agriculture and women continued to struggle to reap something from the land, livestock gained in importance compared to cultivation where sufficient land was available. This development further marginalized women within the household, as cattle were the sole preserve of men.[41] By investing their money in cattle, men limited women's access to their income. These resources thus remained out of the wives' economic sphere. Cattle were in this context a special-purpose money.[42]

Of course, becoming an *umnumzane* and a rural man of standing came with social obligations. Moodie explains that "*ubudoda*, the essence of manhood, had to do with competent and benevolent management of the umzi, aiding in homestead decision-making, settling disputes, and generous sharing of homestead resources with guests and visitors."[43] Dock workers were aware of these expectations and tried to live up to them. They invested in cattle and in their land, and they supported their kin. Many were particularly concerned with the well-being of their mother, especially if their father was polygamous or may for other reasons not have given their mother the support they believed she deserved. Young men could thus achieve *ubudoda* by earning wages as migrant laborers. There was a deep irony in becoming a respected rural man and *umnumzane* by going through the often humiliating and alienating experience of working in a racist industrial context, where they were "boys" and not men. To claim their spot at the top of the rural gender hierarchy, African men had to accept a position at the bottom of the urban racial ladder.

Urban employment was therefore at the same time a source of humiliation and of pride. The Durban docks, like any other workplace in South Africa, and the city itself were profoundly shaped by racism. Zulu Phungula, clearly aware of its effects, challenged the racial segmentation of work that kept African wages artificially low when he claimed entitlement to the same wages as white workers.[44] Moreover, racism was not the only issue dock workers encountered. Dock work is a tough and dangerous job, and while the interviews did not indicate the same interpersonal violence that was rife on the goldfields, Nhlanhla

Sokhela did mention verbal abuse: "Izinduna were shouting—you know, to ensure their dignity."[45]

These workers took pride in doing this job, emphasizing their masculine strength and collectivity by referring to themselves as *onyathi*. Dock workers also used gendered language in laying claim to higher wages. Phungula used a language of responsibility as fathers and husbands to lament wages that were inadequate for workers to fulfill their familial responsibilities as breadwinners. He proclaimed the indignity of having to bring their wives and children to the city because their wages were insufficient to keep the rural homestead afloat; this was their failure as providers, as *umnumzane*. In the city, their wives brewed beer to supplement the household income, and children, torn away from the moralizing influence of rural society and left to their own devices, became petty criminals.[46] In making this argument, he cleverly appealed to white fears about permanent African urbanization and undisciplined African youths.

Dock leaders claimed entitlement to living wages not only as fathers but also as loyal and respectful "children" of the white government. Phungula hijacked the government's racial paternalist discourse that portrayed the government as a father to African children who can count on generosity and just care in return for loyalty and obedience. He characterized the government as a father failing in its responsibility as provider: "We thought that our father would not be against our being given [8s] a day. . . . It is a shame that there are some of your children and you do not like to see them properly fed. It is a shame for a parent not to see that his child is properly clothed."[47] Workers strategically both asserted their masculinity as fathers and breadwinners and claimed dependence as the government's children.

The ability to buy into rural patriarchy also depended on workers' ability to control their wives' movements and behavior while they were away in the city. Without women's productive and reproductive labor, the homestead would crumble; there would be no *umuzi* for the man to head. The prospect of their wives leaving the Reserves for the cities or leaving their husbands for men who were present in the rural areas threatened migrants' ability to achieve rural status and *ubudoda*. Consequently, many migrants were anxious about what their wives were up to in their absence and subscribed to a very conservative and inflexible understanding of custom; many also supported official attempts to tighten restrictions on female autonomy and mobility.[48] Yet it was not just their waning authority over women that threatened migrants' ability to become *abanumzane*. As the impoverishment of overpopulated

Reserves continued and accelerated after the mid-1950s, it became ever more difficult and even impossible to build a viable patriarchal homestead. For growing numbers of African men, migrant labor was no longer just a phase in life that allowed them to establish an *umuzi* before they retired as rural patriarchs; it became a lifelong and alienating reality. Nevertheless, most dock workers continued to strive for this increasingly unattainable ideal.

Women in the Rural Areas

The household is a crucial economic institution. It is through household membership that people gain access to all-important economic resources, including land, labor, and capital. This should not blind us, however, to the love and affection involved in "keeping house"[49] in rural Natal. The love of a woman for her family can easily obscure the exploitation of her labor, conflating her physical labor, as she cares for the household, with her emotional labor, as she cares about the household and its members.[50] Nevertheless, love, affection, and mutual respect were important in the marriages of our interviewees. Thandiwe Mcanyina emphasized her love and affection for her husband and fondly remembered the times when he was home: "We would sit together and I would make food for him. We would then end up watching the [sunset] together." She was equally fond of his mother, for whom she had a lot of respect and whose affection and agricultural skills she greatly missed. The relationship between a wife and her mother-in-law was certainly not always antagonistic.

Yet the homestead did not only offer women love; it also offered them and their children socioeconomic security and stability that was difficult for unmarried women to achieve in apartheid South Africa. In the absence of legal rights for African women, who were considered minors under colonial law, their security depended on being attached to a man who reliably sent home wages and gave her access to land. Many women thus conformed to a "patriarchal bargain" in which they remained loyal to the *umuzi* and worked within the patriarchal system as long as it delivered a sufficient return in the form of land, access to men's wages, and security.[51] Indeed, the liberal individualism that values independence, autonomy, and freedom above all cannot be considered universal. James Ferguson argues that women and men in southern Africa frequently value and declare their dependence on (rather than independence from) chiefs, husbands, or employers.

Here, dependence is not solely considered a negative state.[52] When Zulu Phungula appealed to the paternalism of his employers and of government officials as fathers who should provide for their children, he declared workers' dependence on them. When wives, mothers, and fathers asked the native commissioners to help find their migrant sons or husbands who had absconded from their rural families and to help ensure their remittances, they strategically appealed to their dependence on migrants' wages.[53] Yet such "declarations of dependence" are not merely ploys to gain access to certain resources; they also address a strong need for social belonging.[54]

Conscious and subconscious considerations of economic and social security, the promise for men to one day become patriarchs, as well as a certain agency women and youth could achieve within the patriarchal order, do of course help us better to understand the relative conservatism of these men and women. However, such practical interests cannot on their own "explain away" their conservatism and loyalty to the patriarchal homestead. Love for one's partner, children, kin, and in-laws, a fondness for the rural life and culture in which they grew up, the need to maintain relations with the *amadlozi*, and so on, are all significant parts of this equation. A political economy of gender and patriarchy should not preclude other considerations.

While the gendered inequalities of the patriarchal homestead of the 1950s were very real, most interviewed women did not consider this a particularly harsh period of their lives. Most remembered the time when they managed the household while their husbands or fathers worked on the docks as a better time. Families were more likely to stay together, they needed less money, and men could still find jobs. This stability was part of the reason why they never abandoned their patriarchal marriages. Women in better-off households were thus more likely to value their rural existence and to remember it fondly; however, women from poorer homesteads were more likely to remember the hardship. Fikile Mlotshwa's husband left her and her daughter, Ningi, only to return sick after six years. She struggled but still found support with her parents-in-law. Talent Gumbi, the youngest of eight children, was more interested in the conveniences that the city offered, especially education, and ended up moving to Durban. Of course, women did not submit to the patriarchal homestead only because it offered stability. Women too valued rural society in its own right and were strongly invested in maintaining their links with the *amadlozi*, which almost all interviewed women brought up.

Although women declared their dependence, the physical absence of migrant men from their rural homesteads opened up spaces for female initiative and qualified independence. Travel and communication were difficult, and it was impractical for absent men to be actively involved in the day-to-day running of the homestead. Women were therefore the de facto homestead heads, while many men were merely "transient visitors, strangers even, in their own communities."[55] Mothers and wives were in charge of the everyday management of the household, which strengthened the female position within the domestic sphere. While some men insisted that they made all the important decisions, others acknowledged that their wives or mothers were in charge of cultivation and the household. Men left decisions to women because women were actually present at home and had more skills and experience in domestic and agricultural affairs. Most men did, however, insist on their decision-making prerogative when investments or the use of their wages were involved, for example to enclose their land. Since men were generally the ones bringing in cash, they considered any sizable cash transactions to be their prerogative. Cash was thus earmarked for the use by the male migrant; that is, of course, except for any cash that wives earned and did not tell their husbands about. Women conceded authority to their men when it came to the rituals necessary to connect with the ancestors.

Women too could have *ubudoda*. In de facto running the household, they could display those qualities expected from an *umnumzane* and that define *ubudoda*. Especially women past childbearing age could gain such respect and status. When a couple married, the new wife would generally move in with her in-laws until the husband can build his own *umuzi*. In this living arrangement, which was often fraught with conflict, the mother-in-law assumed authority over her son's wife. She was the expert and deserved respect for her age. Indeed, several workers mentioned that their mothers made all major decisions at home. For the newlywed wife, this could be a difficult time.[56] On the one hand, Thembeni Phewa indicated some tension with her mother-in-law, and Talent Gumbi remembered her mother working hard for her in-laws. On the other hand, Fikile Mlotshwa and Dudu Dumakude were grateful for the support they received from their in-laws when their husbands respectively absconded and started drinking. Thandiwe Mcanyina remains quite fond of her now late mother-in-law. Women did not only find support with their in-laws but with a wider network of kin, something they found sorely lacking in the city. This too was a reason to remain loyal to the patriarchal homestead economy; however, increasing poverty eroded such support networks over time.

This relative independence of women in domestic affairs should not blind us to their dependence on men. Even though some homesteads did comparatively well, virtually all were ultimately dependent on migrant wages. Rural life could thus be harsh and insecure. If a man stopped sending money—because he was injured, killed, sick, robbed, unemployed, or because he found another woman in the city—the consequences for the rural household could be devastating. This happened to Fikile Mlotshwa, who had to beg, rely on odd jobs, and eventually take a job at a local hotel. For this job she had to leave her house and children at 5 a.m. only to return at 9 p.m. In the rural areas, women often had to take the least desirable jobs, such as those on white farms. Of course, they did this work on top of their domestic labor.

Moreover, life without their husbands could be lonely. Thandiwe Mcanyina feared that her husband could cheat on her and thus went to the city to check up on him; fortunately, she discovered that her fears were unwarranted. She was always happy when he came back home. It could also be difficult to fend off other men. Late marriage, gender imbalances, and the often drunken advances of returning migrants put great pressures on married women, who had to balance their own sexual needs, expectations of virtue, and loneliness.[57] Moreover, women's pivotal role as the often very skillful managers of the rural household was not matched by their social or legal status. Women had to make decisions in the absence of the *abanumzane*, but there was always the possibility that the man would disagree with the decision or consider such female initiative a threat. Some men did insist on their own authority to make decisions, even when they were not around, which could lead to indecision and stress.[58] Dudu Dumakude's husband, for example, would get drunk and then aggressively challenge the decisions she and his mother had made together.

Many women did not limit themselves to their expected domestic roles: they did not just run the household and cultivate the land while waiting for remittances to make up the income deficit. Some, of course, set up small businesses based on selling the pilfered goods the migrant workers sent home. Many women also took the initiative to sell some produce when they had a surplus, and they advised each other on such commercial strategies. Others sold chickens or made raffia bags to sell.[59] Most sold to neighbors who had less land and less produce, but some also sold in the rural towns or to rural stores. Women in the more successful households used the small profits from such ventures to diversify their earnings, for example, by investing in a tea room or in small livestock for breeding. Such diversification increased women's control over the household's resources, but they remained dependent on the wages and goods migrant men sent home. Their autonomy remained male dependent. Moreover, most continued to recognize the homestead head's authority when it came to major decisions.

Most men acknowledged that such initiative helped the household to survive, as Galo Mtolo did: "My wife started selling to the neighbors and later also to some stores in the area; and we kept that money for developing the land, but also for planting and helping here and there . . . you know." However, even though women seldom used the money they earned this way for personal needs but rather spent most of it on household consumption, their initiative could lead to conflict. Small-scale rural commercialism gave women access to their own cash income, for which they would otherwise be dependent on male wages. Takulu Kheswa considered it stealing from him when his wives sold produce without his consent, especially when they did not surrender their earnings to him.

Within these households, largely unspoken yet very real struggles took place over authority and access to resources. Men invested their wages in cattle in part to keep the money out of the hands of their wives, but some women had their own access to cash income. Rural commerce was the female sphere, and absent men had few ways to control women's access to and use of any money earned that way. Indeed, the household is not an undifferentiated unit of decision making. Different members do have common interests, for example in ensuring that the household survives, thrives, and is reproduced, but they also have differing priorities. Thus, even when household members cooperate, they can also conflict with each other. The central dynamic of the household, Amartya Sen notes, is thus not just cooperation but cooperative conflict.[60] This synthesis of cooperation and conflict reflects Kwame Gyekye's discussion of the two-headed crocodile in Akan art. Gyekye uses this art motif to illustrate that individuality and communalism are not antithetical in African social thought. The two heads of the crocodile symbolize individuality, and the single body stands for common interests. The heads struggle and compete with each other over food, yet they have only one stomach; therefore, they have the same basic interests.[61] Household members similarly struggle over resources and priorities, but they are also bound by their common interests in helping the household to survive, reproduce, and prosper. Rather than undivided decision-making units, these households are "amphibious" clusters of individuals linked together in cooperative conflict.

A clear trend emerged from the interviews where men were generally more interested in cattle while women were more often concerned with immediate consumption. Men did not only try to keep resources out of the hands of women by investing in cattle; cattle were also what gave them a tangible presence in rural society. As opposed to cash, livestock could be seen, and cattle allowed men to marry and gain dependents. Moreover, the social sanction against selling cattle except in exceptional circumstances meant that cattle were a good way to save and accumulate. Cash resources, on contrary, tended to drain quickly in the face of immediate pressures for everyday consumption. While the interviewed men measured their success by the size of their family and their herds, the interviewed women took pride in the fact that their "children never went to bed hungry,"[62] even if they themselves sometimes did. Moreover, where men always mentioned cattle, women were more interested in livestock that met consumption needs more directly, for example, goats, pigs, and chickens. This does not mean that women had no interest in cattle; most preferred marriage with *ilobolo* and were concerned about the rituals that ensured their connection with the ancestors, which often required cattle.[63]

Though the sample of female interviewees was small, it seems that there were generational differences in women's attitudes toward rural life. Younger women were more likely to be attracted to the conveniences of the city and felt greater needs for nonessential forms of consumption, such as cosmetics and new or fashionable clothes. Because of the accelerated impoverishment of the Reserve economies after the mid-1950s, they were also more likely to have grown up in less well-off homesteads. The more impoverished the patriarchal homestead was, the less it had to offer these women. The patriarchal bargain thus came under increasing stress. This generational difference was also reflected in attitudes toward education. Older women thought of education as something for boys and thought that girls would turn into *izifebe* if they became too smart for their own good. The younger generation, however, was very interested in education. The availability of schooling was part of the greater attraction that the city had for them. This generational divide is in line with Mark Hunter's findings on gendered investments in education in uMlazi, a large African township southwest of Durban. He argues that it was in the 1960s that African women rather than men became the greater proponents of education.[64] Women for whom the rural household no longer promised stability and socioeconomic security sought to improve their chances of urban employment by taking advantage of their expanded access to primary education, which resulted from the 1953 Bantu Education Act.

Women in the City

South African colonial policies made it very difficult for African women to gain legal rights to the city. Although many women were struggling in the Reserves, neither the state nor African patriarchs would allow them to build a new future for themselves in the city. Thandiwe Mcanyina, for example, had to leave her job after getting married, because her husband did not want her living in the city. There were several reasons why both state officials and male elders would want to limit women's mobility. Women performed the bulk of the agricultural labor, and when women left for the city the viability of the rural homestead was threatened. A collapse of the homestead economy would force the state to confront the impossibility of maintaining "white" cities and the migrant labor system, and it would force African men to acknowledge that their desired rural patriarchy was no longer viable. Moreover, restricting the movements of women also ensured that young men would return to the rural areas to find a wife.[65] Of course, women also had interests in maintaining access to land and remittances, as economic opportunities for single women in the city were sparse.

Rural poverty, however, slowly eroded patriarchal controls. The city offered prospects for a different future, even if this future was not necessarily easier or more secure. The urban environment did not free women from patriarchy but locked them in a different gendered and racialized hierarchy. Legal residence in the city depended on their husbands, forcing women once again into relations of dependence.[66] Despite the many obstacles in their way, women did move to the city illegally. However, without legal access to formal housing, they ended up in informal settlements like uMkhumbane. In this periurban world women were somewhat shielded from both rural patriarchy and the strict bylaws and pass laws of the city. There, they could achieve some autonomy by engaging in informal economic activities. The sexual and racial division of labor in Durban excluded women from most formal jobs other than domestic service, which was a particularly undesirable occupation with long hours, low pay, and few opportunities for socializing. Most formal employment also kept women away from their children.

There were some thriving Shebeen Queens, who were successful brewers and sellers of illicit liquor and beer. In fact, many prominent entrepreneurs in the early informal settlements were women.[67] However, even for the more successful female entrepreneurs urban life could be a struggle. The reality for most urban women was one of poverty and constant fear of being endorsed out, that is, being rounded up and sent back to the rural areas. Many urban women thus had to gain access to men's earnings to survive. This could mean that they ended up in dependent relationships with migrant men and had to count on their generosity, often while having occasional intercourse with other men who would also offer some financial support.[68]

There were also more mutually beneficial relationships between dock workers and their urban partners, for example when they teamed up to engage in commercial activities (see chapter 2). These women generally did not get direct access to dock workers' wages but rather to pilfered goods to sell or a client base of the man's colleagues. Such partnerships could but did not always involve a romantic or sexual relationship. How the proceeds from these businesses were shared is not entirely clear and seems to have differed. Mandla Xaba claimed that *he* "made good money selling food," but it was his partner who did the actual selling. Yet she must have received something in return to continue with their arrangement. Moreover, as she was the one actually running the business, it is possible that he did not know exactly how much they earned. She likely could have pocketed her fair share of the proceeds without his knowledge. Others paid their partners in cash or in kind. These women's households were separate from the households of the migrant workers, yet they were dependent on each other. This cooperation was mutually beneficial but did not imply identical interests or a unified strategy. Township women wanted to feed their children and diversify their income, while dock workers wanted to send money to their rural homestead or buy cattle. Most dock workers did not consider urban women as potential wives, yet they were willing to work with them to bolster their rural homesteads. Township women thus played an important role in the reproduction of the dock workers' households, but they did so to ensure the sustainability of their own households.

Women's commercial activities, however, were continuously undermined by the state's offensives against unlicensed traders and brewers, and by the endorsing out of unattached women. As early as the 1920s, women protested the government's attempts to eradicate the informal economy. Side by side with dock workers, female brewers challenged the Durban Municipality's attempts to extend their beer monopoly into the fringes of the city by erecting a municipal beer hall in the Sydenham area. They protected their livelihoods and protested government policies that threatened these. Such threats were also a principal reason to oppose the extension of pass laws in the 1950s.[69] Simply staying put and continuing to live their urban lives and run their businesses was a political statement in itself. African women's presence challenged the official ideal of a white city to which single African men migrated for work.[70]

In this hostile political and socioeconomic context, household structures became flexible. Women formed nonconventional households to cope with the contingencies and insecurities of urban life and changed their strategies of household formation to adapt to changing circumstances. The structure of the household became more fluid: women teamed up with migrant workers to get access to their resources, engaged in multiple relations to secure financial support from several men, or formed female-linked households.[71] Women often sent their children to the rural areas to be raised by their kin, as they considered the city an unsuitable environment for children or had employment that did not allow them to be around for them. Thus, they created rural households that skipped a generation, like the Phewa households: there are grandparents and grandchildren, but the generation in between resides in the city, trying to earn a living.[72] Rural households had therefore changed. While homesteads did continue to resemble the rural Zulu *umuzi*, the *imizi* of the 1950s were certainly not those of the nineteenth century. In the politically and socioeconomically challenging context of apartheid South Africa, African households both in the city and the countryside had to be flexible and adapt to changing circumstances.

Conservatism and Innovation

In a society where authority and access to resources depended on age and gender, women and young men bore the brunt of the labor responsibilities in the household. For young men, however, there was the promise that one day they could make it to the top of this hierarchy, even if the rewards for their patience and loyalty to the patriarchal household became progressively less tangible. Dock and other migrant workers bought their way into this rural hierarchy by leaving the rural areas to work in Durban. They invested their wages in cattle for *ilobolo* and used their earnings to establish their *umuzi*. Through these actions they could become respected men with *ubudoda* at home. By sending remittances, they also kept the homestead alive. They thus reproduced the gendered and generational relationships of their patriarchal society. However, they could not recreate their homesteads as unchanging or unchallenged institutions.

Women generally accepted their position in the *umuzi*, yet this cannot simply be seen as the result of innate conservatism or a false consciousness. Conforming to gendered norms and even appealing to them did have concrete advantages in the form of remittances, access to land, and a network of kin to fall back on. Especially to women with children and other dependents, such comparative security was a major benefit. Of course, women's relative conservatism cannot be reduced to considerations of socioeconomic security. Both men and women felt a strong ideological pull from rural society; they wanted to remain connected to the *amadlozi* and often preferred rural life. Moreover, love and affection for their family and their partner, as well as a sense of obligation, significantly influenced women's loyalty to the rural patriarchal household.

Furthermore, this conformity did not imply an unquestioning acceptance of these norms. Women eked out a qualified independence within the rural household or in the periurban areas. In doing so, they engaged in an unspoken but continuous struggle with other members of the household over resources and authority. Being the de facto household heads, women made most decisions in the running of the household, although men often insisted on their decision-making prerogatives concerning sizeable cash spending. Many women gained access to cash independently from their husbands by engaging in small commercial enterprises, and they invested in chickens, goats, and pigs rather than cattle. Men, on the contrary, preferred to invest in cattle, not just to reproduce the lineage but also to keep resources out of the hands of women, who were more likely to use it for everyday consumption needs. While migrant men tried to rebuild and prop up a fading patriarchal order, women both pushed its boundaries and appealed to its gendered norms to gain access to the homestead's resources.

The internal dynamics of the household were thus always subject to change; relations of power and gendered and generational expectations were constantly appealed to and struggled over. The actual household, while continuing to resemble a traditional Zulu *umuzi*, became something more flexible and fluid; the household adapted to changing contexts. Women performed roles traditionally performed by men, eked out some autonomy, and gained access to resources independently from the homestead heads. Households also came to rely on informal trade and even on urban women outside the household. It was in the cities, however, that the fluidity of African households emerged most clearly. To manage the insecurities of urban life, African women formed female-linked households, sent their children to the rural areas, and found multiple ways to tap into the earnings of African men, including having multiple partners or engaging in commercial partnerships.

5

Cleaning the Wharves

Pilferage, Bribery, and Informal Trade

Durban's dock workers defy easy classification either as radical proletarian dock workers or as conservative migrant laborers who "exhibited a distinct unwillingness to join an uprooted proletariat," as Patrick Harries argues for Mozambican miners.[1] Work in Durban's port, however, cannot simply be divorced from the experiences of dock workers around the world, as many of the work and hiring processes at the Point were notably similar to those elsewhere. This chapter discusses two important ways in which the livelihoods of Durban's dock workers resembled those of thousands of dock workers in London and New York, Liverpool and Mombasa, Shanghai and Tanga. First, like dock workers all over the world they bribed foremen and supervisors, and they used their social connections to get the best jobs. Second, they pilfered without shame. Although none of the interviewees was explicitly asked about this, about half mentioned that they regularly engaged in pilferage. Half is thus a conservative estimate.

Different commentators have considered these activities crimes, acts of resistance, or both. In particular, there is a substantial literature on theft and pilferage by laborers and the dispossessed as a form of informal resistance against proletarianization and the disciplinary power of employers. Friedrich Engels famously discusses crime in the context of the industrial revolution as an early, primitive, and individual form of protest, which was later superseded by more mature, collective forms of resistance, including formal trade unionism and the rise of workers' parties.[2] Eric Hobsbawm similarly assumes a historical progression in forms of resistance in his influential *Primitive Rebels.* He argues that the "social bandits" of early capitalism were often people who were not born into this new political and economic system; they were only just starting to learn the rules of the new order. These rebels engaged in prepolitical resistance; they challenged the enclosure of their commons, of their collective user rights, but did not have a collective revolutionary vision to challenge or reform the capitalist system that was taking shape.[3] These accounts paint theft as an essentially reactive and defensive, prepolitical form of resistance, not as a creative and strategic one.

This model of social banditry is rooted in an account of economic and political change based on European experiences, but Hobsbawm considered it a "universal and virtually unchanging phenomenon."[4] Indeed, James Scott describes pilferage, arson, sabotage, gossip, character assassination, and the like, by poor Malaysian peasants as the "weapons of the weak." These are everyday and covert forms of resistance employed by the subordinated population, which are less risky than overt rebellion but often do not fundamentally challenge socioeconomic structures as such; rather, the peasantry push and explore the limits of what is allowable in their social and political context in order to minimize their disadvantage. In Scott's account, resistance includes "*any* act(s) by member(s) of a subordinate class that is or are *intended* either to mitigate or deny claims . . . made on that class by superordinate classes . . . or to advance its own claims."[5] Critics note that such a broad definition of resistance can result in almost any act by the poor or the repressed being read as an act of resistance and therefore risks downplaying the structural limits to such resistance.[6]

In his later writings, Hobsbawm found that the evolution of a social banditry was not easily traceable in sub-Saharan Africa and India.[7] Charles van Onselen did his part to fill this gap with an extensive study of banditry during the first decades of the development of the gold mining industry on the Rand.[8] For Ralph Austen too, the concept of social banditry is useful in the African context because it forces us to think about the social meaning of crime as an expression of alternatives to the values of the dominant stratum of society in a context where precapitalist and precolonial social values are still very much alive.[9] Indeed, in the rapidly and dramatically changing contexts of early capitalist Europe, modernizing southeast Asia, and colonial Africa proletarianization was (and is) an ongoing project. In such societies, one can fruitfully consider certain crimes as reactions to dispossession and to the criminalization of once common user rights. What was a property crime to those in power was a right to the poor, for example, the collection of firewood and kindling, poaching of small game, the use of grazing lands, and the gleaning of the harvest.[10]

However, in this chapter I argue that pilferage and bribery on the docks were not merely opportunistic and reactive deeds in response to proletarianization but rather crucial elements in carefully constructed livelihood strategies. Dock workers actively strategized, and many used the opportunities for pilferage and entrepreneurialism that their employment in the harbor offered to achieve independence from wage labor. These technically criminal acts made the entrepreneurial strategies discussed in chapter 2 possible and thus facilitated workers' retreat from the labor market.[11]

Pilferage

Certain user rights have yet to be completely criminalized. This is the case even in the West, where the erosion of these rights has a much longer history than it does elsewhere. This is particularly true in employment relations. Almost everybody gets part of their wages in kind: these are the invisible wages. Such payment in kind can be nonmaterial, for example, in the form of work satisfaction or prestige, or material in the case of tips, short changing, perks, and pilferage.[12] Pilferage falls in a grey zone between theft, which is clearly illegal, and a perk. Strictly speaking, pilferage is not part of the workers' remuneration and thus not a right. More often than not, however, some small-scale pilferage is condoned by employers and supervisors, largely because it is too difficult and too expensive to police and because it is usually limited to small quantities and low values. Many forms of pilferage are considered a customary right by the workers and, within certain limits, even by employers: white-collar workers can use office printers, phones, and supplies for reasonable personal needs; servers can take home unfinished bottles of wine; and workers in industrial bakeries can often take home a loaf of bread. The catch for the worker is that the employer has the authority to define a certain act as a perk or theft and can even do so after the facts.[13]

Pilferage and theft from ships and warehouses is nothing new. Patrick Colquhoun documented dockside theft in London at the end of the eighteenth century and Gerald Mars wrote a fascinating anthropological study of pilferage in the port of St. John's, Newfoundland.[14] Mars discusses how it happened, the need for trust and cooperation, and the moral considerations at work. Dock workers around the world have for centuries considered small-scale pilferage for personal consumption a just part of the compensation for their labor, as indeed it would have been in precapitalist societies before bourgeois morality and the state labeled it theft.[15]

Of course, we do not have to look at St. John's or eighteenth-century London to find evidence of forms of theft that were not considered wrong by the "perpetrators." Young Zulu boys grew up stealing sugar cane and other agricultural produce for a snack while herding livestock.[16] When these young men migrated to the towns to work as domestic laborers, they would live in the servants' quarters of white households. There, they would often entertain their kin and *abakhaya*, give them food from their employers' kitchens, and even provide them with accommodation. White householders denounced this practice as sponging and theft. However, what was considered thievery by the employers was viewed as perfectly normal social mores by the workers: it was socially unacceptable to them not to offer this form of hospitality to their *abakhaya*.[17] Even when the appropriated items were neither food nor accommodation, pilferage could still be considered perfectly acceptable by the workers and even by supervisors. Harries notes that African miners on the Rand stole tools such as iron files, knives, piping, and copper and iron wire, and also pilfered by-products of gold mining: "What the mineowners saw as pilfering seems to have been condoned by many Europeans who, only a generation previously, had considered 'chips,' 'clippings,' and 'sweepings' and other by-products of the work process as a legitimate part of the wage."[18] Durban's dock workers were thus neither the only dock workers nor the only African workers who pilfered and considered this a legitimate part of their compensation: a right rather than a crime.

Dockers in colder climates would usually hide their loot under layers of clothes and in special pockets in loose-fitting garments, in order for it not to show.[19] However, in Durban's subtropical climate this was not an option. There was no good excuse for any excess clothing, especially not in the often uncomfortably hot hold of a ship, yet Durban's dock workers did pilfer. They mostly used the sacks they brought with them to work, which could easily hide small amounts of pilfered goods. Eric Ryland, a former stevedoring employer, noted that security at the port was not a real concern and that searches of workers' bags and belongings were not a regular practice. Workers could thus use their bags to pilfer small quantities of cargo without much trouble.

Durban's dock laborers were most interested in taking loose foods like salt, sugar, beans, rice, samp, and flour. This limited the portion of their wages they needed to spend on consumption in the city and shielded them from rising food prices. Doda Ndaweni recalled that he "did not use much [of his wages] for consumption, because, you see, that time there were plenty of broken bags of different foods, like flour, maize meal, beans, sugar, et cetera. And, if you take it, it was like you were cleaning the wharves."[20] Others confirmed that picking up loose food for your own consumption was generally allowed. Indeed, at the Durban office of the South African Container Stevedores there are pictures of workers picking up spilled sugar in Maputo with as caption "cleaning the docks." It would thus seem that employers did in fact accept this practice in good humor.[21] Pilferage could actually be useful to port authorities and shipping employers as it did help cleaning the holds and wharves, much like gleaning helped cleaning the fields.[22] A certain amount of spillage was expected, especially in the case of bagged cargoes, which included many food items. A certain amount of bags were expected to break during the loading and unloading of the cargo, and shipping insurance covered this risk. Shippers and traders considered this loss to be part of the costs of transportation. Moreover, employers regarded these small losses to be more the customers' problem rather than their own, as long as these remained within certain limits and did not hurt their reputation.[23]

While the losses resulting from this form of "crime" were negligible for employers and customers, the impact of these opportunities on the livelihoods of workers and their households was substantial, especially for those workers who did not stay in one of the company compounds and did not receive free meals.[24] Being able to pilfer allowed workers to minimize the portion of their wages they spent on consumption in the city. The less money they spent in the city, the more they could send home. Zulu Phungula illustrated in 1941 the sizeable difference that free food could make when he told officials that he spent 2s per day on food and earned only £1 (£1 is 20s) in a regular week.[25] After spending 14s per week on food, there would have been very little money left over for other urban expenses, let alone to send home. Of course, not everybody could work on ships that carried foodstuffs, and sometimes the bags did not break. In the latter case, one could of course always break some on purpose, as at least one interviewee regularly did.[26]

Dock workers did not consider this criminal behavior, and they talked openly about it, despite the fact that they were not explicitly asked about pilferage. Yet not everybody was entirely unconcerned about the morality of theft. Mzo Mzongo considered it part of the reason why the docks were a bad and corrupt place, as workers there "were stealing and swearing at each other." He thought it was a place for "naughty workers." Other workers, however, and even supervisors and employers did not generally share his concerns. For Eric Ryland, the worst that workers could steal was perhaps a few tools, but the supervisor should just make sure that there were none lying around. No one would really miss a few pounds of beans or rice on a whole shipment, and it does not seem that employers or the state ever considered it a priority to combat these forms of pilferage. Only a few complaints about theft can be found in the archives, despite the fact that pilferage was clearly very common, and these complaints were mostly received in the context of specific crises, such as the withdrawal of the Water Police from the harbor and the wartime blackouts.[27] To the extent that opportunities to pilfer allowed people to live off otherwise insufficient wages, pilferage could also relieve some of the upward pressure on wages and could thus be in the interest of employers.[28] This was of course only the case if such thefts remained within bounds.

Cargo thefts only made it into the newspapers when larger and more valuable items were stolen, for example when a white railway checker stole twelve cases of whisky, eight drums of white lead, a case of oil, one case of starch, twenty-one drums of creosote, and attempted to take a further 153 bags of sulfur.[29] Theft on the docks was thus not always as innocent as just cleaning the wharves. Some African dock workers also stole bigger and more expensive cargoes, in these instances of course without the same tacit acceptance of employers. Guns and generators were especially popular among the larger items. Generators were mostly used to water the land and were thus an investment in agriculture. Guns were usually sold at hefty profits. Eight interviewees said they had stolen a generator and five that they had stolen guns; one had done both.

Such examples of more extensive pilferage did not just require a culture of acceptance, that is, a workplace culture that did not consider pilferage illegitimate, but also the active cooperation and complicity of people who had the authority to write clearance notes and to adjust inventories or who were less likely to be searched even when leaving the harbor with a large amount of goods. In practice, this required the complicity of an *induna* or, even better, a white supervisor. Many supervisors and *izinduna* were so involved in pilferage that they were frequently the ones to introduce other workers to this practice:

> The other activity that I undertook was stealing cargo. I was introduced to this when one day the white foreman told me to take a box full of guns and put it in the company *bakkie*, and we took it to his home. When he opened it, there were twenty-four guns and he gave me three of them and warned me not to tell anyone. That woke me up and I got spoiled. I

> then did this on my own, with my own connections. I took and sold a lot of things from the ships and this earned me a lot of money.[30]

Those higher up in the workplace hierarchy often pilfered on a larger scale, but they were not planning to carry the loot to their *bakkie* themselves. Therefore, they needed the assistance of a worker they trusted or could bribe on what Gobile Mbhele called a "shut-up basis." The complicity of white supervisors made it difficult for the police to catch thieves, as supervisors were even less likely to be searched than African workers. Moreover, they had the authority to write clearance notes.[31] Galo Mtolo confirmed that "the foremen also told me to take that there and if the foreman sent you, no one would say anything. That was stealing and they gave me these things [the stolen goods]. I sold them and kept the money."

However, the initiative did not have to come from the person with authority. When Amos Sibiya saw something he liked, he would take it to the supervisor who would then give it to him. This was only possible if there was a prior relationship of trust and complicity between the two. No less than twelve workers mentioned that they gained access to cargoes through the complicity of white supervisors. One supervisor was a particularly active pilferer and was mentioned by several interviewees. His nickname was Nkomiyahlaba, "The Cow That Gores."[32] Moreover, workers also doctored clearance notes written by white supervisors for reuse. As such, the supervisor's authority could be used without his consent, which was of course a riskier practice that could result in the worker getting fired or even being arrested.[33] Yet only one of the interviewees for this research was ever arrested for theft. He was part of a gang of professional thieves based in Sikotheni, an area of uMkhumbane: "The ships were loading and off-loading different cargoes. Therefore, I started stealing and after a while I made connections with Sikotheni thieves who taught me to steal cargo and also to identify it while it was still in the boxes. Therefore I started stealing until, luckily, they were caught while I wasn't there. But, they said I was with them and then the police came and arrested me."[34]

It is not surprising that this gang was active in uMkhumbane, as the settlement was a notorious center for the fencing of stolen goods.[35] The fear of being arrested, however, was enough to scare other workers away from more extensive pilferage and other illegal activities. Cacile Khozana stole one generator but then got scared, and he never stole again. Lungani Xulu retired when somebody told the police where he usually sold *dagga*, and Bhekinkosi Zimu when some of his colleagues were arrested and informed the police about his activities: "Mr. Dlams, you see about stealing cargo: some other workers got caught doing that and were arrested. They then started pointing out other thieves. That is when I went into retirement." Others did not engage in any pilferage at all out of fear of arrest. Under the apartheid regime, many Africans living in cities experienced arrests for trivial and administrative offenses, particularly for pass law violations. They were thus familiar with the resulting trauma, and most did not care to repeat it, even if the fact that so many Africans were regularly arrested meant that imprisonment did not carry much stigma.[36]

That dock workers regarded a certain amount of pilferage as acceptable did not mean that everything was tolerated. They did have a sense of right and wrong, but that sense differed from the legal definitions of theft and crime, just like beer brewers, *dagga* sellers, and domestic servants stealing food from their employers broke the law but did not consider what they did to be immoral or illegitimate.[37] Pilferers on the docks did generally operate within self-imposed limits, which were enforced by the group and a deep-seated moral economy.[38] The concept of a moral economy, as popularized by British historian E. P. Thompson, signifies the continuing influence of precapitalist norms, social relations, and user rights in the early capitalist economy.[39] Actions that were strictly speaking illegal were thus seen as legitimate by the majority of the population as long as these fell under a common but implicit understanding of behavioral norms and collective rights.[40] This concept has most famously been used and expanded in the South African context by T. Dunbar Moodie. He interprets the moral economy as "encompassing mutually acceptable rules for resistance within systems of domination and appropriation. On the mines, the moral economy sorted out those aspects of compound life that dominant and subordinate groups could take for granted as inevitable from those which would be contested by workers, often with fierce outrage, or forbidden by management outright."[41]

Moodie uses moral economy as an interactive and contested concept, shaped both top-down and bottom-up. The acceptance of pilferage was part of a similar moral economy. While theft is mostly an individual act, it required a labor culture that both accepted its legitimacy and set limits. There is little evidence in this period of attempts at clamping down on pilferage, but there were seemingly mutually accepted limits to the quantities and types of cargo that one could take. There was some self-regulation.[42] Dockers in Durban made a clear distinction between taking spilled food items and, for example, taking generators. While the majority was engaged in pilfering loose food, only a minority stole guns or generators. Interviewees used words that can be translated as theft or stealing (*ukweba, ukuntshontsha*) when talking about bigger items but did not generally do so when it was only food that was being taken. In the latter case, they were only cleaning the wharves.[43] This implies not a monolithic common value system but rather a set of commonly accepted but also loosely defined norms within a labor culture with roots in a noncapitalist rural society.[44]

One important difference between the moral economy of Durban's dock workers and that of other dock workers around the globe was that the selling of pilfered goods was considered acceptable. In other ports this was usually not seen as a legitimate practice: if pilferage was not for personal consumption, it was no longer a right but a crime. This was not the case in Durban. Interviewees did not appear to find the selling of these goods in any way reprehensible, as they talked openly about the businesses they built on the selling of pilfered merchandise. Doda Ndaweni, for example, "ended up selling those loose foods and people were buying it because it was cheap and plenty. That made me end up not using my wages for consumption and sending home good money to buy cattle." Likewise, Sosha Masikane "was collecting broken bags of sugar, beans, rice, and all that I found there, and I sent it home to sell and eat." Bheka Dlaba, who was once arrested for his part in organizing the 1958 strikes, first started selling pilfered goods in uMkhumbane. His prices were "small and the quantities were big," and there was a township woman who sold the goods for him: "As soon as I saw that the job was proceeding, I spoke to one city girl to sell it for me and paid her with food stuff to raise her children. I avoided making her my girlfriend because I did not like city women." Later, he also sent salt and sugar home for his wife to sell. His coorganizer, Dumile Sibiya, also pilfered food and sent the goods home for his wife to sell.

However, not everyone was equally likely to engage in pilferage. All but one of the casual workers mentioned that they engaged in pilferage, but only about one-third of all permanent workers mentioned this. Permanent workers usually lived in employer-owned compounds where their lives were constantly scrutinized, which complicated pilferage, and where they received free meals, which reduced the need for it. Working most days, they also did not have much time to manage a side business. When the casual labor system was abolished in 1959, pilferage also became less attractive and more complicated for the former casual workers who became part of a permanent labor pool.

Bribery and Networking

To base a business on pilferage, one has to secure predictable access to pilferable goods. Moreover, dock workers required some sort of risk management strategy to pilfer bigger items or larger quantities of goods. They could do both by making the right connections with complicit *izinduna* and white supervisors, with other pilferers, and even with the police. Maintaining good relations with people who could provide access to the "good stuff,"[45] that is, items that could easily be pilfered and that could be sold in the townships or at home, afforded one access to considerable income opportunities. Making and maintaining these connections through bribes, selling *dagga*, and everyday social interaction was an important part of these workers' livelihood strategies.

Mtukatshelwa Phewa, whose aunt sold pilfered goods in Chesterville, bribed both police and *izinduna* to make this business possible:

> [The police] first disturbed me. Then I thought to sort this out by visiting the police station with something the police wanted and they left me alone after that. Even when some policemen wanted to come to me or to raid the whole area, I was informed by my connection amongst them. Then, I just closed the shop. . . .
>
> I knew that *izinduna* and other gangs used to go to the beer-hall after work to drink *utshwala*. Now, I used to buy a lot of beer for them and they became my good friends, like the police. I knew what they loved, like meat and drinking, and that's what I did to sort someone out.

Later in his life, he also gained access to land to build his *umuzi* through the connections he made as a trader. The man from whom he sometimes rented a *bakkie* arranged this for him. This man was Mdu Jama, who was a dock worker as well and who cooperated extensively with Phewa. Jama too made regular visits to the police station to keep the policemen happy and to bribe them.

In general, it seems that those dock workers with commercial businesses on the side were often well connected and relied heavily on these networks. For Jama, his car was a major asset in maintaining these useful relationships; it made him into the equivalent of a "blue-eyed boy"[46] among *izinduna* who had access to goods but no means to transport them: "White supervisors did not like me after hearing that I had a car, but *izinduna* liked me for it. Because, if they had something special to remove from the docks, I was there for them." Another way to make valuable connections was by selling good-quality *dagga*. Several interviewees had *izinduna* and supervisors among their clientele, which resulted in significant benefits, such as promotions and better pilferage opportunities.[47] Lungani Xulu took care of another practical need by paying bus drivers in kind for transporting pilfered "flour, salt, rice, samp, tins of fish," and more to his rural home, where his wife sold these in their tea room.

Apart from turning a blind eye to and assisting in pilferage, *izinduna* could also hire certain people before others. As elsewhere, casual hiring lent itself to nepotism and bribery. This hiring system gave intermediaries considerable autonomy in taking on certain people and not hiring others. It was thus important for *togt* workers to be liked and preferred by the *izinduna*, and bribing them was a way to mitigate the insecurities of casual dock labor. It was certainly important to be a good worker so that you would be able to help the gang get the job done. Nevertheless, buying beer, selling good *dagga*, and generally being well-connected helped as well, not only to be hired yourself but also for the people you know. Godidi Msomi explained that he "had to do something for the *induna* so that he takes my people, the people I know from home and from Lamontville, before taking others on the line."

The difference between using one's social network to find jobs and bribery was not always clear cut. A bribe was often an extension of the social relations that African workers had used for over a century to get access to jobs. Buying an *induna* some beer could be seen as bribing him, but one could also just be maintaining a friendship. As Linda Cooke Johnson notes, "Corruption on the docks was . . . not necessarily *malum in se* or *in prohibitum*. It often began with preferential hiring for family, friends, and reliable workers and then extended to economic kickbacks, theft, increasing corruption, bribery, and extortion."[48] Bribing *izinduna* also signals recognition of their authority: the bribe symbolizes the acceptance by the worker of the intermediary's power to hire, fire, and discipline.

Keletso Atkins has extensively described the social networking involved in finding employment. She discusses how Africans found and evaluated work for each other through kitchen associations in the nineteenth century. Mphiwa Buxton Mbatha also explains how workers arranged for their kin and *abakhaya* to be hired in the 1950s.[49] Only a small minority of interviewed dock workers did not land their jobs on the docks through similar contacts. In this context, the maintenance of these social networks, which was especially important for casual workers, easily spilled over into bribery.

Keeping the *izinduna* happy was important in order not only to be hired but also to get the most desirable jobs. Casual workers could present themselves for hiring at those ships that carried sought after cargoes. Mzwakhe Sosibo explained that "if you are a casual worker, you face to be hired where you know there is cargo that you want to steal." Of course, having the right connections would allow one to be hired on such ships more regularly and reliably. Casual labor and bribery thus enabled more systematic pilferage, which in turn was the basis of many small businesses. Mdu Jama pointed out that strict regulations for permanent workers and the fact that these laborers could not choose on which ship to work would have inhibited his pilferage. He thus chose to remain a *togt* worker. Others remarked that casual labor gave them the freedom to work on their side businesses, which were in turn supplied by pilferage.[50] There was thus a clear correlation among casual labor, pilferage, and starting a small commercial business. All casual laborers interviewed had some commercial business on the side, compared to less than half of the permanent workers.

"Crime" as Resistance

Since the 1980s and 1990s, many Africanists have written about these "crimes" as informal and everyday forms of resistance.[51] They did so in part to rectify the often too-exclusive focus on formal strikes, unionization, and open rebellion by a radical historiography of labor and resistance.[52] This change was also inspired by a similar shift toward a focus on everyday forms of resistance in the literature on slavery in the Americas, for example, in the work of Eugene D. Genovese or Herbert G. Gutman.[53] Interpreting these activities as acts of resistance infuses them with a sense of agency for African workers or for slaves in the Americas, thus making these actions into more than just coping mechanisms or examples of socially unadjusted behavior. These acts can of course fruitfully be regarded both as survivalism and as resistance, but shifting the emphasis from one to the other can give these acts completely different meanings, from desperation to empowerment.[54]

Theft and criminality could also serve as markers of masculinity, as it did for urban youth gangs.[55] An element of bravado was often present in dock pilferage around the world, and workers would brag about extraordinary feats of pilferage and trickery.[56] Indeed, particularly successful pilferers could become folk heroes, much like Hobsbawm's social bandits.[57] However, Durban's dock workers did not seem to place much, if any, emphasis on this meaning of pilferage. They related being a man to having cattle, being married, and becoming an *umnumzane*, but not to pilferage or crime. Their strength, their perseverance, and the collective nature of their work, captured in their moniker *onyathi*, were important to their self-image as well. Most dock workers, whether they engaged in pilferage or not, did not identify with *tsotsi* (thugs, robbers) or *amalaita* gangs; they even mentioned the presence of such gangs as an important reason to dislike the city.[58]

Like Hobsbawm and Thompson, who saw theft and poaching as reactions to the enclosure of common user rights, Robin Cohen and Bill Freund both read theft in colonial Africa as a reaction to still-ongoing processes of proletarianization and dispossession.[59] However, Freund departs from Hobsbawm's concept of social banditry by not constructing the same historical evolution in forms of resistance: "Theft . . . can play a major role alongside the more conventionally developed forms of working-class protest; indeed, it can provide an effective vehicle of protest when and where conventional forms fail. Far from being crude or fruitless, theft can be an effective economic response by proletarians to the totalizing surplus demands of corporate capital."[60]

While theft is an individual form of resistance—although pilferage also requires a common culture of acceptance and thus transcends the merely individual act—it does not therefore exclude collective action and a working-class consciousness. Indeed, despite their commercial ventures based on pilferage and despite not having the right to unionize, dock workers in Durban were also a particularly strike-prone group of workers and often well organized. Hence, theft does not exclude political action and is not devoid of a consciousness of their shared exploitation. Indeed, Freund argues that "the distinction between theft and *re*-appropriation may be less important than their similarities."[61] The "re" in reappropriation implies a conscious resistance to dispossession and surplus appropriation. Therefore, theft and pilferage carry the potential for political action as well.

Examples of such consciousness from around the continent are numerous. Freund notes that northern Nigerian tin miners considered theft "merely a modest recompensation for the expropriation of land and difficulties faced by Birom farmers; it expresses the belief that wealth has been appropriated unjustly by outsiders."[62] Dock workers in the Tanzanian port of Tanga, according to Frederick Kaijage, viewed pilferage as "an attempt at a justifiable redistribution of resources,"[63] and Charles van Onselen writes that pilfering miners in Southern Rhodesia "sought to gain compensation for what they had been denied through the system."[64] Zulu Phungula was equally aware of the injustice of the low remuneration for the hard work dock workers performed. In a meeting with officials, he argued that "what increases the number of ships is because we get so little money." In the same meeting, another dock worker noted that for the same job Africans were paid less than whites.[65] These dock leaders fought inequality as well as low wages and poor working conditions, but this consciousness alone does not make pilferage into political resistance. To the extent that pilferage helped clean the wharves and allowed workers to live off wages that would otherwise be insufficient, these practices could even be advantageous to employers. Pilfering was an individual action for individual gain, but it was justified by shared sense of injustice at the hands of employers and the apartheid authorities.

Some of the literature on informal resistance has inherited the conceptualization of these forms of resistance as essentially reactive from Hobsbawm and Engels. Cohen, in his classic essay on hidden forms of resistance discusses these according to the specific aspects of the process of proletarianization against which they were a reaction. Theft, for Cohen, was a reaction to the psychological adjustment that sociopolitical and economic changes forced onto the workers.[66] Scott too implicitly assumes the reactive nature of informal resistance. By presenting the peasantry as essentially protesting and resisting new rural social relations, he leaves little room for peasants who may not just have been fighting these changes but who were also active participants in them and who were trying to adjust to and maybe even prosper in a changing context.[67] For Durban's dock workers, bribing and pilferage were not just reactive but also active and strategic acts that were part of wider livelihood strategies. As Allen Isaacman and his coauthors emphasize about informal resistance to forced cotton production in Mozambique, this was "not a knee-jerk reaction . . . it was a carefully considered decision."[68]

Indeed, pilferage and bribery were central to the economic strategies of many workers interviewed for this research. Dock workers in Durban used pilferage as a basis for small-scale enterprises, and a large number of the interviewees had some sort of commercial activity on the side as an alternative and supplementary source of income. Most frequently this meant that they pilfered loose food that their wives would sell in the rural areas or that women they knew would sell in the townships. Even if their rural businesses outgrew what they could realistically pilfer, they had acquired the seed capital for these stores by selling pilfered goods. Pilferage and bribery were thus at the root of these commercial endeavors. Free merchandise and little or no overhead costs facilitated the success of these businesses.

For a good number of workers, entrepreneurial activities allowed them to become self-employed, withdraw their labor from the urban wage labor market, and retire from Durban much earlier than was the norm in the 1950s. There was indeed a strong congruence between having a business on the side and being able to retire early from the docks, as was noted in chapter 2. The real act of resistance to proletarianization may thus not so much be the actual pilfering but rather the permanent and early withdrawal from the labor market. Hence, pilferage was part of these broader livelihoods, part of a strategy to become independent from wage labor. The use of pilferage in such strategies was sometimes consciously planned and sometimes more haphazard, but it was never purely reactive.

Such strategies were possible because these migrant laborers worked on the docks and in the holds of ships, where they had easy access to cargoes. Their workplace was very difficult to police, and the system of casual labor, as Mdu Jama noted, allowed them the flexibility to present for hiring only at ships carrying desirable cargoes or to choose not to work one day in order to spend their time and energy on their commercial business instead. The nature of dock labor thus enabled these strategies, but with the institution of a hiring monopoly in 1959 and of containerization in the 1970s these opportunities disappeared. The demise of *togt* labor ended many of the freedoms dock workers had, as they no longer had the choice to work on specific ships or not to present for hiring. These developments also allowed for workers' lives to be policed much more closely, as they were forced into the employers' compounds. Containerization, moreover, meant that dock workers handled fewer loose goods and could thus not pilfer as easily.

Furthermore, individual action by workers does not have to exclude collective action, nor is there a clear-cut historical progression from "primitive" individual action to "mature" collective struggles. In fact, not only did Durban's dock workers combine participation in strikes with individual resistance, for example, in the form of pilferage and the eventual withdrawal of their labor, but some prominent dock leaders of the 1930s and 1940s also had commercial aspirations and showed concern for the interests of African traders. Similarly, Bheka Dlaba and Dumile Sibiya were actively involved in working-class action and were arrested for their role in organizing the 1958 dock strikes, but they also used their jobs on the docks as the basis for small businesses that enabled their early retirements from urban wage labor.[69]

Moreover, practices of pilferage and bribery could also lead to and inspire collective action when the labor regime that made these possible and the moral economy of the port were under threat.[70] Thus, dock workers fought attempts at decasualizing labor in the port, as well as efforts to increase employers' control over the work process or over compound life.[71] Pilferage and small-scale entrepreneurialism were not in themselves political, though they were at least partially justified by a political consciousness based on experiences of injustice, but they could lead to collective and more explicitly political action when these practices were challenged by the state or by employers.

6

Buffaloes on Noah's Ark

Reimagining Working-Class History

An organizer known as Mkhumbikanowa, or "Noah's Ark," played a prominent role in the labor unrest that rocked Durban's harbor in 1958–59.[1] Several interviewees still remembered him in 2009. Noah's Ark attempted to keep Durban's dock workers, or buffaloes, safe from exploitation and repression. He used biblical imagery, as Zulu Phungula had done before him. Both presented their struggles as a story of suffering and redemption. Phungula argued that Africans lived in hell even though they had helped to build up the British Empire higher than the kingdom of heaven. They too wanted to share in the milk and honey.[2] Both Phungula and Mkhumbi, short for Mkhumbikanowa, strove to redeem African workers, to lift them out of their hell, and to protect them from the rising tide of poverty that threatened to engulf them.

Mkhumbikanowa was of course a nickname. Like most other organizers, he did not use his actual name, as victimization of labor leaders was common practice. Mr. Mkhwanazi recalled that "it used to happen when these strikes occurred, when we chose people to represent us, we would hear that they are detained."[3] Similarly, while these strikes did have organizers, there were no identified spokesmen who could be singled out and fired, arrested, or expelled from the city. In the context of apartheid, a strike was not just a conflict between employers and workers; it was a direct challenge to the racial and political order. In the eyes of the authorities, it was something to be repressed. Zithulele Chemane recalled that "you would be arrested if you were against the white people." Unfortunately, the use of a nickname did not keep Mkhumbi safe. He was arrested and banned from working on the docks. As we shall see, however, such bans could not always be enforced.

Dock workers around the world have a long-standing reputation for being uncompromising and strike-prone working-class radicals. Durban's port laborers are no exception. From the first *togt* boycotts in the 1870s to their refusals in the 2000s to handle Israeli ships and weapons destined for Zimbabwe's Mugabe regime, these workers have used their strategic position in global networks of exchange and communication to express their grievances. The classic explanation for such radicalism comes from Clark Kerr and Abraham Siegel, who argue that, like miners, sailors, and loggers, dock workers often formed isolated and tight-knit communities. These dock communities lack socioeconomic differentiation and neutral elements that could act as mediators and break up broad-based solidarity.[4] While this explanation is very useful, it is also insufficient. It is true that dock workers often form their own communities with strong solidarity, but frequently they also have close connections with other sections of the working class. Especially in colonial settings, dock workers were often much less isolated from other workers than those in Europe or North America.[5] In Durban, many dock workers lived at the Point, yet they also regularly visited the informal settlements surrounding the city, where they drank, danced, and talked. Moreover, the port was the city's main source of gossip and news about international affairs.

David Hemson links this long history of working-class militancy to the "unvarnished nature of exploitation in the docks."[6] He convincingly argues that Durban's dock workers had a well-developed working-class consciousness and that Zulu Phungula was their proletarian hero; his radical style and uncompromising militancy made him impossible to co-opt and thus the type of leader dock workers gravitated toward. Yet the preceding chapters suggest a more complicated political identity. These workers were not unambiguous proletarians, and neither were they the conservative rurally oriented migrants the Mayers write about. They combined both rural and urban sources of income and used the opportunities their urban employment afforded them to accelerate their return to their rural homes. These dock workers were indeed strike prone and took action over pay and workplace issues, but they also defended the rights of African traders and engaged in informal trade themselves. Today, trade unions across the continent struggle to reach out to informal workers and to organize across the formal/informal divide.[7] For the dock workers in this book, however, and for their organizers, there was seemingly no contradiction between collective organization as a working class and individual entrepreneurial strategies, or between their commitment to rural life and using urban opportunities to their advantage.

Workers' industrial and political activism thus involved an idiosyncratic mix of fighting for working-class issues and actions that seemingly do not fit into the image of radical proletarians. This includes a strong ethnic nationalism that was also fervently anti-Indian. Though their political consciousness contained many ideas that are not purely proletarian, we should not deny these workers their working-class status and agency either.[8] We cannot reduce the identity of these workers to that of working-class radicals, or rural conservatives, or an entrepreneurial petty bourgeoisie; rather, we need to emphasize diverse and even seemingly contradictory interest and identities. Durban's dock workers were rural, Zulu, African, working class, entrepreneurial, permanent or *togt* workers, masculine, old or young, and dock workers.

In this chapter, I revisit a more traditional concern of labor history, namely working-class action and organizing. If these workers are not a traditional working class, as I have argued in the preceding chapters, why did they engage in forceful working-class action so frequently? And, how do we account for this seemingly contradictory mix of proletarian radicalism and more conservative petty-bourgeois concerns? The answer can be found in the life histories and livelihoods of these workers. My argument thus comes full circle: we have seen how an account based essentially on dock workers' working-class radicalism cannot fully capture their experiences and identity, and now we come back to their working-class activism.

Durban's dock workers were not the typical wage laborers that are often implicitly assumed in labor history. They were not the male breadwinners for a family of dependents who happened to live in the countryside; their wages were seldom their households' only source of income and sometimes it was not even the main source of income. We thus should not study their dock labor in isolation from the other economic activities taking place within their households. An approach to labor history that focuses mainly or only on wage labor, which is often the unstated norm, fails us here. The rural economy remained important, and most households were engaged in some small-scale commercial business. These businesses were frequently run by women and made possible by dock pilferage. Moreover, these different sources of income were not independent from each other. In particular, their entrepreneurial strategies were made possible by their dock labor. As such, their interests as wage laborers and as petty entrepreneurs cannot be dissociated. By breaking out of the constraints of traditional labor history and looking at wage labor in the context of other economic activities that take place within the household, the contradictions in dock activism become more comprehensible. Where chapter 3 has focused more on the rural-urban links, this chapter is mostly concerned with the links between formal wage labor and informal entrepreneurialism.

A Long History of Dock Militancy

Durban's first industrial action took place in 1874 when the vast majority of *togt* workers, including dock laborers, left Durban. They refused to offer their labor to protest the imposition of *togt* regulations designed to limit the economic independence of casual workers. This new law required *togt* workers to register, pay a registration fee, and accept work at a predetermined rate. On the day that these regulations took effects, there were scarcely any workers to be found in the harbor. In the late 1870s and early 1880s, dock workers walked off the job several more times, as the labor shortages caused by the Anglo-Zulu War afforded workers more agency and bargaining power.[9]

At the turn of the century, new labor shortages resulting from the Anglo-Boer War once again allowed workers to demand better pay. When the postwar boom subsided, however, the conditions for militancy deteriorated as labor shortages turned into a surplus. Apart from some limited skirmishes between 1918 and 1920, working-class action returned to the docks only in the late 1920s with the spread of the ICU. The depression of the 1930s suppressed workers' militancy, but in the late 1930s their silence was broken several times before the Second World War brought a new period of intense conflict under the leadership of Zulu Phungula, as well as increased government intervention in the port's labor relations. The second half of the 1950s was marked by a last wave of strikes before decasualization and monopoly hiring curbed the power of dock laborers and muted their militancy. During these different waves of activism, Durban's dock workers organized themselves with little or no outside assistance and often in the face of government oppression.

While wages, employment, and workloads were usually the main stakes in these conflicts, workers stopped work for other reasons as well. In March 1920, for example, one thousand *togt* dock laborers went on strike over a variety of issues, including wages but also food and compound regulations.[10] Workers considered accommodation and rations part of their compensation, and demanding more and better food was thus also a form of fighting for better remuneration. The racial paternalism of housing and feeding one's employees thus also brought living conditions and food into the realm of employment relations.[11] Employers and officials, however, did not always recognize these as legitimate reasons for industrial action. In August 1956, 250 stevedores walked off the job to demand the dismissal of their compound manager, who had disallowed a ritual that would have brought outsiders into the compound. In the eyes of the government, the workers had no reason to strike as their grievance was not related to the workplace. Officials helped the company to recruit strike breakers.[12] Not only the size and quality of the rations were at stake but also the right of compound dwellers to brew their own *mahewu*, a conflict that played a role in the 1929 beer boycott.

Strikes about accommodation and rations were actions in defense of mutually understood and unwritten expectations resting on the employer and supervisors. These included the provision of a certain standard of housing and nutrition, as well as tolerance for established practices, such as the brewing of *mahewu* and the performance of certain rituals. When these expectations were unfulfilled, workers considered it legitimate to take action. These strikes were not so much evidence of a radical working-class consciousness as they were actions in defense of the status quo. These were reactions to the breach of the moral economy of the docks. At other times workers defended their privilege within the working class rather than fighting as a class. Stevedores recognized the value of their skills and occasionally refused to do the unskilled work of regular jobbers, including bunkering coal and carrying timber.[13]

Other conflicts revolved around workplace control and the conditions of hiring. In November 1956, some five hundred *togt* workers demanded that seventeen workers who had just become permanent laborers continue to receive the same daily wages as casual workers. Officials discerned a plot to sabotage the phasing out of *togt* labor, and employers complained that "what the labourers failed to appreciate was the security which the new conditions gave them."[14] There were significant advantages to permanent labor for the workers, above all the security of employment, but not everyone was willing to give up the relative freedom and better daily remuneration of casual employment. By demanding the same pay for permanent labor as for *togt*, workers contested the terms of employment. Employers were at least partially right when they argued that workers preferred *togt*, as some certainly did.[15]

Casual laborers and employers also had different conceptions of time. Workers considered their shifts finished either at the end of the day or when the ship for which they were hired was fully loaded or unloaded, even if that was before the regular end of the day. For employers the shift ended at 5 p.m., even if workers finished the ship early, in which case they were required to work on another ship for the rest of the day. Dock workers were thus regularly accused of insubordination when they demanded their pay after the ship was finished and refused to work until 5 p.m. Employers eventually accepted the workers' interpretation, and by the 1950s it was usual practice to let workers off with full pay if the job was done early.[16] Permanent workers also defended their control over workplace and hiring practices in 1948 when they challenged new SAR&H regulations. These rules equated unauthorized leave or returning from leave late to a resignation and penalized starting late or taking unauthorized breaks. Moreover, leaves of more than three months would now result in a dismissal. These regulations breached long-standing practices and limited workers' freedom to return to their rural homes, thus upsetting the balance between rural and urban life. Dock workers protested this attempt to increase employers' control over their lives on and off the job. They refused to appoint a delegation in order to prevent victimization and insisted that the new regulations should be withdrawn immediately and completely. They only resumed work after management promised to reconsider.[17]

Struggles over workplace control were also about how much work had to be done in one shift. In the late 1950s, workers enforced a new standard to determine their workload. While before they had to work until either the ship or the shift was finished, they now worked until they had reached the required tonnage, measured in number of ropes, or crane loads. If they reached that number of ropes early, they could either collect their pay or continue to work and get paid overtime. Dumile Ndlovu explained that "we were informed that we should work this much tonnage in an eight hour shift. For example, a rope carries forty eight bags. Now, tonnage determines how many ropes a gang should do in eight hours. After that, we found out that we were doing too much work, so those who worked fast finished the job in three or four hours."

In the hard to police workplaces on the docks, especially in the holds of ships, dock workers had a relatively high level of control over the labor process. Supervision was notably difficult and inefficient, and the relation of mutual dependence between workers and *izinduna* gave dock workers some leverage. Even before wresting concessions from the employers, workers set the pace of work through forms of informal resistance to employers' control. Workers rested on the job and slacked off, which was frequently condoned by *izinduna* who understood that this was necessary to recuperate. Go-slows could also be used as a form of collective action, for example, as retaliation against unfair treatment at the hands of *izinduna* or white supervisors. One of Sideris's informants specified that "this happened especially when a white foreman quarelled [*sic*] a lot. . . . The workers didn't like working with a foreman who fought with them. So they decided to work very slowly. They made the work go slower if he made too much noise."[18] Of course, pilferage and informal trade were also hidden and informal forms of resistance to a political and economic system that tried to keep Africans dependent on poorly paid wage labor.

Finally, dock workers engaged in political protests as well. In 1930, Durban's dock workers were among the most enthusiastic participants in the CPSA's pass burning protests. The year before, dock workers had boycotted the municipal beer halls and refused to pay their taxes. The target of these protests was the official apparatus of racial and class domination rather than wages or working conditions. Both the pass system and the municipal brewing monopoly were central to the government's control over African workers. Laborers saw their employers and the state as cooperating in their oppression, and their grievances in the workplace could thus not be separated from the political context.

The boycott of an Italian ship, named the *Perla*, in 1935 showed that dock workers were aware of international politics as well; it was also evidence of a nascent racial consciousness.[19] Despite an oversupply of labor during the Depression, workers refused to load frozen meat destined for Italian troops involved in the invasion of Ethiopia. The Italian aggression was the main subject of conversation at the Point, and some were even willing to take up arms against the Italian army: "If war breaks out in Abyssinia, we want to go there and fight on the Black side. . . . If we can do anything to stop the White man treading down the Native in Abyssinia as he has done in other parts of the world, we will do it. It is the last Native kingdom and it must survive."[20] The workers received moral support from the CPSA and multiple antifascist organizations.[21] However, the lack of union organization, as African trade unions were illegal, made this boycott impossible to sustain.

Dock workers engaged in collective action for a variety of reasons, and their identity was at least partially formed by their rural experiences. Dock workers did fight for their interests as workers, but their consciousness was more diverse than a focus on working-class activism or rural and ethnic conservatism alone can capture.[22] Especially the idiosyncratic mix of working-class action and informal entrepreneurialism, noted in chapter 1, is of interest in this book. Dock workers and their leaders stood up for the interests of African traders as much as for those of African workers.

Three Leaders from the Workers' Own Ranks, 1930s and 1940s

Many *togt* laborers at the Durban docks resided in the municipal Bell Street *togt* barracks at the Point. From the 1930s onward, the inmates elected representatives to serve on the Native Advisory Board, which was established as a response to the 1929 beer hall boycott and riots. This board consisted of four white councillors and ten Africans, and as its name suggests it had only an advisory function. Its stated goal was to serve as an outlet for grievances and to act as a buffer between the African masses and the authorities.[23] Durban's African elites promptly embraced this board, and workers initially welcomed it as a first step toward municipal representation.[24] Quickly, however, workers came to see the NAB as mostly ineffective.

In the 1930s, residents at the Bell Street barracks elected Dick Mate and Amos Gumede as their consecutive representatives on the board. In the 1940s, Zulu Phungula was their leader. As opposed to the middle-class Africans claiming to represent African workers, such as A. W. G. Champion and John L. Dube, these were leaders from their own ranks. Mate was elected in 1931, but not without a struggle. When the board was first established, Magcekeni Matsoni represented *togt* workers at Bell Street.[25] The MNAD had appointed him, but the inhabitants of the barracks expressed their displeasure at this appointment. They petitioned the board to replace Matsoni with an elected representative and explained that they did not know him and never voted for him. He also refused to meet with them or to give an account of his activities on the board.[26] However, the MNAD did not replace Matsoni, and the workers took the initiative. On July 26, they informed the board that they had elected Dick Mate to represent them.[27] The native welfare officer objected that NAB representatives were not supposed to be elected, but subsequent records of the board's meetings indicate that Mate did in fact replace Matsoni.

Over the next two years, Mate advocated for the rights of both *togt* workers and African traders. On November 3, 1931, he wrote a letter to the town council after the assistant of an African butcher at the Bell Street Native Market was arrested for delivering meat to a white person. A proposed bylaw prohibited trade between Europeans and Africans, but Mate insisted that this measure had not yet been passed.[28] Significantly, he did not challenge the segregation of urban trading but objected to the fact that traders were punished before the proposed bylaw took effect. In August 1932, he complained on behalf of African entrepreneurs about a white trader setting up shop across the street from the barracks. He argued that this trader "would compete with the [African] table and stall holders" in the compound.[29]

Wages were equally on Mate's agenda, especially when a rumor went around that the authorities were planning to reduce the prescribed *togt* rates. This was an especially troubling prospect for casual workers who did not receive rations from their employers, including the workers at the Bell Street barracks. Indeed, the SAR&H had already cut wages by 20 percent, and workers feared that other employers would follow suit.[30] The next NAB meeting discussed casual wages, but the board's white chairman denied that the municipality had any authority over private-sector wages. Mate disagreed; he "expressed the view that as togt labourers were more or less under the control of the [Durban] Corporation, certain representations should be made to the Government on their behalf in connection with such reduction to wages, more especially as he understood that the Corporation had itself not reduced the wages of its employees."[31] While most *togt* workers did not work for the city, Mate correctly pointed out that the municipality did have significant influence over their pay and work conditions. Durban's *togt* bylaws required casual workers to register and set wage rates at which workers were obligated to accept employment, thus outlawing bargaining over wages. He exposed the hypocrisy of the municipality disavowing its responsibility. The chairman consequently agreed to make informal representations to the employers "as guardian of the natives."[32] Mate left one more trace in the archives in December 1932 when he applied prematurely for a license to open a store in the yet to be established uMlazi Glebeland township.[33] Clearly, being a dock worker and fighting for increased wages did not preclude entrepreneurial ambitions or an intent to become independent from wage labor.

The next year, on July 30, the barrack dwellers elected Amos Gumede as Mate's successor; he was reelected unopposed in 1935.[34] The grievances he brought to the NAB concerned issues of both traders and *togt* laborers living in the compound. In 1934, he brought up the poor quality of the sleeping bunks and complaints about Indian hawkers plying their trade outside the barracks. These hawkers were "detrimentally affecting the Native traders within that institution." Moreover, Africans could not compete on a level playing field, as they were only allowed to sell inside the compound. When the police complained in 1936 about *togt* workers congregating at the corner of Bell and Prince Streets, inconveniencing white residents on their way to the beach, Gumede defended their right to assemble there. If casual workers failed to find a job in the morning, he argued, they would have to wait around to see if more jobs became available later in the day.[35]

We know little about Mate and even less about Gumede, though it is clear from the limited archival record that they were receptive to the needs and interests of both African small-scale traders and workers. Zulu Phungula left a much bigger imprint on dockers' memories, the archives, and historiography. Hemson discusses Phungula's activism extensively, yet this chapter focuses specifically on the tension between working-class identity and other identities that fueled his militancy. In 1939, dock workers elected him to represent the Bell Street *togt* barracks. Like most dock workers, he was from rural Natal, more specifically the iXopo District (see map 1.1). These rural origins have been linked to his style of activism. A former Communist Party activist called him "stubborn like a peasant."[36] Hemson's more generous portrayal was that Phungula possessed a "peasant-like independence."[37] However, Phungula did not have much security on the land, which leads Hemson to the conclusion that he, like other migrants with insufficient returns from the rural economy, fought "to force open the possibility of becoming part of the urban proletariat."[38]

Phungula's leadership signaled a shift from respectfully petitioning the authorities to more radical working-class action with a strong political undertone. He was a charismatic leader, and his discourse invoked a sense of injustice and outrage at workers' misery, pride in being Zulu, and biblical imagery. Under this "very brave and strong organizer," as Sidumo Chiliza characterized him, Durban's dock workers went through one of their most militant phases. Increased shipping and a high demand for dock labor during the Second World War both bolstered their bargaining power and complicated activism as the government declared stevedoring a controlled industry under its wartime Emergency Regulations. This brought labor relations in the harbor directly under central government authority.

The many strikes and other actions that Phungula, and others with him, organized despite these regulations are not the only evidence of his industrial and political militancy. In discussions with authorities and employers, he made radical demands that revealed the political nature of their struggles. Dock workers demanded 8s per day in 1941–42, which represented a 100 percent increase, but Phungula asserted that they ultimately wanted 25s, the same as white employees. While these demands were in the first place about bread-and-butter issues and rooted in a strong economism, Phungula was not only looking for gradual increases (albeit at a very steep grade) but also challenged the racial structure of wages itself. He did not merely argue that their wages were insufficient but claimed equality and equal pay with white employees.[39] He rejected the idea of a rural wage subsidy and free social security in the Reserves, which legitimized low African wages, and demanded provisions for old age and illness.[40] His insistence that the government could not send striking dock workers home because their homes were in Durban, was particularly significant. This assertion of full urban and proletarian status, with which most workers would probably have disagreed, challenged a central premise of the migratory labor system and its use of cheap African labor. Acceptance of the fact that these workers and their households principally relied on urban wages for their survival would have undermined the structure of wages in Durban and increased shipping costs.[41]

He expressed workers' sense of injustice and contended that "the government and the employers agree among themselves that Natives should not be paid and yet we natives have helped to build up the British Empire far above the Kingdom of Heaven," and that Africans "should also have a share of the milk and honey that abound in this country."[42] He also articulated the political nature of their struggle when he accused the government of withholding the increased wages employers had promised on the condition that the government would stipulate them. Employers had indicated a vague and uncommitted willingness to pay higher wages but argued that it was the government's responsibility to determine these pay rates. African wages were set by *togt* bylaws and by the wage board, not through collective bargaining. Moreover, the fact that stevedoring was a controlled industry during the war allowed employers to portray labor relations as purely a legal matter over which they had no control.[43] Employers were in this case not the object of the workers' ire but rather the state for not legislating these higher wages. Just like Mate years earlier, Phungula argued that while the government did not directly employ these workers, it did regulate pay and work conditions. These were thus a political matter.

Phungula's preference for forceful working-class activism instead of peasant action was once again very clear in his calls for a general strike in 1948–49, after he returned to Durban from his five-year exile. In his 1948 "Report of Our Workers in Natal," he decried the shortage of Reserve land but did not advocate for a rural solution to this problem. The report addressed both workers' and peasants' issues, but its demands were for significantly higher wages rather than for more land or agricultural assistance.[44] In late 1948, Phungula repeated his demand for a 25s daily minimum wage and called for a general strike in support of this claim. Despite some enthusiasm among workers, his strike call was unsuccessful, as other labor organizations considered his demand too radical for them to support.[45] Yet, he did not give up on the idea of a general strike. After the January 1949 anti-Indian pogrom, in which dock workers played a prominent role, he asked African workers in Durban to stay home on May 1, 1949.[46]

This strike was fairly successful on the docks, where Phungula had a strong influence; it was certainly more successful than the six to eight hundred strikers that the newspapers reported. In particular, Bell Street *togt* workers walked out in great numbers. There was, however, no significant disruption of work beyond the harbor area.[47] The South African Police (SAP) concluded that Phungula was to blame for agitating the workers by making excessive wage demands, and he was exiled once more, this time for ten years.[48] This is his last appearance in the archives or the literature. Phungula was probably well aware that he could be banned from Durban again, but Hemson points out that he was always "prepared to make sacrifices, to suffer the consequences of his actions, and to return to battle again."[49]

His exile did not end resistance on the docks. While the first half of the 1950s did bring a slump in labor activism, it reemerged without his leadership. The leaderless nature of their continued resistance indicates that informal organization survived repression and the onslaught on their formal leaders. Indeed, workers' organization was driven underground but did not disappear. Of course, Phungula was the most prominent but not the only organizer; for example, the July 1942 strike was organized by a ten-member committee. Thus, even after removing the most charismatic and well known of these leaders, an organizational memory would have remained. Phungula was a different leader than the union strongmen in Dipesh Chakrabarty's work. While he was charismatic, organization and militancy did not rely mostly on his personal power and influence.[50] A memory of him did survive, however, and one of the demands of strikers in 1954 was for his return.[51]

It is clear from this brief overview of Phungula's activities as a dock leader that he championed a proletarian radicalism: he advocated for and organized strikes, made demands for substantial wage increases, and argued strongly against the idea of a rural wage subsidy. However, an account focused only on industrial action and proletarian consciousness may not provide a complete picture. Apart from a working-class consciousness, he also espoused strong appeals to Zulu identity and an outspoken anti-Indian discourse. In fact, his epithet Zulu derived from his tendency to address meetings with "Zulu" or "*Bayete* Zulu" (*bayete* is a salute).[52] Nevertheless, Hemson attributes the 1949 anti-Indian pogrom, which Phungula supported and is discussed in more detail in chapter 1, to the failure of a working-class strategy.[53] In this account, nationalist and racial violence was a surrogate for frustrated working-class action. I argue that that we need to consider Phungula's economic nationalism and his appeal to Zulu identity as integral and central to his political ideas. South African progressive scholars have frequently either ignored nationalism or dismissed it as false consciousness. This was partially in rejection of apartheid's emphasis on race and nation, and partially rooted in a Marxist tendency to prioritize class. Yet nationalism has been and continues to be a very real force in South African history and politics.[54]

An emergent nationalism did not only take root among the African middle class, which is the focus of most accounts of African nationalism. Bill Freund notes that "Phungula, who was a supporter of the 1949 violence against Indians to some extent, was able to combine an antagonism to the bosses [and] demands for a place in the city for black workers, with a concept of Zuluness. It is not only among individuals such as Champion, who liked to write about the resuscitation of the 'Zulu nation' that this sort of concept prevailed but also among the most revolutionary."[55] It is this tension between working-class identity and other sources of consciousness and activism that is most of interest in this chapter. Freund's invocation of A. W. G. Champion is significant. Champion emerged in the 1920s as the leader of the Natal branch of the ICU, the ICU *yase* Natal, and was once considered a dangerous radical and the main representative of Durban's African workers. However, the ICU's politics were often ambiguous; after the 1929 beer hall riots, Champion joined the NAB and rebranded himself as a moderate and respectable member of the African elite.[56] The union's leadership mostly consisted of the aspiring African middle class and generally eschewed a language of class-based solidarity and working-class action. Rather, it preferred a discourse of nationalism, middle-class respectability, and Garveyite self-help. The leadership did not generally support industrial action, favoring litigation and petitioning over confrontation, and advised union members to petition the authorities rather than to strike.[57] Champion could even be quite condescending to African workers, characterizing them as untrustworthy.[58] He was not alone in this condescension. Much of the African nationalist elite subscribed to a civilizational discourse in which the majority of Africans were considered indolent and incapable of self-improvement due to moral failings. The nationalist elites saw themselves the civilized, educated, and industrious Africans, separate from the ordinary Africans who were yet to be civilized through the dignity of labor.[59]

This brief discussion indicates some of the important differences between Phungula's and Champion's political and organizational ideas. Significantly, the ICU's strategies did little to guarantee lasting organization among workers, and the union collapsed quickly after 1929.[60] However, there were also notable parallels. Both believed in a form of economic segregation where Africans would buy from African traders rather than from whites or Indians. Mate may have been amenable to commercial segregation as well, as he did not protest a bylaw segregating urban trade but only its premature implementation. Both Champion and Phungula considered cooperative societies a route to economic independence and a source of opportunities for African entrepreneurs. Their economic nationalism contained a strong anti-Indian rhetoric and should be understood in the context of the emergence of a racial and Zulu ethnic consciousness in the first half of the twentieth century.[61]

In the 1930s, Champion urged Africans to "smash Indian traders" and to become "trustees of their own wealth," and he argued in favor of segregation so that only Africans would be allowed to trade with Africans.[62] Similarly, Phungula stressed in his evidence to the commission investigating the 1949 pogrom that Indians did not have "any claim to this country." He accused the National Party of not living up to its promise to send Indians back to the Indian subcontinent and to bring more complete segregation after their 1948 election victory on the platform of apartheid.[63] Both leaders advocated African self-reliance through cooperative societies where Africans buy from Africans and avoid commercial exploitation at the hands of Indian and white traders. Champion was inspired by Garveyite ideas of self-help, and the ICU organized the All-African Cooperative Society. African American and black Caribbean sailors had been spreading the ideas of Marcus Garvey and the Universal Negro Improvement Association in the ports of Cape Town and Durban for decades, putting their intellectual stamp on the early ANC and ICU.[64] Champion also stood to gain personally from calls to support African businesses, as he was an entrepreneur himself. He established several businesses in the late 1920s that benefitted from his association with the ICU and that may even have been funded with union dues.[65]

Whether or not Phungula was familiar with the ideas of Garvey and the Universal Negro Improvement Association is unclear, but he did try to establish a cooperative movement among African workers in 1941–42.[66] Later that decade, he once again put his weight behind a cooperative venture; after the 1949 violence he petitioned the town council not to replace the disrupted Indian bus services with municipal buses. Such replacement, he argued, would keep African workers from purchasing buses themselves and running them as a cooperative business. He also collected money for this undertaking.[67] There was an African cooperative society at Maydon Wharf (see map 1.2) in the mid-1940s as well.[68] Because of its location in the harbor, dock workers would probably have been involved in this. Furthermore, the ICU leadership and Zulu Phungula were not the only Africans interested in cooperative societies and economic segregation.

In the late 1940s a similar ethnically chauvinist and segregationist discourse, centered on a vision of a New Africa, emerged in uMkhumbane. This mostly Indian-owned area was a place where both Indian and African informal entrepreneurs could thrive, as the city's control over it was limited. This was also where African women could eke out an independent livelihood beyond the grasp of authorities through brewing, retailing, and other businesses. The millenarian and populist belief in a rejuvenated African society had a strong anti-Indian component to it. As is often the case with millenarian ideas, the emergence of a new and just society was predicated on a cleansing violence. If uMkhumbane were to become this New Africa, Indian ownership had to disappear, and the land had to be expropriated.[69] Pushing out Indians of course also meant that the African traders' competitors would disappear.

Africans were hardly the only ones advocating economic segregation in the interest of their own petty entrepreneurs. Afrikaner nationalists made appeals to customers to support Afrikaner businesses and for these businesses to deal with Afrikaners only.[70] The cooperative movement in uMkhumbane, closely associated with New Africa, equally encouraged economic segregation. While urging acceptance of the industrial order, this movement argued that the African working class and petty bourgeoisie had to unite to protect their common economic and commercial interests. They had to unite not to engage in industrial or political action but to escape commercial exploitation at the hands of Indian and white traders and to support African businesses instead. This would help Africans to become economically independent. S. S. L. Mtolo, quoted by Iain Edwards, captured the enthusiasm about cooperatives: "It swept through people so quickly. It was so obvious. People needed to live together so that they could help each other. That's self-help. Everyone always knew that they were being cheated in the city. No-one needed to tell them that. But how to stop that . . . that had always been something people did not even think about. You just tried to live along. But the co-operatives changed all that."[71]

Indeed, the economic nationalism of Champion, Phungula, and New Africa was shared by a broad cross-section of the African population. As Phungula advocated for cooperative African bus services and collected money for this purpose, workers boycotted Indian-operated buses. This boycott was supported by the Natal branch of the ANC, led at that time by Champion, but not by the national ANC; and it forced authorities to grant eleven certificates to African bus operators. All recipients of these certificates were established entrepreneurs with links to the NAB.[72]

Just like the cooperatives run by the ICU in the 1920s, however, the cooperative societies of the 1940s turned out to be more in the interest of African traders than of African workers and the poor. Their appeals for racial unity did not stop entrepreneurs from taking advantage of their involvement in cooperatives. Idealism made room for greed, and by the 1950s it had become clear that those running these societies were interested in little else than profits.[73] While uMkhubane's interest in these societies reached its peak in the late 1940s, there is striking continuity in the interest in cooperatives between the ICU, Zulu Phungula, and the New Africa movement.

New Africa and other cooperative movements likely inspired Phungula's attempts at establishing a cooperative society in the early 1940s and his enthusiasm for cooperatively owned and operated African bus services in 1949, and vice versa. After all, Africans in Durban's informal settlements relied extensively on the harbor as their source of gossip and news, and some would take up stevedoring shifts from time to time.[74] Dock workers also visited uMkhumbane and other periurban settlements on weekends and whenever they were free to drink and socialize: uMkhumbane was an important center for African working-class culture, a hub for recreation and illegal (but not necessarily illegitimate) activities.[75] Dock workers like Phungula would thus have been familiar with this discourse of economic segregation and with the interests and grievances of African traders. Like Mate and Gumede, he was not only concerned with the interests of dock workers as workers. Indeed, his remarks to the commission investigating the 1949 pogrom illustrated his ethnic chauvinism and his concern for advancing the interests of African over Indian traders. While these anti-Indian feelings are not reducible to economic interests, economic and political resentment was a factor. This cannot simply be dismissed as false consciousness or a surrogate for thwarted class-based activism but needs to be seen as integral to the political thought of these workers.

Organization in the 1950s

After Zulu Phungula's second banishment, workers' organization on the docks went underground. There were few major labor conflicts in the first half of the 1950s until, on July 1, 1954, thousands of *togt* stevedores and hundreds of permanent workers walked out in demand of 15s per day, instead of 10s 3d.[76] They had learned from the victimization Phungula had suffered and did not appoint spokesmen. They shouted in unison, "The man we want back to speak for us has been taken away. We are still looking for him. We won't have spokesmen."[77] Workers did have a collective and organizational memory of their actions, and organization took place informally. Officials looked for a scapegoat and found one in the ANC, which was rapidly becoming the main African political organization after the defiance campaign of 1952. For the district commandant of the SAP there was "little doubt that this organisation had much to do with bringing about the stoppage of work."[78] However, there seems to be little evidence for this claim beyond a letter of support from the ANC and eleven other organizations.

According to the *Natal Mercury*, there had been an undercurrent of restlessness among the three thousand *togt* laborers in the port for some time. Workers had been agitating for better wages for six months.[79] Employers offered a nonnegotiable 9d increase, which the workers rejected. An amicable solution was unlikely and became impossible when S. D. Mentz, the chairman of the government's Central Native Labour Board (CNLB), became involved. Mentz was unwilling to compromise and believed that "there should be a showdown."[80] He considered this strike the first test of the Native Labour (Settlement of Disputes) Act, which was meant to eliminate the remnants of African trade unionism. The employers' 9d offer angered him, as he believed this offer would encourage further claims and inspire other African workers to make similar demands. He thus refused to settle the dispute.[81]

Striking was illegal for African workers but as mostly casual workers they did not technically strike, they merely did not offer their labor for hire. Therefore, they did not do anything illegal and could not be dealt with by the police and courts. Mentz conceded that the strikers had not committed any offense and considered this evidence that they received legal advice from outside agitators.[82] Once again, officials did not consider it possible for dock workers to organize independently. The CNLB and employers had to look for other ways to force the stevedores back to work. They reminded workers of the conditions of their stay in the compounds, which stated that the workers had to be on first call for the company that houses them. The workers were thus threatened with eviction. This paternalist system of housing benefited the workers by limiting the need to spend their wages in the city, but it also afforded the employers greater leverage. However, there was substantial juridical doubt whether the strikers could be evicted from the compounds.[83] The workers played hardball as well; they turned down offers for 9d and 1s 9d increases. However, a labor surplus and the threat of eviction weakened their position, and most workers eventually returned to work. They insisted, however, that they returned only because it was the CNLB's condition for negotiations. Workers assured a journalist from *Advance* that they would not be satisfied until they receive the same 15s per day as black dock workers in other South African ports.[84]

There was also a generational element to dockers' militancy. In this instance, some older workers claimed that they had tried to stave off a strike but that "the majority of the workers were young and irresponsible."[85] Two years later, three older stevedores managed to avert a strike and convinced their younger colleagues to petition the authorities instead. They were "tired of warning these young men."[86] Older workers often had more dependents and household responsibilities and could ill afford to lose pay; they were also more likely to rely on their wages alone, as workers with a side business generally retired earlier. Moreover, traditional age-based hierarchies characteristic of rural Zulu society had been recreated in the urban world of labor. Older workers thus felt that they were entitled to the obedience and respect of the younger men who instead flouted the authority of both their elders and their employers.[87] Conservative elders experienced this behavior as deeply disrespectful and unbecoming to Zulu culture. Indeed, the seemingly audacious independence of young Africans in the city was a long-standing concern of both African patriarchs and colonial authorities.

The latter half of the 1950s brought several more strikes over living conditions and freedoms in the compounds, and over the future of casual labor.[88] The years 1958–59 were particularly tumultuous in Durban and on the docks, leading one official to label the city a "strategic centre for subversive elements" in Natal.[89] Strikes in early 1959 sealed the fate of casual labor on the Durban docks, which employers and the government had come to see as expensive, undisciplined, and strike prone. The instability of *togt* labor also complicated attempts at segregating the city more completely. For workers, casual labor meant unpredictable earnings but also a degree of freedom and comparatively higher daily wages. The late 1950s also brought increased political resistance to apartheid from the ANC and the South African Congress of Trade Unions, in which Durban's dock workers participated enthusiastically.[90]

In April 1958, these two groups organized a stay-at-home as part of the £1-a-day campaign. Durban's dock workers complemented this strike with an overtime ban. Authorities went to great lengths to dissuade Africans from participating in the general strike; they received assistance from Champion, who urged workers not to participate in industrial action, as he had done many times before. The stay-at-home was a mixed success at best, and the ANC called it off after just one day. However, Durban's dock workers were once again very willing to put down their tools and did respond well to the strike call. As a result, most shipping was suspended. At the end of the first day, when the ANC called off the general strike, dock workers decided to boycott overtime until they received £1 per day.[91] The workers exploited the industry's reliance on overtime and could not be prosecuted or expelled from their compounds because overtime was, in theory, voluntary. The ban had some success, as they received a moderate raise of 1s 6d to 14s, up from only 8s 6d in 1952.

The next strike finally tipped the balance in favor of decasualization. In February 1959, regular stevedores asserted their equality and status against *izinduna*. A Wage Board Determination had awarded a raise to these African foremen but not to the general workers. It was this inequality that caused dock workers to walk out. The conflict started with about two hundred workers at just one company, but quickly laborers at other firms joined them. News travels quickly on the docks, and by the end of the day between 1,000 and 1,500 stevedores were on strike. According to the SAP the strike was spontaneous, and the spokesmen refused to give their names.[92] Their inability to identify these spokesmen illustrates the employers' lack of knowledge of and control over their workforce. As they outsourced hiring to *izinduna*, they did not know enough about their own workers to identify or to effectively and directly discipline them.

In response, stevedoring companies decided to hire laborers on monthly contracts only; they thus did away with *togt* labor. All strikers were dismissed but the majority was reengaged under the new permanent labor scheme, which guaranteed a weekly wage of £3 regardless of fluctuations in shipping and employment.[93] In March, the last conflict for a decade broke out over compensation for injuries during overtime. Workers once again engaged in an overtime ban during a busy period. This new interruption of normal operations convinced employers that their current workers were too strike prone and that the problem could only be solved by replacing the entire labor force.[94] Convinced that stevedoring was an unskilled job, the employers were confident that "the new stevedores will be as capable as the old gangs within four or five days."[95] I found no information on performance or accidents after this strike, but the experience of a similar mass dismissal in 1969, when the pace of work dropped and the number of injuries increased, seems to negate this claim.[96]

Several interviewees participated in the strikes of the late 1950s, and some were even involved in organizing them. The interviewees in particular remembered gaining concessions from the employers on tonnage, that is, how much work had to be done in one shift. Of course, money was also a prominent issue, as discussed by several interviewees. Sergeant Ngcobo, an *induna,* thought that *togt* workers used to strike frequently because they wanted to earn enough money to only have to work three days per week.[97] However, finding out from ship crews that they worked harder and for less money than in other ports seems to have been a more important motivation.[98] Dockers learned from crews how much laborers worked in other ports in the region and that they were being "robbed in tonnage," as Dumile Ndlovu put it. They also found out how much others were paid and learned about strikes in other ports. Strike waves could thus spread easily along the coasts of Africa through these networks of communication. Ship crews retained their role in the spread of activism and resistance, a role they have played for many centuries.[99] Zulu Phungula also referred to soldiers and foreign crews who were astounded by the poverty of Durban's dock workers to claim international solidarity and to express the injustice of their situation.[100] However, this solidarity was not absolute and crews occasionally acted as strike breakers, loading and unloading cargoes when stevedores were on strike.[101]

The interviews also offer an important corrective to the view that dock workers would strike at the drop of a hat. Several interviewees mentioned that there were talks and negotiations before strike action was undertaken, and there are documented meetings where workers explicitly stated that they chose to "make representations" instead of striking.[102] These talks were often enough to avoid a strike. Moreover, workers did not necessarily consider themselves to be on strike if they were not working while their representatives were negotiating. Mabhalane Dlamini, for example, noted that their leaders were in talks with management and that "therefore they don't want anyone to do their job until that is solved."

As opposed to Mate, Gumede, and Phungula, the leaders from the late 1950s have not clearly been identified in the archives. The attempted 1949 general strike was, as far as the record show, Phungula's last political appearance. After his second banishment in 1949, he never appeared in the newspapers or the archives again. However, some interviewees claimed that he was the organizer of at least one of the strikes in 1958–59, but they knew him under his actual name, Mzamo Phungula. During this time, Phungula operated under different nicknames to prevent victimization, just like Mkhumbikanowa, who was mentioned at the beginning of this chapter. The details they knew about him make it likely that this was indeed Zulu Phungula. They remembered him as a good and experienced worker, who was respected by the *izinduna* and by other laborers. He had a sharp mind and was trusted by the workers. Eventually, Mzamo Phungula, Zodwa Tenza, Bheka Dlaba, and Dumile Sibiya were arrested for organizing a strike and released after workers collected money to pay the fine.[103] This account is similar to the account of Mkhumbikanowa that was given by some other interviewees.[104] Mkhumbi too was arrested and released after workers paid his fine. Moreover, he continued to work on the docks after his arrest, even though he was banned. Because of the limited knowledge employers and authorities had of the workforce, it was possible to work on the docks without being known to do so. This could explain how Phungula too could possibly have returned without drawing the attention of the authorities.

These interviews also gave some insight into organization in the absence of trade unions. Lihlo Shange explained that there was a dock worker who was "announcing from Q shed to M shed, and one from M wharf, one to fifteen minutes before the start of the shift that there was something going on and that the dock workers should be ready to drop their tools." Others found out through meetings and by talking to colleagues; most people would not have found out from workers announcing the strike on the day itself. Sidumo Chiliza noted that "Phungula and a few of us went to talk to colleagues and also organized meetings with workers." These meetings would mostly have taken place at the Bell Street barracks, which had the greatest concentration of *togt* stevedores and was the traditional center of dock militancy. Mr. Xulu remembered talking about a strike among the workers: "(How did you go on strike?) We did not go to work. (Who said you shouldn't go?) We talked among ourselves that we shouldn't go to work."[105] About the actual strike, workers recalled gathering at the employer's offices and singing.

Of course, these strikes invited a strong response from the employers. After the March 1959 strike, all stevedores were fired and replaced by new workers, believed to be untainted by militant ideas.[106] However, if all stevedores were replaced, it would have been impossible for the interviewees, except those who worked for the SAR&H, to have worked on the docks both before and after 1959, yet most did. Durban's dock employers did not know enough about their labor force to actually implement such measures. This changed after the decasualization of dock labor, a process to which the implementation of monopoly hiring was key. Durban followed a global trend of phasing out casual dock labor. The core changes were the same as elsewhere: a restricted supply of labor, centralized hiring, predetermined hiring patterns, and reduced autonomy for gang leaders to choose their own workers.[107] After decasualization, stevedoring employers in Durban and elsewhere had much more control over the hiring, firing, and disciplining of workers; they increased their control over the workplace and the labor process. However, decasualization in Durban was also a specific and unique process. In many ports, the end of casual labor went hand in hand with unionization. This was not the case in Durban, as Africans were denied these workers' rights.[108]

The end of *togt* labor should also be seen in the light of a colonial African trend of stabilization of urban African labor. Workers who did not work a regular job for a white employer and who had some freedom to start a side business or to live where they wanted, conflicted with officials' ideal of the urban African worker. Policy makers preferred a steadily working male wage laborer with respect for authority either residing in a planned and orderly township with his nuclear family or living in a hostel and maintaining his family in the rural Reserve.

Contradictory Interests?

Dock workers and their leaders both engaged in militant working-class action and stood up for the interests of small-scale entrepreneurs. This may seem peculiar, contradictory, or in the case of their leaders even disingenuous. Do the interests of traders really correspond to those of their customers? Does a strategy of individual advancement not preclude class-based solidarity? And do the unequal power relations between entrepreneurs and their working-class customers, or between landlords and tenants not complicate such unity? After all, Champion's concern for the rights of African workers ebbed away after he was co-opted into the NAB and became an establishment figure. He tried to dissuade workers from taking action and used the union to provide customers and possibly funds for his own petty-capitalist enterprises. The political leadership of uMkhumbane's cooperative movement, which mostly consisted of shack lords and small-scale entrepreneurs, also advocated acceptance of the industrial order. This leadership avowed radical politics yet betrayed the interests of workers and the poor in return for the municipality's recognition of their leadership and control over housing. They talked about radical change but did not follow up with their actions.[109] The classless discourse of African unity suited African elites who stood to gain from economic segregation and the leadership roles to which they could lay claim, but it obscured divisions between men and women, smaller and larger traders, landlords and tenants, laborers and entrepreneurs, and so on.

Commercial aspirations and advocacy for the interests of African traders are not always compatible with the interests of workers. However, while the sincerity of the leadership of uMkhumbane and the ICU is questionable, Mate, Gumede, and Phungula did fight with and for the workers. Both Mate and Gumede defended the interests of Durban's dock workers in the NAB, and one cannot simply interpret their association with the powerless advisory board as selling out. They consistently defended the interests of their constituency of African dock workers, but also of traders, especially compared to the other African members of the board. How involved they were in strikes and other working-class action is less clear, but that Phungula was at the forefront of these is well documented. Dumile Sibiya and Bheka Dlaba, two leaders of the 1958–59 strikes, also engaged in small-scale businesses selling pilfered food. They would thus likely have been receptive to traders' concerns as well.

The radical politics of these dock leaders were not a smokescreen or mere rhetoric. Their actions give us little reason to doubt the sincerity of their commitment to workers' concerns, despite also campaigning for and even having entrepreneurial interests. They did not just appeal to workers to gain a popular following, increase their profile in the eyes of authorities, or secure their political positions. Small-scale entrepreneurs were often as poor as most workers and encountered the same indignities as other Africans in the city. As such, Durban's African workers and petty entrepreneurs had much in common, and class distinctions were not always very pronounced.[110]

More than half of the interviewed dock workers combined wage labor with informal commercial enterprise, though their businesses were for the most part significantly smaller in scale than those of Champion and other prominent members of Durban's African middle class. These dock workers were not so much part of a petty bourgeoisie as they were African migrant workers trying to combine different opportunities into a sustainable livelihood. However, many did have entrepreneurial ambitions and used these opportunities to become independent of wage labor. Thus, we cannot look at either their commercial activities or their wage labor in isolation from their broader livelihood strategies. Dock workers' households combined urban labor and the homestead economy with small-scale commercial enterprises run by the dock worker himself or by others within or even outside the household. Not only did these households have more than one earning strategy; there also were close links among these sources of income. Employment on the docks enabled commercial small and microenterprises in the townships, in the compounds, in informal settlements, and in the rural areas.

This straddling of formal employment and the informal economy can help us make sense of the seemingly contradictory interests and actions of dock workers and their leaders. Mate, Sibiya, and Dlaba were not the only wage laborers aspiring to be entrepreneurs. They fought to improve the working conditions for both shore workers and stevedores, but the household strategies of many workers did not just revolve around their dock labor. Their politics reflected that fact. It is not just that these workers wore two hats, one as laborer and one as self-employed entrepreneur, and could defend their interests in either capacity. There was a functional relationship between both activities. As such, better wages, the continuation of the casual labor system, and shorter hours would benefit them not only as workers but also as members of households that relied on small-scale entrepreneurialism. Higher wages resulted in more resources to invest, and shorter hours meant that they could spend more time on their commercial activities. Actions in defense of the casual labor system were also in defense of the opportunity to offer their labor specifically to those companies that worked ships with interesting goods or to take a day to work on their business. When dock laborers with commercial interests and ambitions stood up for workers' rights, this was not just because they were laborers as well but also because dock labor enabled these commercial strategies. Moreover, actions to defend the rights of African traders appealed to a sense of injustice about racial restrictions and to the aspirations of many workers.

When seen from the perspective of laborers and households straddling the formal and the informal economies, the nationalist violence of 1949 and Phungula's support for it become more than just a substitute for a failed general strike. For many of these dock workers, Indian traders were competition and symbolized the economic and political marginalization of Africans. This marginalization fed into their anti-Indian nationalism. In this pogrom, African petty accumulators evicted their Indian competition, and African tenants evicted their landlords. Similarly, the beer hall boycott and riots in 1929 started when *togt* workers boycotted an Indian shop across the street from the Bell Street barracks. Workers believed that the shopkeeper was behind the crackdown on the brewing of *mahewu* in the compound, as this represented competition for his business.[111]

Many dock workers were or aspired to become petty traders, and the support for traders' rights by Mate, Gumede, and Phungula should be seen in this light. However, the end of the casual labor regime drastically curtailed the opportunities that their dock employment offered. In the decades that followed, apartheid policies continued to close off many commercial opportunities for Africans, and different levels of government carried on their legislative attacks on African traders, and especially on women engaged in informal trade.[112]

These workers clearly did not subscribe to an unambiguous working-class identity, and few labor historians would adhere to an unquestioning notion of proletarian consciousness. Several historians have noted the complex interplay between working-class action and forms of Zulu nationalism. However, discussions of these workers' nationalism in relation to their livelihoods are scarce, and scholars have often paid more attention to the nationalism of the African petty bourgeoisie. This chapter has discussed the idiosyncratic mix of working-class action and concern for the interests of African small-scale entrepreneurs. The apparent contradiction between these different interests was not evidence of insincere appeals to the working class by an African petty bourgeoisie, and Zulu nationalism was more than a surrogate for frustrated working-class action in a context where Indian traders were a safe outlet for Africans' anger at employers and the state. Though nationalism is irreducible to economic considerations, dock workers did have divergent interests rooted in livelihoods that straddled waged employment and informal entrepreneurialism, as well as the rural and the urban. These interests cannot be separated from workers' industrial and political activism. Since these small-scale commercial businesses were often made possible by employment on the docks, these different activities were not merely separate sources of income but rather integral and connected parts of wider livelihood strategies.

Conclusion

Durban's Dock Workers in Global Perspective

There is a contradiction at the core of the lives and livelihoods of Durban's dock workers. These migrant laborers performed the hard work necessary to connect South Africa and the subcontinent to global markets. Working in South Africa's largest harbor, they handled most of the country's imports and exports. They were thus crucial to the integration of southern Africa into global networks of trade, communication, and capital. Discourses on globalization, which often conflate globalization and financialization,[1] seldom pay much attention to labor, except when performed in sweatshops or offshored from the West.[2] However, it was the hard work of transport laborers around the world, as well as that of industrial, agricultural, and other workers, that enabled the expansion of global trade and capitalist exploitation. Nevertheless, as African rural migrants under apartheid, Durban's dock workers did not reap rewards commensurate with their seminal role in servicing the country's international trade, neither in legal status nor in economic compensation. Not only were these workers shortchanged, their livelihoods also did not reflect the global connectedness that their labor made possible. Rather, their social and economic lives were thoroughly rooted in local rural economies and remarkably disconnected from the global networks of trade and communication they served. Thus, while the recent turn to the Indian Ocean world offers many exciting new perspectives in South African historiography, I was more interested in looking inland to the workers' rural homes and households.

Thinking about ports and shipping can too easily lead us to prioritize cosmopolitanism and global connections over withdrawal and exclusion from the world of shipping and global mobility. Yet the latter phenomena were at least as important to the lives of these dock workers. Likewise, academics and policy makers have often tended to find their ideal subjects, regardless of whether these are proletarian radicals or neoliberally celebrated entrepreneurs, among African workers and the African poor (see the introduction). Both of these accounts of African labor rely on a similar assumption that global connections and the spread of capitalism somehow flatten social relations.[3] Consequently, both accounts assume the applicability of either understandings of wage labor based on Western experiences of commodified work or of a universal market rationality and innate entrepreneurialism embodied by *Homo economicus*. Durban's dock workers, just like many African workers and entrepreneurs both today and in the past, do not fit into such universalist concepts of socioeconomic relations.[4]

This book is in many ways an example of an Africanist writing back to labor history and to the literature on entrepreneurialism, both of which generally fail to consider African social realities on their own merits. In my view, African history forces us to reconsider common understandings of what labor is and to dispense with accounts of an innate and universal entrepreneurial spirit.

Global Shipping, Local Lives

Durban's dock workers did not live in isolation from the cosmopolitan world of shipping. The harbor was the geographic, economic, and social heart of the city: it was often from the docks that people learned about new trends and styles, international affairs, strikes, wages and labor practices, and politics. It was the center of news and gossip for Africans in the city, and stevedores and shore workers could interact with sailors from around the world. For example, it was through the ports of Cape Town and Durban, where black sailors from the Americas interacted with African workers, that Garveyism spread in South Africa.

As Frederick Cooper notes, the news of strikes and wage increases also traveled between ports. Strikes in Durban could thus inspire similar actions in other African ports and vice versa. Talking with ship crews offered opportunities to compare labor practices and wages with those at other harbors; this was strategic knowledge in the struggle for better work conditions. When Durban's dockers learned about the counting of ropes in other ports, they knew that they were being "robbed in tonnage" and demanded the same standards. News about world politics also traveled. The attempted boycott in 1935 of the *Perla*, a ship supplying the Italian troops in Ethiopia, was testament to harbor workers' awareness of international affairs.

There is thus no doubt that dock workers were linked into the global networks of exchange that were serviced by the port. However, the limited extent of these connections is perhaps more noteworthy than the fact that they existed. Despite working in a global industry, the lives of Durban's dock workers did not exude the cosmopolitanism that many other dock workers around the world exhibited;[5] their lives were remarkably locally rooted. As important as the connections to global networks of trade and communication were to these workers, their disengagement from them shaped their lives at least as much. Under apartheid, African workers could not travel or mingle freely with others. Their generally limited command of English also complicated interactions with ship crews. The "educated people," that is, those few who had received enough schooling to carry on an extended conversation in English, were therefore the ones who found out that they worked more than their counterparts in other ports.[6] Moreover, they received meager wages, even if these were often comparatively better than those of other African workers in Durban, and could thus not afford many of the imported consumer goods they unloaded on a daily basis.

Apartheid authorities restricted the residence, mobility, and social life of Africans in the city. Furthermore, authorities equally limited the freedom to go about the city for ship crews, and especially for their nonwhite members.[7] Sailors and dock workers thus could not simply meet and gossip in dockside bars. However, urban segregation was always less than complete, and the lives of casual dock laborers were especially difficult to police. Many continued to live in servants' quarters, informal settlements, downtown parks, or on the verandas of dockside sheds. On days that they could not find work, they would hang around town or on the beach, which the police considered loitering and a nuisance. On weekends they, like many other workers in the city, would often make their way to informal settlements to illegally drink and attend parties. The government continuously struggled to regulate this unwanted behavior but only managed to significantly increase its control over dock workers after phasing out casual labor in 1959.

Apartheid policies that made Africans into strangers in the supposedly white city thus complicated dock workers' engagement with international networks of trade and exchange. Nevertheless, the rural orientation of these workers' lives was not just the result of urban segregation. All interviewed dock workers came from the rural areas and retired to the countryside. Leaving the city and urban wage labor to return to rural life was always their goal. Apartheid policies narrowed their options, but their commitment to a rural conservatism is irreducible to government policy. The white minority government did try to preserve the system of oscillating labor migration—throughout the second half of the twentieth century this increasingly meant dumping an

African surplus population in the countryside via forced removals—but African migrants themselves also built and upheld this system. Migrant labor allowed them to become homestead heads and to take up their position in the rural patriarchal order, even if that came at the cost of many years of unfulfilling and exploitative urban labor. Indeed, many workers defended labor migration. Consequently, the violence that accompanied the transition to democracy resulted at least partly from the threat that the political programs of the ANC and the Congress of South African Trade Unions (COSATU) presented to the migrant labor system.[8]

Access to rural land and livestock had sociocultural and emotional significance, as one could not establish an *umuzi* and become a homestead head without it. Even for women, who performed the bulk of domestic labor under rural patriarchy, marriage through *ukulobola* and retaining their bonds with the *amadlozi* were important. Land also offered a limited form of economic and social security in workers' otherwise very insecure lives in which illness, unemployment, or an accident could easily leave them without money or other resources. African workers did not enjoy social security benefits and could claim only very limited compensation for workplace accidents, which were hardly rare occurrences among dock workers. Moreover, they had no employment security and could not legally invest in urban property. Amid this uncertainty, access to land under communal tenure was an asset and a source of stability, a home to which one could always return.

The rural homestead was also the place where African workers could bolster their masculine self-image. In the city, African migrant men had no power and were subject to racial paternalism, but the often-denigrating experience of urban wage labor allowed them to marry and build their *umuzi*, in other words, to buy into rural patriarchy. Dock workers and other migrant laborers were thus not simply striving to recreate a rural idyll; they were also keeping a patriarchal system alive in which they had the power and recognition they lacked in urban South Africa. Nevertheless, as we have seen in chapter 4, we cannot reduce men's and women's continued commitment to rural life, despite all its problems, to mere calculations of security or achieving rural status; social, cultural, and emotional considerations were equally important. To be a respectable *umnumzane*, furthermore, men had to be away from the homestead to earn wages. This meant that women became the de facto homestead heads, the ones in charge of the everyday management of the homestead. As the men were far away and had no convenient means of communication, their wives or mothers often had considerable autonomy.

This could lead to conflict and struggles over the household's resources, as men and women frequently had different priorities.

While dock workers were strongly committed to a rural life and future, they did not isolate themselves from urban society and the advantages that it did bring. They used the opportunities their urban labor offered to achieve an early rural retirement. They strategically combined wage labor with Reserve agriculture and pastoralism and with petty entrepreneurship. These mixed livelihoods made them more successful than most African migrant workers in retiring early to the rural areas. Especially those who had small commercial businesses on the side managed to leave urban employment comparatively quickly. Dock labor was particularly suited to such strategies, as some of the most successful businesses started with the selling of pilfered goods. Moreover, casual labor paid relatively well, giving workers the chance to invest and take some risk in business. It also offered the flexibility to offer their labor only on ships that carried desirable goods or to take a day off to devote time to their businesses. It was thus precisely their position at a strategic node in the global networks of trade and communication that made their very locally oriented lives possible.

Dual Economies

At the core of my argument in this book is a recognition that in the livelihoods of Durban's dock workers and their households, wages tell only part of the story. These livelihoods did not just rely on a male breadwinner and his pay packet. Income from Reserve agriculture and pastoralism, as well as from informal trade, was equally important to the economic strategies of these households. A history of dock laborers in Durban thus needs to focus on the intersections between the rural and the urban spheres, and between the formal and the informal economies. I do not argue this merely for the sake of historical accuracy. My case for linking these through the study of the household is also an argument about how we should understand the South African economy.

In the literature on development, there is a long-standing tradition of considering non-Western economies as existing in two separate spheres. The dualist modernization theories of the 1950s and 1960s, for example, assumed that two discrete economies coexisted in developing countries. In this account, modern productive economies formed "islands of development" that absorbed labor, that is, population, from the unproductive traditional economies. Development took place when the former increasingly absorbed and displaced the latter.[9]

These modern economies were generally urban and industrial, and the traditional economies were rural subsistence economies. Today, South African policy makers still write and talk about the existence of two economies in South Africa: a first and a second economy. Former president Thabo Mbeki in particular was a major proponent of this discourse.[10] Jacob Zuma's government has undertaken some limited attempts at formulating a more coherent policy approach to the informal economy, yet it largely continues to treat this sector as separate from the formal economy.[11]

The assumption of two structurally disconnected economies allows the South African government to trumpet the success of its macroeconomic policies, as the first economy performs comparatively strongly and has delivered satisfactory GDP growth rates for some time. Because the first or formal economy has, at times, performed relatively well and did more or less react to the government's policies and incentives as expected, policy makers do not consider the enduring poverty in the second economy to be evidence of the failure of their successive macroeconomic programs (RDP, GEAR, AsgiSA, NGP, NDP).[12] Hence, the reasons for the lack of success in the structurally disconnected second economy, which includes the informal economy, are presumed to be internal. Separating the poor and the unemployed in a separate economic sphere helps avoid the conclusion that the prosperity of one section of South African society comes at the expense of the rest of the country.[13] While certainly not as crudely dualist as the two economies discourse, Jeremy Seekings and Nicoli Natrass's influential argument that a new underclass has emerged in South Africa, consisting of those excluded from access to formal-sector wage resources and opportunities, does equally assume that there is a fundamental socioeconomic divide that separates two sections of the country's economy and population.[14]

Focusing on the intersections between the formal and the informal, between the employed and the unemployed, and between the rural and the urban, can help us challenge this conceptual disconnect; yet critiques of the dual economy discourse are nothing new. As far back as 1972, Harold Wolpe urged us to study the South African economy as a whole rather than as existing in separate spheres.

Market Society as a "Stark Utopia"

Durban's dock workers-entrepreneurs thus cannot simply be subsumed under concepts of wage labor derived from Western experience. Moreover, this account of households relying on entrepreneurial activities in the face of persistent official attempts to quell unlicensed African trade seems to confirm neoliberal claims that overextended and intrusive governments stifle people's innate entrepreneurial spirit. Few dock workers, however, strove to become part of an entrepreneurial petty bourgeoisie; rather, they used these strategies to escape dependence on urban wage labor and to hasten their return to their rural homes. Most did not continue their investments in their businesses after they achieved that goal. They preferred instead to invest in cattle and in dependents. Colonial officials and later development specialists often thought of such "unproductive" investments as irrational and wasteful, yet there was sound reasoning behind them. Its logic, however, was not a universal market logic.

Cattle were of course a productive investment. They were a source of milk, meat, and draft power for ploughs. Moreover, breeding and selling livestock earned several dock workers some decent money, as they had built up their herds as a form of self-reproducing capital that carried them through their rural retirement. Nevertheless, cattle were more than commodities to be bought and sold or a source of meat and other animal products. Cattle played an indispensable social role in African communities across southern Africa. Young men needed access to cattle to marry and to become homestead heads, cattle provided a symbolic presence at their rural homes for absent migrant workers and thus a public claim to continued belonging to the rural society, and the practice of *ukusisa* fostered clientelistic relations. Money simply cannot fulfill the same social functions.

The value of cattle therefore is irreducible to their monetary exchange value or to the milk they produce. Cattle are not simply subject to a formalist and reductionist market valuation; in other words, they cannot be reduced to numbers. Land too had sociocultural significance beyond its value as a productive asset.[15] Land provided continued access to rural society and allowed migrant workers to build their *umuzi.* Building their own homestead and leaving the paternal *umuzi* established a man as an *umnumzane* and was an important marker of manhood and adulthood.

Rather than being irrational, decisions that value land and cattle beyond their market price or productive potential follow a different economic logic, one that is irreducible to a purportedly universal market logic. Karl Polanyi reminds us that there is no "rational" universal market logic that can be dissociated from the sociopolitical sphere. The economic sphere is always embedded in social relations.[16] The self-adjusting market that would necessarily be at the heart of a disembedded market society "implied a stark utopia" that "could not exist for any length of time without annihilating the human and natural substance of society."[17] Polanyi thus argues against a tendency to assume a universal economic rationality where values derive purely from a market logic and are devoid of social or cultural value;[18] he names this tendency *formalism*. Against this formalist tradition, he posits a *substantivist* approach to economic anthropology that considers economic behavior as "interwoven with the general fabric of social, political, and religious life."[19] Hence, the pursuit of financial gain becomes just one of many considerations.

The more-than-monetary value of cattle is perhaps most pronounced in the practice of *ukulobola*. Not only are cattle worth more than their monetary exchange value; marriage is also more than a private decision between two autonomous individuals. Marriage through *ukulobola* is an investment in affines and thus in a social and economic support network. The relationship with affines and kin is ultimately a social rather than a biological one, and the circulation of cattle shapes and maintains these relationships. Building and maintaining these social networks of support also requires forms of labor that cannot be subsumed under either waged work or entrepreneurial labor and that do not adhere to a market logic. In fact, central to the production and maintenance of such social relations is a gift economy, which is irreducible to a market economy or even a strict system of reciprocity.[20] The making of claims on those who have resources or the fostering of relations with people who may be able to help you when you are down on your luck, that is, the maintenance of networks of support, are forms of *distributive* labor that are often crucial to the survival of the poor. We cannot dissociate these forms of labor from their social context or reduce them to mere calculations. As such, my argument is not only that the study of labor needs to overcome the rural-urban and formal-informal divides but also that we have to look beyond market considerations. To do full justice to the livelihoods of dock workers and their households, labor history should not only consider waged, agricultural, domestic, and informal labor, but also the very important distributive labor.[21]

It would therefore be a mistake to assume that Durban's dock workers were gifted with an instinctive and universal profit motive, which is of course a key characteristic of the *Homo economicus*. The pursuit of financial gain, while important for the survival of households that are dependent on cash income, was less a goal in itself than the means to achieve a goal that was at least partially culturally and socially determined: namely, the return to their rural homes. This is not to say that people were not looking for gains but rather that money was not the only measure of these gains; cattle, affines, the status of *umnumzane*, and so on, were equally part of this consideration. I do not suggest that these households existed in a precapitalist nonmarket utopia. This was neither a purely market society nor its antithesis, a society entirely devoid of money and markets, neither of which can ultimately exist.[22]

Moreover, we cannot see dock workers' entrepreneurialism as somehow separate from their wage labor, as these activities were crucially dependent on their employment on the docks. Opportunities to pilfer and the flexibility of casual dock labor made these strategies possible. If they had not worked on the docks, they may never have engaged in this small-scale trade. Consequently, informal trade was a creative way in which dock workers took advantage of the opportunities their employment offered in order to break their dependence on wage labor, more than it was the outcome of any entrepreneurial essence. To escape rural poverty and dependence on unpleasant urban employment, dock workers' households strategically combined different economic activities, which included wage labor, cultivation, animal husbandry, pilferage, small-scale trade, the commercial labor of women who were not part of these households, and non-market-based distributive (rather than productive) labor.

The Elusive *Homo Economicus*

Durban's dock workers did not fit very well into accounts either of radical proletarians forming a militant working class or of innate entrepreneurs imbued with an individualistic profit motive and a universal "propensity to truck, barter, and exchange."[23] These essentially Eurocentric categories have limited purchase in this context, and even in the West their wholesale applicability is often questionable. Moreover, this is not only the case for 1950s Durban, as the *homo economicus* tends to be elusive throughout much of Africa.

This hypothetical "economic person" is generally attributed to John Stuart Mill, who for the sake of economic analysis reduced the motives of this abstract decision maker to a narrow range of relatively simple motives—the most important one being monetary profit.[24] Mill undertakes an "ethology" of this hypothetical person but also acknowledges that one can never entirely separate these motives from other interests and that this model has geographical and historical limitations.[25] However, he sees such exceptions only as the result of secondary *disturbing causes*, as aberrations to a general law.[26] As such, the ideal of a universal human who behaves in certain predictable ways remains unchallenged. This human just has to be recovered from the messy real world with its irrational impulses and disturbing causes of geography, culture, and history—lived reality is a layer of uncertainty to be peeled away to reveal the abstract rational and predictable economic human. This recovering of a rational *homo economicus* from a messy and irrational lived experience parallels the modernist divide between a rational modern economy and an irrational traditional economy, with the former inevitably displacing the latter.

The concept of the *homo economicus* or Lionel Robbins's formulation of economics as a *science* of choice relies on a hypothetical subject who operates in a market society and makes choices according to a market rationality.[27] Such models assume the universality of a specific disembedded market economy that only matured in the West in the nineteenth century. This market society, Polanyi reminds us, "alone was economic in a different and distinctive sense, for it chose to base itself on a motive only rarely acknowledged as valid in the history of human societies, and certainly never before raised to the level of a justification of action and behavior in everyday life, namely, gain. The self-regulating market system was uniquely derived from this principle."[28] The assumption of a universal *homo economicus* or of the applicability of the purportedly normative "free" wage labor relationship, modeled on Western history, ultimately relies on an ethnocentric perspective.[29] Decisions about consumption, production, and the distribution of resources—in other words, economic behavior—cannot be reduced to a universal, formalist market logic. Labor, moreover, is human activity and therefore essentially social. One cannot fruitfully consider labor, consumption, and distribution outside of their social, political, and cultural contexts. This is why Polanyi's substantivism focuses on livelihood, that is, on the place of economy in human society, and not just on a formalist focus on the market: "To study human livelihood is to study the economy in this substantive sense of the term."[30]

A *substantive* reading of the economic sphere is of course nothing new to the literature on Africa. There are numerous examples of workers who do not quite behave like wage laborers and of economies that do not operate along the lines of a universal market economy. In *Marginal Gains*, Jane Guyer shows how profits in Atlantic West Africa were made in the interstices between two different economic systems with different ways of valuation.[31] Sara Berry's *No Condition Is Permanent* discusses how and why African farmers and rural dwellers often behave irrationally, at least if judged through a formalist market logic. Economic and sociopolitical motives are not mutually exclusive or somehow separable. Economic investments are inseparable from seemingly unproductive investments in the social networks that allow one access to crucial resources, such as land, labor, necessary permits, or support in times of need. Consequently, investing one's surpluses in the maintenance of these networks—that is, in status, political access, dependents, and the like—is not irrational; these are investments in the means of negotiation over such access.[32] These are investments in wealth in people rather than wealth in things (see chapter 4).

In short, Eurocentric assumptions about the working class or the neoclassical and equally ethnocentric understanding of the *homo economicus* as an individual decision maker with a predominant (if not exclusive) interest in maximizing monetary profit, do not work very well in much of sub-Saharan Africa. The decisions regarding their livelihoods that dock workers and other members of their households made were never purely economic and market driven, and these cannot be divorced from their social, cultural, and political context. As such, these decisions are social as much as they are economic. These workers were both wage laborers and entrepreneurs, just as they were husbands, African, Zulu, fathers, homestead heads, and so on. Their lives and livelihoods, however, are irreducible to any one of these categories.

Thinking about Labor beyond the Global North

The importance of recognizing that Durban's dock workers were neither typical proletarian workers nor innate entrepreneurs, of course, exceeds the context of 1950s Durban. Africanist perspectives on work force us to reconsider the meaning of labor—and, importantly, to do so without falling back on neoliberal clichés of innate entrepreneurs. Labor includes all those activities that we undertake to survive, reproduce, flourish, or entertain ourselves. Yet, when we study labor, we tend to reduce it to wage labor or at least to forms of labor that are recognizably commodified, such as cash cropping, slavery, or commercial labor.[33]

Both southern African and international labor history have focused largely on wage laborers. Formal wage labor, however, remains an exception in the Global South, where workers fit uneasily into accounts of proletarian labor based on the Western experience. Furthermore, even among those in formal wage labor and even in the West, labor relations often do not resemble a one-man-one-job pattern, particularly as precarity is increasingly the new normal.[34] The nascent yet substantial field of global labor history has done much to move beyond the traditional focus on the supposedly normative labor relationship based on "free" wage labor. Marcel van der Linden in particular has brought various forms of forced and dependent labor into the picture. Indeed, the exploitation of labor takes on many different forms under capitalism.[35] While taking important steps to move beyond free wage labor, however, this literature still focuses mostly on forms of labor that are easily recognizable as commodified.[36] In his impressive *Workers of the World*, van der Linden has very little to say about labor in the informal economy or about Africa, except on the topics of slavery, transport workers, and South Africa.[37] He focuses on commodified labor that directly or indirectly produces for global capital and on labor that is in the process of being commodified. If these workers are not wage laborers, they are slaves or cash croppers, or they are engaged in the reproduction of commodified forms of labor. In this account of global labor history, capitalism—and with that Europe and its offshoots—remains the touchstone for studying labor.[38]

Global labor history has achieved much by moving beyond national histories and a narrow focus on wage labor, yet more remains to be done. Van der Linden transcends traditional labor history by broadening his scope to all forms of commodified labor, which includes the work done by "women (and sometimes men) who through subsistence labor reproduce commodified labor."[39] However, as Belinda Bozzoli notes, it is unsatisfactory to reduce the social role of women to reproducing wage laborers.[40] Indeed, we should not merely discuss domestic labor in its function of the reproduction of commodified labor but as integral to the social and cultural networks that constitute the household. Capitalism does not just articulate with the rural subsistence economy so that the latter can serve the function of reducing the cost of labor in the former. Rather, capitalism interacts and conflicts with this noncapitalist economy, redrawing social and domestic relations in the process.[41] As such, a focus on commodified labor draws attention to one side of this equation and risks constructing the domestic sphere as merely serving the needs of capital rather than as a site of struggle and conflict in its own right. Informal, reproductive, and distributive labor should be seen as necessarily part of the study of labor, not because it reproduces and subsidizes wage labor but because these forms of labor are integral parts of people's lives and livelihoods.

Franco Barchiesi has thus rightly questioned what place African workers could occupy in van der Linden's approach to global labor history.[42] Even Durban's dock workers, who I argue in the introduction are prime candidates to suit this conception of labor as connected to global markets and as recognizably commodified, are in reality a poor fit, as this book shows. Common approaches to the study of labor either ignore vast numbers of African workers (that is, everyone who works and not just those whose labor is recognizably commodified) or consider their work only to the extent that it reproduces commodified labor. Moreover, van der Linden's emphasis on workers producing for global markets is problematic in light of James Ferguson's convincing argument that "Africa's participation in 'globalization' . . . [has] been a matter of highly selective and spatially encapsulated forms of global connection combined with widespread disconnection and exclusion."[43] Capital leapfrogs most of the continent, *l'Afrique inutile*, to touch down in those few places it is interested in, the islands of development that have now largely become mining or oil enclaves. A focus on commodified labor and on global markets thus risks neglecting much of the continent.

Significantly, it is not just in Africa that much of the labor people actually perform is not recognized as such. Many readers will be familiar with the feminist critique that the wage labor system tends to undervalue the mostly female labor of reproduction and with the arguments for wages for housework.[44] However, the hard work of the poor and the destitute is equally underappreciated in many studies of labor. After all, it requires a lot of work to beg or to steal, for a homeless person to stay cool in a Durban summer or warm in a Moscow winter, to foster relationships with better-off kin and acquaintances or with volunteer caregivers, to evade police brutality, and more. Being "out of work" is hard work. However, if we acknowledge all this work as labor, we might be less tempted to see forms of redistribution as charity and more likely to see these as a fair compensation for their work. One does not see charity where one sees work.[45]

Epilogue

The mixed and complex livelihood strategies discussed in this book relied on some of the important advantages that casual dock labor offered. The work was hard, dangerous, and irregular, and, as Africans, workers received a fraction of the pay that their white colleagues received for generally much lighter work. However, these African migrant dock workers were also paid better than most Africans in the city, and the flexibility of casual dock labor, as well as their access to cargoes from which they could pilfer, allowed them to diversify their livelihoods. Many also lived in places where apartheid authorities could not police their lives as closely as they wanted to.

Many of these advantages disappeared in and after 1959, when dock labor was decasualized. Workers' ability to use their bargaining power on a daily basis disappeared with the establishment of a hiring monopoly, they were increasingly forced into compounds, and they no longer had the flexibility to choose when to work or for which ship to show up to for hiring. After more than a century, the city's authorities and stevedoring employers had finally succeeded in exerting their control over this notoriously independent group of workers at the heart of the regional economy. In the preceding decades, these workers had walked off their jobs regularly, protesting their wage rates, working conditions, and pass laws, or defending the moral economy of the docks. In the decade after decasualization, however, hardly any significant industrial action took place. The introduction of shipping containers in the 1970s, reducing the sector's reliance on manual labor and making pilferage much more difficult, further undermined the agency of dock workers.

Just as migrant labor had turned from a source of opportunities into a form of compulsion and a cause of impoverishment, many of the opportunities that casual dock labor offered disappeared after the 1950s. The agency afforded by the strategies described in this book were ultimately tenuous and vulnerable. Apartheid authorities' relentless attempts at rooting out independent African economic initiatives won out in the end. Nevertheless, such small-scale African businesses never entirely disappeared and would eventually develop into what became known as the "informal economy." While a comprehensive array of repressive apartheid-era measures kept this sector small compared to the rest of the continent, it was never completely suppressed.

The term "informal economy" was coined in the 1970s, when it became increasingly clear that much of the newly decolonized world would not fit into a Eurocentric model of modernization based on formal wage labor, the creation of the modern industrial man, and government regulation of trade and industries. "Informal economy" or "informal sector" thus often came to stand for any economic activity that did not fall within the "traditional" scope of formalized regulation and labor relations. The differences in the experiences of dock workers engaging in small-scale trade in the 1950s and informal workers today, however, illustrate the importance of looking at actual practices in the sector and at how they changed over time, as well as at how the formal and informal economies relate. Such a perspective should warn us against celebrating an uncomplicated agency rooted in informal businesses.

Harold Wolpe paid scrupulous attention to the social reproduction of labor, and his legacy remains important when considering the history of the informal economy. Just as traditional economies were not separate from the capitalist economy and subsidized low African wages in the latter, the informal sector fulfills much the same role today. Many South African workers manage to survive on otherwise insufficient wages because the cost of housing, goods, and services in the informal sector is low and because they have access to informal sources of income. The informal economy thus reduces the upward pressure on formal-sector wages; informal trade also provides the unemployed with opportunities to make some money and acts as (inadequate) poor relief and social security.[1] Thus, while informal trade was a source of agency for dock workers in the 1950s, today it is mostly a source of exploitation.

The literature on the informal sector does not always pay much attention to history, especially not in South Africa, where the sector is often mistakenly seen as a postapartheid phenomenon. Nevertheless, the differing contexts of dock workers diversifying their livelihoods in the 1950s and millions trying to survive through informal labor today highlight the importance of a historical perspective. In the 1950s, South Africa was not yet plagued by mass unemployment, and commercial competition in most townships and rural areas was very limited. These two advantages have now disappeared. There are millions of unemployed, and many of them try to make a living through informal trade, which leads to fierce competition and razor-thin profit margins. Today, most people do not find the same opportunities in the crowded informal sector as Durban's dock workers once did; they do not pull themselves up by their bootstraps but rather struggle to survive. With this historical context in mind, one is less likely to see in informal entrepreneurship a source of agency and independence than changing strategies to cope with growing unemployment and an ever more competitive informal market.

This combination of towering unemployment and a crowded survivalist microenterprise sector can lead to tensions. Just as resentment of Indians' commercial success fed into the 1949 pogrom, the relative success of African foreign nationals in the informal economy fuels the xenophobic violence that broke out throughout South Africa in May 2008 and that has periodically flared up since then. Both rioters and others expressed their frustration at foreigners making a living while up to 60 percent of young South Africans are unemployed. Many see foreigners as taking scarce jobs and business opportunities away from citizens.[2] South Africa has a largely extractive economy, and, consequently, the poor often deem access to jobs, resources, and opportunities a zero-sum game. Hence, they believe that the success of foreign nationals comes at the expense of South Africans.[3]

This violence is unfortunately not new to South Africa or other African countries. The nationalist and exclusionary violence of 1949 foreboded the dangers of nationalism about which Frantz Fanon would warn. Fanon recognized as early as 1961 that postcolonial Africa had a problem of "ultranationalism, chauvinism, and racism."[4] His emphasis on nationalism as both necessary and dangerous remains painfully relevant today. To overcome colonialism and racism, a national consciousness is needed as a unifying force, bridging the racial, ethnic, and other divides that imperialism fosters. Yet if this nationalism is not transformed into a consciousness of social and political needs, "then it leads to a dead end."[5] However, as the ANC took over from local activists and trade unions after its unbanning, it increasingly sacrificed social transformation to political power. The party built its hegemonic project on appeals to national liberation and popular nationalism. It thus linked liberation to *nation*, while the majority of the population was denied a much-anticipated better life.[6]

Trade unions have struggled to come to terms with this toxic mix of towering unemployment, growing numbers of people trying to make a living in the informal economy, and xenophobia. Xenophobic violence exposed the failure of organized labor and the left to address effectively the frustrations of the poor. As the country's main trade union federation, COSATU's stance on foreign workers has been contradictory.[7] It has condemned the xenophobic attacks, organized humanitarian assistance for the victims, and expressed concern about the exploitation of undocumented foreign workers. However, COSATU officials have also portrayed foreigners as driving down conditions for South African workers and even as stealing their jobs.[8] Most importantly, the federation has no coherent strategy for organizing some of the most vulnerable workers: foreign nationals, contract laborers, and informal workers.

In South Africa and elsewhere, trade unions have found it difficult to organize across the formal/informal divide or to reach out to precarious contract laborers. As a result, they have often come to represent a comparatively privileged group of workers, namely those with secure formal employment and protections under the law. There are inherent difficulties in organizing informal workers, as their lack of stable formal employment relation does not suit the traditional trade union model. Moreover, their interests can differ from those of the union's other members.[9] Durban's dock workers in the 1950s, however, saw no contradiction between working-class organization and defending the rights of informal traders. There are issues today on which unions have built alliances with informal workers and the unemployed as well, including service delivery, resistance to privatization, shack dweller rights, and job creation. Many formal-sector workers are still poor and live in households and communities with those who are even more vulnerable; on these issues, they have shared interests. Moreover, formal-sector workers too are increasingly engaged in precarious forms of labor that mirror informal-sector labor practices.[10]

It is only if we consider how formal and informal economies interact in the daily lives of the poor that we can overcome the artificial division between the two and start thinking about the South African economy as a whole, rather than as existing in two separate worlds; this is a necessary first step to building solidarity with and among the poor across both sectors.

Notes

Introduction

1. Lambert and Morrell, "Domination and Subordination in Natal," 80.

2. "Boycott: Durban Dockworkers Block Arms to Zimbabwe"; Padayachee, "Sending Arms to Zim 'a Recipe for Conflict'"; "Dock Workers to Boycott Israeli Ship."

3. The grammatically more accurate *izinyathi* is also used. Paul La Hausse also mentions *ozinyathi* as a variation in "Message of the Warriors," 21.

4. Hemson, "In the Eye of the Storm," 166.

5. Hemson, "Class Consciousness."

6. Morris, "Stevedoring and the General Workers Union," parts I and II; Baskin, "GWU and the Durban Dockworkers"; Dubbeld, "Breaking the Buffalo."

7. On dock worker radicalism and work practices elsewhere, see Hill, *Dockers*; Mills, "The San Francisco Waterfront"; Wellman, *Union Makes Us Strong*; Taplin, "Dock Labour at Liverpool."

8. Taplin, *Dockers' Union*; Broeze, "Militancy and Pragmatism."

9. Oberst, "Transport Workers, Strikes and the 'Imperial Response.'"

10. Waterman, "Concept of the 'Semi-proletarianised Peasantry'"; Cooper, *On the African Waterfront*; Luke, "Dock Workers of the Port of Freetown"; Jeffries, *Class, Power and Ideology in Ghana*; Cooper, *Colonialism in Question*, chapter 7.

11. An excellent but inevitably dated review of this literature can be found in Freund, *African Worker*. For a more up-to-date overview of South African labor history, see Freund, "Labour Studies and Labour History in South Africa."

12. See Davie, "Strength in Numbers"; Hemson, "Class Consciousness," 1.

13. For a brief biography and overview of his remarkable career, see "David Hemson."

14. Many argue today that the negotiated transition to democracy in South Africa has largely failed to address inequality, as social and economic demands were sacrificed for deracialization and political power in a Faustian bargain. See, for example, Bond, *Elite Transition*; Saul, *Liberation Lite*; Kasrils, "How the ANC's Faustian Pact Sold Out South Africa's Poorest."

15. Seekings, "Rise and Fall of the Weberian Analysis."

16. Wolpe, "Capitalism and Cheap Labour-Power"; Legassick, "South Africa." Though Legassick's paper was published after Wolpe's article, it was presented earlier and referenced by Wolpe. For examples of the liberal scholarship Wolpe and Legassick criticized, see Wilson and Thompson, *Oxford*

History of South Africa; Horwitz, *Political Economy of South Africa*; Houghton, *South African Economy*.

17. Wolpe, "Capitalism and Cheap Labour-Power," 434. Emphasis in original.

18. For example, Webb, "Vanishing Lands and Migrant Labour." Jonathan Crush concisely explains why it was often believed that working-class unity was difficult to achieve among African migrant laborers in "Migrancy and Militance."

19. Hemson, "In the Eye of the Storm," 158.

20. See Callebert, "Transcending the Dual Economy."

21. Good overviews of these critiques can be found in Christopher Saunders, *Making of the South African Past*, chapter 18; and Seekings, "Rise and Fall of the Weberian Analysis."

22. Saunders, *Making of the South African Past*, 189.

23. Bozzoli, "Marxism, Feminism and South African Studies"; Bozzoli, *Women of Phokeng*; Beinart, "Worker Consciousness, Ethnic Particularism and Nationalism"; Delius, "The Ndzundza Ndebele."

24. Moodie, *Going for Gold*; Harries, *Work, Culture, and Identity*. See also Crais, *White Supremacy and Black Resistance*.

25. Atkins, *The Moon Is Dead!*

26. Von Holdt, *Transition from Below*; Edward Webster and von Holdt, *Beyond the Apartheid Workplace*; Alexander et al., *Marikana*.

27. The liberal anthropologists of the Rhodes-Livingstone Institute are prime examples of this liberal tendency, cf. Gluckman, *Malinowski's Sociological Theories*. Ferguson provides an excellent overview of this scholarship in *Expectations of Modernity*.

28. Potts, *Circular Migration*; Ferguson, *Expectations of Modernity*.

29. See also Callebert, "Rethinking the Underclass."

30. Hemson, "Class Consciousness," 351.

31. See Cooper, "Work, Class and Empire."

32. Berry, *Fathers Work for Their Sons*, 108.

33. Goebel, "Our Struggle Is for the Full Loaf."

34. Cf. Grown and Sebstad, "Introduction: Toward a Wider Perspective on Women's Employment," 941.

35. Mosoetsa, *Eating from One Pot*.

36. Chirwa, "'Theba' Is Power."

37. Similarly, Jeff Guy and Motlatsi Thabane do not regard workers' strategies as just a matter of leadership, organization, and resistance but also of personal struggles by workers to gain control over their lives: "Basotho Miners, Ethnicity and Workers' Strategies."

38. Philip and Iona Mayer's *Townsmen or Tribesmen* is a good example of portraying African migrants as rural traditionalists. However, this dichotomy returns even in more recent scholarship, for example in Mahmood Mamdani's *Citizen and Subject*.

39. See, for example, Lucassen, *Global Labour History*; Marcel van der Linden discusses the necessity to move beyond "free" wage labor in *Workers of the World*,

yet has fairly little to say about informal labor or about Africa outside of South Africa. For a critique of how global and global labor history discuss African labor and trade, see Callebert, "African Mobility and Labor in Global History." For debates about the nature of global labor history, see Brown, "Scholarly Controversy: Defining Global Labor History."

40. There are of course notable exceptions, for example, in a special issue of *Africa*: James and Hull, "Popular Economies in South Africa."

41. Penvenne, *Women, Migration and the Cashew Economy*, 3.

42. Guyer, "Household and Community."

43. Sen, "Gender and Cooperative Conflicts."

44. Mark Hunter, *Love in the Time of AIDS*, 3. Emphasis in original.

45. Guyer, *Marginal Gains.*

46. Birla, *Stages of Capital*, 235.

47. Polanyi, *Great Transformation.*

48. O'Laughlin, "Review Essay: Livelihoods."

49. Mosoetsa, *Eating from One Pot*, 129–36.

50. Vansina, *Oral Tradition as History*, especially chapters 1, 4, and 6; Kynoch, *We Are Fighting the World*, x–xi; Beinart, "Labour Migrancy and Rural Production," 81.

51. White, *Comforts of Home*, 21.

52. For a discussion of the distinction between words and voices in African oral historiography, see Cohen, Miescher, and White, "Introduction: Voices, Words, and African History."

53. The literature on the Indian Ocean world does not regularly include South Africa, but recent work has brought some change. Hofmeyr and Williams, *South Africa and India*; see in particular Jonathan Hyslop's chapter titled "Steamship Empire." See also Kaarsholm, "Zanzibaris or Amakhuwa?"

54. Similarly, the mobility afforded by the Freedom Railway in Tanzania became central to the livelihoods of traders and farmers living along the line. See Monson, *Africa's Freedom Railway.*

55. Nesvåg, "Street Trading from Apartheid to Post-apartheid."

56. Moyo, *Dead Aid*; de Soto, *Mystery of Capital.*

57. Organizing across the formal/informal divide is more difficult today. Trade unions across the continent have tried to reach out to the unemployed and to informal workers, but generally with limited success. See Lourenço-Lindell, *Africa's Informal Workers.*

58. Chakrabarty, *Provincializing Europe*, chapter 2.

59. Gillian Hart, *Rethinking the South African Crisis.*

Chapter One

1. Freund, "City Hall and the Direction of Development," 12. See also Jones, "Port of Durban."

2. A good overview can be found in Crush, Jeeves, and Yudelman, *South Africa's Labor Empire.*

3. Smuts, foreword to *Reaction to Conquest,* vii–viii. For another example, see van der Horst, *Native Labour in South Africa.*

4. E.g., Wallerstein, "Three Stages."

5. Sithole, "Zuluness in South Africa," xiii.

6. Beinart, *Political Economy of Pondoland*; Delius, *Land Belongs to Us*; Delius, *Lion amongst the Cattle.*

7. Beinart, "Labour Migrancy and Rural Production"; David Webster, "Origins of Migrant Labour," 261.

8. Walker, "Gender and the Development of the Migrant Labour System," 179; Guy, "Women in Labour."

9. Bundy, *Rise and Fall*; Beinart, "Labour Migrancy and Rural Production," 88.

10. Van Onselen, "Reactions to Rinderpest in Southern Africa"; Ballard, "Repercussions of Rinderpest."

11. Carton, *Blood from Your Children*; Beinart, "Labour Migrancy and Rural Production," 86; Walker, "Gender and the Development of the Migrant Labour System," 184–85. On the limits to the invention and manipulation of tradition, see Spear, "Neo-traditionalism and the Limits of Invention."

12. John Lambert, "Impoverishment of the Natal Peasantry"; Mahoney, *Other Zulus,* especially chapter 3.

13. MacKinnon, "Land, Labour and Cattle," 46, 58.

14. "Report of the Department of Native Affairs for the Years 1945–7," U.G. 14-'48, 5.

15. Cf. Mike Davis, *Late Victorian Holocaust.*

16. Harries, *Work, Culture, and Identity,* 7–8, 16.

17. Simkins, "Agricultural Production in the African Reserves."

18. Union of South Africa, *Handbook of Agricultural Statistics,* 53.

19. Simkins, "Agricultural Production in the African Reserves."

20. Cowen and Shenton, "Origin and Course of Fabian Colonialism."

21. Guy, "Shaka's Shadow," 220. One of the most influential studies on indirect rule is Mahmood Mamdani's *Citizen and Subject.* Anne Phillips, however, sees indirect rule more as the result of a "makeshift settlement" than as a coherent ideology or blueprint for colonial rule; see *The Enigma of Colonialism.* Thomas McClendon makes a similar argument about Natal, arguing that the establishment of indirect rule was "more improvisational than systematic," in *White Chiefs, Black Lords.*

22. Heydenrych, "Port Natal Harbour," 46–69.

23. From 1.5 million tons in 1895, shipping reached an initial peak of over 4 million tons per year in 1904, in the wake of the Anglo-Boer War, after which tonnage fell back to 2.3 million in 1909. By 1928 a new peak of 5 million tons was reached before the depression of the 1930s precipitated another slump. By 1960, however, the Durban harbor handled over 9 million tons per year.

Colony of Natal, *Census of the Colony of Natal, April 1904*, 911; Horwood, *Port of Durban*, 141.

24. Lumby and McLean, "Economy and the Development of the Port of Durban," 29.

25. Taplin, *Dockers' Union*, 12–17.

26. KCAL, Nolan-Wackernow-Ward papers, KCM 1883, "Minutes of a Meeting with Representatives of Shipping Companies," October 28, 1903; Ingpen, *Horizons*, 50; *Port Natal: The Coaling Station*, 3, 30;

27. SAB, ARB, vol. 3315, file 1196/5/2, part 1, "Report on Conditions of Employment of Stevedoring Workers," August 1956; Harries, "Plantations, Passes and Proletarians," 395–97; "Lazy Zanzibaris," *Natal Mercury*, May 31, 1904, 10; Sicard, "'Zanzibaris' in Durban." Note that the Zanzibari community in Durban did not come from Zanzibar, but from northern Mozambique.

28. PAR, SNA, vol. II/4/1, "Summary and Index of Evidence of Natal Witnesses Given before the Native Affairs Commission, Section: Native Labour," n.d. [1903–5].

29. Colony of Natal, *Report of the Native Affairs Commission, 1906–7*, 30.

30. DAR, 3/DBN, vol. 1/2/11/1/10, Native Administration Committee minutes, April 14, 1950; "500 Natives Stop Work at Docks," *Natal Mercury*, November 2, 1956, 7; "Strike at Durban Docks," *Natal Witness*, November 3, 1956, 5.

31. KCAL, Marwick papers, KCM 3073, untitled document, 11.

32. SAB, ARB, vol. 3315, file 1196/5/2, part 1, "Questionnaires to Stevedoring Employers," [1956].

33. Cooper, "Dockworkers and Labour History," 527–28.

34. Dubbeld, "Labour Management and Technological Change," 57, 70.

35. Similarly, on the Rand the unwritten rules of the mines dictated that *izinduna* had obligations to the workers as well as the workers to them. Dunbar Moodie describes this set of mutual expectations as part of a moral economy in "Moral Economy of the Black Miners' Strike," 4. For more on the moral economy of Durban's docks, see chapter 5 of this text.

36. Hemson, "Dock Workers," 91; SAB, ARB, vol. 3315, file 1196/5/2, part 1, "Questionnaires to Stevedoring Employers," [1956]; Vivian Bickford-Smith notes similar processes at work in Cape Town in "Black Labour at the Docks."

37. SAB, ARB, vol. 3315, file 1196/5/2, part 2, Natal Employers' Association to the Chairman of the Wage Board, "Wage Board Investigation—Stevedoring Trade," January 13, 1958.

38. SAB, SAP, vol. 474, file 35/3/49, telegram from DECOMPOL, Port Natal, to COMPOL, Pretoria, "Strike * Dock Labours * Durban = 24/2/59," February 25, 1959; "1,500 Durban stevedores strike—all dismissed," *Natal Witness*, February 26, 1959, 1; "Stoppage at Harbour Continues," *Natal Mercury*, July 3, 1954, 3; "Maydon Wharf Strike," *Natal Mercury*, September 1, 1937, 28.

39. Kearney, "Bamboo Square"; la Hausse, "Cows of Nongoloza"; Swanson discusses fears of disease fueling segregation in "Sanitation Syndrome" and in "Asiatic Menace."

40. See, for example, DAR, 3/DBN, vol. 1/1/1/1/35, Town Council minutes, July 7, 1916.
41. Hemson, "Class Consciousness," 95–99.
42. "Report of the Economic and Wage Commission (1925)," U.G. 14-'26, 38–39.
43. DAR, 3/DBN, vol. 1/1/1/1/35, Town Council minutes, appendix, 1916.
44. SAB, MVE, vol. 1200, file 538/159/1, "Report of Committee of Investigation Appointed to Enquire into Togt Labour Strikes at the Harbour at Durban," October 7, 1942, 26; "Meeting with Representatives of Stevedoring Togt Labourers at Durban," November 20, 1942; KCAL, PNAB, KCF 43, file H3-20, Superintendent of the Bell Street Togt Barracks to MNAD, June 9, 1948; DAR, 3/DBN, vol. 1/1/1/1/27, Town Council minutes, May 5, 1904.
45. Mbatha, "Migrant Labour and Its Effects on Tribal and Family Life," 196.
46. Ambler and Crush, "Alcohol in Southern African History"; Swanson, "Durban System."
47. The role of barracks and compounds as institutions of labor control in South Africa has been discussed most extensively in relation to Kimberley and the Rand. See Moroney, "Development of the Compound"; Worger, *South Africa's City of Diamonds*; Turrell, *Capital and Labour.* Dock compounds in Durban have been discussed in Ross-Watt, "Housing of Bantu Stevedores."
48. Swanson, "Rise of Multiracial Durban," 385.
49. DAR, 3/DBN, vol. 1/1/1/1/25, Council minutes, "On Inspector of Nuisances," September 25, 1901; DAR, 3/DBN, vol. 4/1/2/99, Chief Constable William Alexander to Town Clerk, April 20, 1925; Freund, *Insiders and Outsiders,* chapter 3.
50. Several interviewees indeed lived in servants' quarters or townships. Godidi Msomi, Mtukatshelwa Phewa, Mdu Jama, and Sicelo Mbokazi, interviews.
51. DAR, 3/DBN, vol. 1/2/12/1/2, Minutes of the NAB, June 11, 1936.
52. DAR, 3/DBN, 4/1/2/99 and 4/1/3/166–167, file 19K, 1925–48.
53. Zifo Mzizi, Galo Mtolo, Zithulele Chemane, Doda Nxele, Co Pityana, Nkomozethu Cikane, Bhekinkosi Zimu, Gampu Ngcamu, and Zakhele Mthembu, interviews.
54. Some interviewees also lived in these informal settlements. Dumile Ndlovu, Sihle Zungu, and Bheka Dlaba, interviews.
55. Edwards, "Mkhumbane Our Home," 77.
56. Cole, "No Justice, No Ships Get Loaded."
57. Hemson, "Class Consciousness," 139.
58. The *amakholwa* were African Christian converts. Mission educated and instilled with European values, they were often part of the socioeconomic and political African elite. However, as the promise of equality for "civilized men" gave way to segregation and overt racial discrimination, their fortunes declined. See Etherington, *Preachers, Peasants, and Politics.*
59. DAR, 3/DBN, vol. 1/2/10/1/1, Native Affairs and Police Committee minutes, June 24, 1918; vol. 4/1/2/1138, file 315E, part 1, Mayor Nicolson to

General Botha, Reports of two meetings with employers, August 9, 1918; J. S. Marwick to Town Clerk, "Memorandum from Meeting of Employers of Natives at the Point," September 12, 1919.

60. DAR, 3/DBN, vol. 1/1/1/1/39, Town Council minutes, October 7, 1919; PAR, CNC, vol. 353, file 1919/1555, Chief Magistrate of Durban to Chief Native Commissioner, Pietermaritzburg, "*re:* Unrest amongst Natives in Durban," August 8, 1919; SAB, ARB, vol. 1239, file 1042/1214, Divisional Inspector of Labour to Secretary for Labour, "Stoppage of Work," August 16, 1956; vol. 3315, file 1196/5/2, part 2, Native Labour Officer to Divisional Inspector of Labour, "Dispute: Jack Storm (PTY) Ltd. Stevedoring: Point," [October 1958].

61. Kadalie, *My Life and the ICU*, 62.

62. Dube was also one of the founders and the first president of the ANC, then the South African Native National Congress, before he was ousted by the more radical Transvaal branch in 1917. See Cope, "Zulu Petit Bourgeoisie."

63. La Hausse, "Message of the Warriors"; Beinart and Bundy, *Hidden Struggles in Rural South Africa*, 281–82.

64. Bradford, *A Taste of Freedom*; Hemson, "In the Eye of the Storm," 153.

65. Bradford, "We Are Now the Men."

66. DAR, 3/DBN, vol. 4/1/2/1146, file 323, part 1, "Notice by the Anti-Kaffir Beer Manufacturing League," n.d.

67. Nuttall, "Class, Race and Nation," 58–59.

68. Bradford, "We Are Now the Men."

69. "Reply to Flouting of Authority," *Natal Mercury*, November 14, 1929, 11; "Massed Police at Point Road Barracks," *Natal Witness*, November 15, 1929, 8; "Sudden Rush to Pay Poll Tax," *Natal Witness*, November 15, 1929, 1.

70. SAB, NTS, vol. 7665, file 46/332, "Meeting at Chief Native Commissioner's Office," September 6, 1929.

71. Bradford, "Mass Movements and the Petty Bourgeoisie"; la Hausse, "Message of the Warriors," 26.

72. Marks, *Ambiguities of Dependence*, 103; la Hausse, "Message of the Warriors," 20–31.

73. On the influence of Garveyism in South Africa, see Vinson, "Sea Kaffirs."

74. La Hausse, "Message of the Warriors," 25–29.

75. SAB, NTS, vol. 7665, file 46/332, part 1, Native Riots Commission, minutes of evidence, July 3–13, 1929.

76. Nuttall, "Class, Race, and Nation," 123–24.

77. DAR, 3/DBN, vol. 4/1/2/1146, file 323, part 1, "Commission of Enquiry—Native Riots at Durban," September 13, 1929; SAB, NTS, vol. 7665, file 46/332, part 1, Chief Native Commissioner, Pietermaritzburg, to Secretary of Native Affairs, August 31, 1929.

78. Du Toit, *Capital and Labour*, 114–16; Bonner, "Decline and Fall of the ICU," 114–20; Hemson, "Class Consciousness," 254.

79. La Hausse, "Message of the Warriors," 25–29. On class and status in South Africa, see also James, *Money from Nothing*, 15–22.

80. La Hausse, "Dispersal of the Regiments," 77–102; Hemson, "Dock Workers," 91.

81. Roux, *Time Longer Than Rope*, 153.

82. Marks, *Ambiguities of Dependence*, 85; SAB, NTS, vol. 7666, file 55/332, telegram from USUTU to NATIVES PRETORIA, December 17, 1930.

83. Maylam, "Changing Political Economy," 102–4.

84. Freund, *Insiders and Outsiders*, 57.

85. DAR, 3/DBN, vol. 1/1/1/1/70, Town Council minutes, November 5, 1943.

86. Mahoney similarly argues that Zulu ethnic consciousness was constructed largely from below in *The Other Zulus*.

87. Edwards, "Swing the Assegai Peacefully?"; Edwards, "Mkhumbane Our Home," 44.

88. Hemson, "In the Eye of the Storm," 156.

89. Sideris, *Sifuna Imali Yethu*; Zakhele Mthembu, Sipho Mkhize, Mzenkosi Duma, Sidumo Chiliza, Zodwa Tenza, and Bheka Dlaba, interviews.

90. SAB, ARB, vol. 2854, file 1069/70, "Notes of Interview," May 9, 1941.

91. SAB, MVE, vol. 1200, file 538/159/1, Durban Stevedores' Association to Native Commissioner, July 1, 1941.

92. SAB, ARB, vol. 174, file COM 1/9/1, "Meeting Held at Native Commissioner's Office, Durban," March 11, 1942.

93. Nuttall, "Class, Race, and Nation," 190–93; SAB, NTS, vol. 2222, file 416/280, part 1, Chief Native Commissioner to Secretary of Native Affairs, August 10, 1942.

94. SAB, ARB, vol. 2976, file 1069/197, part 1, Zulu Phungula, "Report of Our Workers in Natal," September 20, 1948.

95. Hemson, "Class Consciousness," 351.

96. For example: "Indians Flee in Terror as Native Mob Runs Amok," *Natal Witness*, January 15, 1949, 1; "Native Mobs Beat Women and Children in Durban," *Natal Mercury*, January 15, 1949, 10. For discussions of these events in African and Indian newspapers, see Soske, "Wash Me Black Again," chapter 3.

97. Edward Webster, "The 1949 Durban 'Riots.'"

98. Soske, "Wash Me Black Again," 122.

99. Mahoney traces antagonism between Africans and Indians in Natal back to the nineteenth century, see *Other Zulus*, 123–25.

100. Soske, "Wash Me Black Again," 120, 129.

101. Edwards, "Mkhumbane Our Home," 49.

102. DAR, 3/DBN, vol. 4/1/2/1054, file 269, part 8, Dick Mate to Town Clerk, August 6, 1932; vol. 1/2/12/1/2, Minutes of the NAB, "Letter from A. P. Gumede," October 10, 1934; vol. 4/1/3/1582, file 323B, part 4, Zulu Phungula to Town Clerk, February 17, 1949.

103. DAR, 3/DBN, vol. 4/1/3/1502, file 290P, part 1, "Report of the Broome Commission," January 31, 1948.

104. Hellmann, "The Importance of Beer-Brewing"; Longmore, "African Poverty and Social Unrest"; KCAL, Bourquin papers, KCM 99/42/30/4, "An

Interim Report of a Survey of Bantu Income and Expenditure in Durban," December 1959.

105. "Nine Ships Lying Idle in Durban Harbour," *Natal Witness*, April 2, 1959, 1; "Kwa Mashu: Point Employers Worried," *Natal Mercury*, March 6, 1958, 2.

106. "1,500 Stevedores Down Tools," *Natal Mercury*, February 25, 1959, 2; "Overtime Ban Hits Shipping," *Natal Mercury*, March 26, 1959, 1; "Drastic Labour Replacement Plan: 11 Freighters Idle in Durban," *Natal Witness*, April 4, 1959, 1.

107. University of the Witwatersrand, Historical Papers, AD 1722, SAIRR Oral History Project, tape 45, interview with Absolom Ngema, November 17, 1982.

108. Lunguza Mbelu and Libho Qoza, interviews.

109. DAR, 3/DBN, vol. 1/2/11/1/10, Native Administration Committee minutes, April 14, 1950; "500 Natives Stop Work at Docks," *Natal Mercury*, November 2, 1956, 7.

Chapter Two

1. Marx, *Eighteenth Brumaire*, 13.

2. The word *umbhunguka* can be translated as "prodigal." This concept is related to the idea of an absconder, someone who abandons his rural family and stops sending remittances. For the similar concept of an *itshipa*, see Philip and Iona Mayer, *Townsmen or Tribesmen*.

3. Lihlo Budu, Lungani Xulu, and Mtukatshelwa Phewa, interviews.

4. Bongeka Faku, interview.

5. Beinart, *Political Economy of Pondoland*; Delius, "The Ndzundza Ndebele."

6. Moodie, *Going for Gold*, 21.

7. Mayer and Mayer, *Townsmen or Tribesmen*.

8. Beinart, "Labour Migrancy and Rural Production," 81.

9. Velile Goba, interview.

10. Mbatha, "Migrant Labour and Its Effects on Tribal and Family Life," 132; MacKinnon, "Land, Labour and Cattle," 230.

11. Wandile Mzamo, interview; Sack, "Izimpohlo," 144.

12. Smith, *Labour Resources of Natal*, 66; University of Natal, *African Factory Worker*, 71.

13. SAB, ARB, vol. 3315, file 1196/5/2, part 1, untitled document, n.d.

14. Wage figures given in these interviews should be treated with caution. This is very specific information for one to remember after fifty years. However, most wage figures were within an acceptable range and in line with those in archival and secondary sources.

15. Cf. Bonner, "'The Great Migration' and 'The Greatest Trek,'" 102; Nattrass, "Migrant Labour and Underdevelopment," 15.

16. Carolyn Brown notes the same contradiction in "Race and the Construction of Working-Class Masculinity."

17. See also Carton, *Blood from Your Children.*

18. Monica Hunter, *Reaction to Conquest,* 60.

19. Beinart, *Political Economy of Pondoland,* 83; Sibisi, "How African Women Cope"; Murray, "High Bridewealth."

20. MacKinnon, "Persistence of the Cattle Economy," 107; Murray, "High Bridewealth," 80.

21. Monica Hunter, "Effects of Contact"; "Report of the Native Economic Commission, 1930–2," U.G. 22-'32, 19. For a discussion of this discourse in more recent times, see James Ferguson, *Anti-politics Machine.*

22. Ferguson discusses the role of cattle as retirement savings in Lesotho in *Anti-politics Machine,* 157–58.

23. Lihlo Shange, Mpho Jaca, Mzwakhe Sosibo, and Mr. Sibiya, interviews.

24. Between 1930 and 1950, the price of one head of cattle fluctuated between £3 and £8. See MacKinnon, "Persistence of the Cattle Economy."

25. Geertz, "Rotating Credit Association," 241–63; on the continuing relevance of *stokvels* in South Africa today, despite increased access to formal financial services, see James, *Money from Nothing,* chapter 4.

26. Thomas, "Rotating Credit Associations."

27. Quoted in Kuper and Kaplan, "Voluntary Associations," 183.

28. Moodley, "Three Stokvel Clubs."

29. Zodwa Tenza, interview.

30. Cf. Francis, *Making a Living,* 84.

31. In 1950, the harbor handled 6,158,000 tons of cargo; by 1960 this number had risen to 9,240,000 tons. Horwood, *Port of Durban,* 141.

32. SAB, ARB, vol. 3315, file 1196/5/2, part 2, R.C. Lloyd to the Minister of Labour, "Wage Board Investigation: Stevedoring Industry," January 10, 1958.

33. Employers' responses to a 1956 questionnaire from the Department of Labour indicate that on average about half of all stevedores worked overtime on any given day. SAB, ARB, vol. 3315, file 1196/5/2, part 1, "Questionnaire to Stevedoring Employers," October 1956.

34. Gedla Lukhozi, interview; Tina Sideris mentions some shortcuts workers used in *Sifuna Imali Yethu,* 25–27.

35. KCAL, Oral History Programme of the University of Natal, KCAV 305, interview with Tunyawa Dlamini by B.T.C. Mkhize, KwaMashu, June 14 and 17, 1981.

36. Hellmann, *Rooiyard,* 26; Krige, "Some Social and Economic Facts"; KCAL, Marwick papers, KCM 8332 (b), "Economic and Wage Commission, Evidence," September 16, 1925.

37. E.g.: DAR, 3/DBN, vol. 4/1/2/99, file 19K, Chief Constable William Alexander to Town Clerk, April 20, 1925.

38. Harries, *Work, Culture, and Identity,* 113.

39. DAR, 3/DBN, vol. 1/1/1/1/73, Council minutes, n.d. [1946].

40. Similarly, Keith Hart notes that Frafra migrants in Accra valued even a low-paid job as an "island of regularity and predictability in a sea of ephemeral opportunities." See Keith Hart, "Kinship, Contract, and Trust," 177.

41. Lunguza Mbelu and Libho Qoza, interviews.

42. Godidi Msomi, Mandla Xaba, and Doda Ndaweni, interviews.

43. Cf. O'Laughlin, "Proletarianisation, Agency and Changing Rural Livelihoods," 520.

44. MacKinnon, "Africans and the Myth of Rural Retirement," 164–66.

45. SAB, ARB, vol. 2854, file 1069/70, "Notes of Interview," May 9, 1941; "Notes of Meeting Held in Native Commissioner Office," May 27, 1941.

46. Harries, *Work, Culture, and Identity*; Moodie, *Going for Gold*.

47. Bonner and Nieftagodien, *Alexandra*.

48. Edwards, "Swing the Assegai Peacefully?," 81.

49. Edwards, "Mkhumbane Our Home," 82.

50. E.g., la Hausse, "Drink and Cultural Innovation in Durban," 78–114.

51. For a critique of how the informal economy is discussed in South Africa, see Devey, Skinner, and Valodia, "State of the Informal Economy"; or Callebert, "Transcending the Dual Economy."

52. Berry, *Fathers Work for Their Sons*; Rockel, *Carriers of Culture*; Roberts, "Nyamwezi Trade"; Coquery-Vidrovitch and Lovejoy, "Workers of Trade in Precolonial Africa"; Keith Hart, "Kinship, Contract, and Trust." While Rockel notes that porters moved from employment into self-employment, he also argues that this pattern may not have been as typical and unambiguous as argued by Roberts and that it became less common as the nineteenth century progressed (56).

53. Edwards, "Mkhumbane Our Home," 197; "Native Market in Sub-let Shacks," *Natal Mercury*, January 21, 1948; "Rack Renting in Slums," *Natal Mercury*, January 26, 1948.

54. Keith Hart, "Kinship, Contract, and Trust," 182.

55. DAR, 3/DBN, vol. 1/1/1/1/74, Town Council minutes, September 6, 1948.

56. DAR, 3/DBN, vol. 4/1/2/1051, file 269, part 2, correspondence between the MNAD and the Native Eating House, May 15–16, 1919; extract from the minutes of the Native Affairs and Police Committee, May 19, 1919.

57. Quoted in DAR, 3/DBN, vol. 4/1/2/1051, file 269, part 2, Overseer Bell Street Native Eating House to MNAD, May 15, 1919.

58. DAR, 2/DBN, vol. 2/1/8, Case 1187/'57; Sack, "Izimpohlo," 207.

59. Moodie, *Going for Gold*, 94.

60. The concern about Africans who are independent from wage labor and from the control of a white employer is a constant theme in the history of the city. Swanson, "Rise of Multiracial Durban."

61. "Cause of Durban Crime," *Natal Daily News*, January 22, 1943; KCAL, PNAB, KCF 21, file H2/CM, 1952–54; KCF 57, file T9, part 3, 1949–51.

62. In a different but comparable context, Rob Davies argues that "this illegality derives from legal institutions embodying the values of the dominant

class and designed to serve their interests. These might not be shared by members of the informal sector, who would therefore regard such activities as legitimate." Davies, "Notes on the Theory of the Informal Sector," 61.

63. E.g., Davies, "Notes on the Theory of the Informal Sector."

64. KCAL, PNAB, KCF 57, file NT1, Native Administration Committee report, August 15, 1956.

65. Hemson, "Class Consciousness," 193–94; Bonner, "Desirable or Undesirable Basotho Women?"

66. A notable recent exception is Dobler, *Traders and Trade in Colonial Ovamboland.* I should note, however, that migrant workers who invested their wages in rural stores in colonial Ovamboland came from a very different background than did Durban's dock workers. They were mostly better off, literate, and educated.

67. Cowen and Kanyanjui, *Some Problems of Capital and Class.*

68. Cowen and Shenton, *Doctrines of Development,* 336.

69. Rockel, *Carriers of Culture*; Jennifer Hart, "One Man, No Chop"; Power, "Building Relevance," 61.

70. Chirwa, "'Theba' Is Power."

71. Legassick, "South Africa," 7.

72. Marks and Rathbone, introduction to *Industrialisation and Social Change,* 2.

73. Keith Hart's 1973 article and a 1972 report by the International Labour Organization on unemployment in Kenya were instrumental in the emergence of this concept. See Hart, "Informal Income Opportunities"; ILO, *Incomes, Employment and Equality.* See also Hart, "Informal Economy."

74. Potts, "Urban Informal Sector in Sub-Saharan Africa."

75. Ibid.

76. Marx and Engels, *German Ideology,* 53.

77. Swanson, "Rise of Multiracial Durban"; Atkins, *The Moon Is Dead!*

78. Davies, "Notes on the Theory of the Informal Sector"; Wellings and Sutcliffe, "Developing the Urban Informal Sector in South Africa"; Bezuidenhout and Fakier, "Maria's Burden."

79. Keith Hart, *Memory Bank,* 151; Mosoetsa, *Eating from One Pot,* 24.

80. Cf. Morris, "Development of Capitalism in South African Agriculture."

81. Wolpe, *Articulation of Modes of Production.*

82. Cohen, "Resistance and Hidden Forms of Consciousness," 15–16; Cooper et al., *Confronting Historical Paradigms,* 238.

Chapter Three

1. Sideris, *Sifuna Imali Yethu,* 4.
2. Hlolomzi Ngcwangula, interview.
3. Zodwa Tenza, interview.
4. Quoted in Sideris, *Sifuna Imali Yethu,* 9.

5. SAB, ARB, vol. 3315, file 1196/5/2, part 2, "Memorandum for Submission to the Wage Board," January 22, 1958.

6. Quoted in Sideris, *Sifuna Imali Yethu*, 10.

7. University of the Witwatersrand, Historical Papers, AD 1722, SAIRR Oral History Project, tape 53, interview with Mr. Zulu, no date.

8. Ingpen, *Horizons*, 50.

9. Beinart, "Transkeian Migrant Workers," 55.

10. SAB, ARB, vol. 3315, file 1196/5/2, part 1, "Questionnaires to Stevedoring Employers," n.d. [1956].

11. Godidi Msomi, Mtukatshelwa Phewa, and Mdu Jama, interviews.

12. SAB, ARB, vol. 174, file COM 1/9/1, "Notes of Meeting Held at Durban with the Stevedores' Association," August 3, 1942.

13. SAB, ARB, vol. 3315, file 1196/5/2, part 2, Onder-Sekretaris to Waarnemende Sekretaris van Arbeid, "I. S. Stuwadoorarbeid: Durbanse Hawe," April 24, 1958.

14. SAB, ARB, vol. 174, file COM 1/9/1, "Notes of Meeting Held at Durban with the Stevedores' Association," August 3, 1942.

15. DAR, 3/DBN, vol. 1/1/1/1/68, Town Council minutes, August 7, 1942; vol. 4/1/3/1354, file 269, part 1, Director of Port and Shipping to Town Clerk, July 20, 1942.

16. Co Pityana and Nkomozethu Cikane, interviews.

17. SAB, ARB, vol. 2854, file 1069/70, "Notes of Interview," May 9, 1941.

18. Cf. Green, "Work Process."

19. Ibid., 570; Hemson, "Class Consciousness," 334, 531.

20. Ingpen, *Horizons*, 50; University of the Witwatersrand, Historical Papers, AD 1722, SAIRR Oral History Project, tape 44, interview with Mr. Ntshangase, November 19, 1982; tape 39, September 23, 1982.

21. SAB, ARB, vol. 1229, file 1042/15/1959, Wage Determination No. 183, February 6, 1959. Wage differentials on the Cape Town docks were similarly limited: SAB, VWN, vol. 4323, file PG 955/27, "Agreement," December 15, 1939.

22. Hemson, "Class Consciousness," 365.

23. Ibid., 394.

24. Zifo Mzizi and Mzo Mzongo, interviews.

25. Cf. Taplin, *Dockers' Union*, 23–24.

26. SAB, ARB, vol. 3315, file 1196/5/2, part 1, "Report on Conditions of Employment of Stevedoring Workers," August 1956.

27. SAB, NTS, vol. 7665, file 46/332, Native Riots Commission, minutes of evidence, evidence by Akob Ally Mahomed, July 5, 1929, and by Mcijelo and Alfred Ngcobo, July 13, 1929; SAB, ARB, vol. 1239, file 1042/1214, Divisional Inspector of Labour to Secretary for Labour, "Stoppage of Work," August 16, 1956. Cf. Moodie, *Going for Gold*, 94–95.

28. "Report of the Native Economic Commission, 1930–2," U.G. 22-'32, 306.

29. SAB, ARB, vol. 1229, file 1042/15/1959, Wage Determination No. 183, February 6, 1959; Hemson, "In the Eye of the Storm," 156.

30. Cf. Wolpe, "Capitalism and Cheap Labour-Power."

31. Edwards, "Mkhumbane Our Home," 109.

32. DAR, 3/DBN, vol. 4/1/3/1502, file 290P, part 1, "Report of the Broome Commission," March 6, 1948.

33. "Drastic Labour Replacement Plan: 11 Freighters Idle in Durban," *Natal Witness*, April 4, 1959, 1; "Docks Return to Normal Routine," *Natal Mercury*, April 7, 1959, 1.

34. DAR, 3/DBN, vol. 4/1/3/3/313, file 45, part 4, Mayor's minute, 1937.

35. DAR, 3/DBN, vol. 1/2/11/1/10, Native Administration Committee minutes, April 14, 1950.

36. Cooper, *Decolonization and African Society*; *On the African Waterfront*.

37. DAR, 3/DBN, vol. 4/1/3/1502, file 290P, part 1, "Report of the Broome Commission," March 6, 1948.

38. SAB, GG, vol. 1574, file 50/1698, "Report of the Inter-Departmental Committee on the Social, Health and Economic Conditions of Urban Natives," March 9, 1942, 7–8.

39. "A Firm Cites Its Own Case," *Natal Daily News*, January 29, 1948; "Immediate Inquiry into Alleged 'Dole Racket'—Dr. Steyn," *Natal Daily News*, February 5, 1948, 1.

40. Hemson, "Dock Workers," 107.

41. Cooper, *On the African Waterfront*, 74.

42. Martin Legassick famously argues that apartheid was not a fundamental departure from supposedly more liberal United Party policies, but rather an adaptation of the already established cheap labor system to a more industrial economy, "Legislation, Ideology and Economy." However, Saul Dubow also warns us against depicting the rise of apartheid as inevitable. He argues that the 1940s was marked by "competing visions of the future" and that none of these were predetermined to be triumphant. Dubow, "Introduction: South Africa's 1940s."

43. Weinhauer, "Power and Control."

44. Hemson, "Class Consciousness," 421.

45. PAR, CNC, vol. 12, file CNC 494/1911, Chief Constable Donovan to Chief Native Commissioner Shepstone, July 4, 1911.

46. SAB, GG, vol. 1574, file 50/1698, "Report of the Inter-Departmental Committee on the Social, Health and Economic Conditions of Urban Natives," March 9, 1942, 37.

47. KCAL, PNAB, KCF 43, file H4-20, Acting Manager MNAD to City and Water Engineer, May 10, 1948. Emphasis added.

48. DAR, 3/DBN, vol. 4/1/3/1355, file 269, part 4, report by Manager MNAD, January 10, 1949.

49. DAR, 3/DBN, vol. 4/1/3/1355, file 269, part 4, Manager MNAD to Town Clerk, August 12, 1949.

50. University of the Witwatersrand, Historical Papers, AD 1722, SAIRR Oral History Project, tape 52, interview with Mr. Maghwasa, n.d.; tape 53, interview

with Mr. Zulu, n.d.; Mbatha, "Migrant Labour and Its Effects on Tribal and Family Life," 151; Ingpen, *Horizons*, 50.

51. Mbatha, "Migrant Labour and Its Effects on Tribal and Family Life," 152.

52. SAB, NTS, vol. 1767, file 60/276, Secretary of the Native Affairs Commission to Minister of Native Affairs, December 12, 1929; Lee, *African Women and Apartheid*, 36; CPSA, *People Overflow*, 4.

53. DAR, 3/DBN, vol. 1/1/1/1/74, Town Council minutes, September 6, 1947; vol. 4/1/2/1052, file 269, part 3, Manager MNAD to Town Clerk, October 23, 1919.

54. SAB, NTS, vol. 2206, file 353/280, "Deputation of Native Employees Received by the Native Commissioner, Durban," August 25, 1937.

55. SAB, NTS, vol. 2222, file 416/280, part 1, "Notes of Meeting Held at Bell Street Barracks," July 29, 1942.

56. For life in uMkhumbane, Lamontville, Clermont, and other townships, see Maylam and Edwards, *People's City*.

57. Cf. Kerr and Siegel, "Interindustry Propensity to Strike."

58. Horwood, "Some Aspects of Urban African Employment," 29; KCAL, Miriam Janisch papers, KCM 90/19/1, "The Family (with Special Reference to the Urban Bantu Family)," [c.1944].

59. Mayer and Mayer, *Townsmen or Tribesmen*; Argyle, "Kalela, Beni, Asafo, Ingoma and the Rural-Urban Dichotomy."

60. Ingpen, *Horizons*, 50; Edwards, "Mkhumbane Our Home," 77. This festive atmosphere on weekends in African townships and informal settlements is captured in Modikwe Dikobe's *Marabi Dance*, 32–33.

61. Cf. Mbatha, "Migrant Labour and Its Effects on Tribal and Family Life," 166–73.

62. Cf. Hellmann, "The Importance of Beer-Brewing."

63. Edwards, "Mkhumbane Our Home," 276.

64. Preston-White, "Women Migrants and Marriage," 170–72.

65. Hellmann, "Social Change among Urban Africans," 173; see also Ashforth, *Witchcraft, Violence, and Democracy*.

66. Cooper, *On the African Waterfront*, 248.

67. Since the vast majority of interviewees lived in Reserves and not as tenants on white commercial farms, this discussion will be mostly limited to life on the Reserves.

68. Gobile Mbhele, interview.

69. Cf. Kark, "Health Implications," 210–11.

70. Reader, *Zulu Tribe in Transition*, 33.

71. MacKinnon, "Chiefly Authority, Leapfrogging Headmen," 569–71.

72. DAR, 3/DBN, vol. 4/1/2/99, file 19K, part 1, Chief Constable to Town Clerk, June 15, 1925; University of the Witwatersrand, Historical Papers, AD 1438, Native Economic Commission, minutes of evidence & memoranda, Box 6, 6312; DAR, 3/DBN, vol. 4/1/2/1131–6 and 4/1/3/1544–9, file 315, Monthly reports of the MNAD, 1916–49; Reader, *Zulu Tribe in Transition*, 32–35.

73. Kark, "Migrant Labour and Family Health," 199.

74. Simkins, *Agricultural Production in the African Reserves*, 17–19.
75. MacKinnon, "Persistence of the Cattle Economy," 101–04.
76. Ngubane, "Consequences for Women," 173–82; John L. Comaroff, preface to *Essays on African Marriage*.
77. Cf. Mafeje, "On the Articulation of Modes of Production."
78. MacKinnon, "Africans and the Myth of Rural Retirement," 165–66.
79. Cf. Hickel, *Democracy as Death*.
80. Chayanov, *Theory of Peasant Economy*; Barnum and Squire, "Econometric Application of the Theory of the Farm-Household."
81. Takulu Kheswa, interview.
82. Guyer, "Household and Community," 99.

Chapter Four

1. Thembeni Phewa, interview.
2. Beinart and Bundy, *Hidden Struggles in Rural South Africa*, 1.
3. For poignant critiques of the relative absence of female perspectives in the historiography of southern Africa, see Epprecht, *"This Matter of Women Is Getting Very Bad,"* chapter 1; Walker, "Gender and the Development of the Migrant Labour System"; Bozzoli, "Marxism, Feminism and South African Studies."
4. Morrell, *Changing Men*; Epprecht, *Hungochani*.
5. In *Women in South African History*, for example, few contributions engage in any significant way with the experiences of rural women who were not involved in politics. More attention is afforded to women who moved to the city and joined trade unions or the ANC Women's League. See Gasa, *Women in South African History*. There are of course notable exceptions, for example, Mager, *Gender and the Making of a South African Bantustan*.
6. Cf. Gasa, "Feminism, Motherism, Patriarchies and Women's Voices," 214.
7. An early study of the strains and conflicts in rural households resulting from colonialism and socioeconomic change, but with limited sustained gender analysis, can be found in Turner, *Schism and Continuity*.
8. Carton, *Blood from Your Children*; McClendon, *Genders and Generations Apart*.
9. Moodie, *Going for Gold*, 158.
10. For a critique of such accounts of gender and patriarchy in South Africa, see Hickel, *Democracy as Death*, 46–51.
11. Wolpe, "Capitalism and Cheap Labour-Power."
12. On the criticisms and legacies of Wolpe's argument, see Sitas, "Wolpe's Legacy."
13. Burawoy, "The Functions and Reproduction of Migrant Labor."
14. Cf. Beinart, "Chieftaincy and the Concept of Articulation."
15. Meillassoux, *Maidens, Meal and Money*; Rey, *Les alliances de classes*.

16. On wealth in people, see Miers and Kopytoff, *Slavery in Africa*; Guyer, "Wealth in People, Wealth in Things."

17. Berry, "Social Institutions and Access to Resources," 42.

18. Bank, *Home Spaces, Street Styles*, 18.

19. Cf. Bonnin, "Claiming Spaces, Changing Places"; Osborn, *Our New Husbands Are Here.*

20. See Landes, *Feminism, the Public and the Private.*

21. Thornberry, "Sex, Violence, and Family"; Hickel, "Engineering the Township Home."

22. For the Zulu homestead, see Guy, "Colonial Transformations and the Home"; "Gender Oppression"; for other southern African examples, see Jean Comaroff, *Body of Power, Spirit of Resistance*; Kuper, *Wives for Cattle.*

23. Connell, *Gender and Power*, 121.

24. Engels, *Origin of the Family.*

25. Guy, "Colonial Transformations and the Home," 31.

26. Meillassoux, "The Economic Bases of Demographic Reproduction."

27. Murray, "Marital Strategy in Lesotho"; Ferguson, *The Anti-politics Machine*, 162–63.

28. Murray, "High Bridewealth"; Beinart, *Political Economy of Pondoland*, 83, 96; Moodie, *Going for Gold*, 39–40.

29. E.g., Jeffreys, "Lobolo Is Child-Price."

30. Vilakazi, *Zulu Transformations*, 27.

31. Murray, *Families Divided*, 154.

32. Pauw, *Christianity and Xhosa Tradition*, chapter 7.

33. All but one of the women interviewed mentioned the importance of these rituals performed by the homestead head. Families today will still turn to the *amadlozi*, especially in times of crisis. However, women have increasingly taken over the role of mediating between the ancestors and the living; see Margaretten, "Parting Homes in KwaZulu-Natal."

34. Cf. Eldredge, *South African Kingdom.*

35. Walker, "Gender and the Development of the Migrant Labour System," 179.

36. Cf. Hickel, *Democracy as Death.*

37. Beinart, *Political Economy of Pondoland*, 98; Coplan, "Emergence of an African Working-Class Culture," 262.

38. La Hausse, "Cows of Nongoloza," 87–89; see also Moodie, *Going for Gold*, 14.

39. Neither in the interviews nor in the archives was there mention of same-sex relations similar to the mine marriages on the Rand. However, uMkhumbane did have a subculture where same-sex intimacy was celebrated in the 1940s and 1950s. Some dock workers seem to have taken part in this subculture. For differing interpretations of these mine marriages see Moodie, *Going for Gold*, 138–40; Harries, *Work, Culture, and Identity*, 200–202; Epprecht, *Hungochani*, 66–67. On same-sex intimacy in uMkhumbane see Louw, "Mkhumbane and New Traditions of (Un)African Same-Sex Weddings," 287–96.

40. E.g., Lihlo Shange and Mr. Sibiya, interviews.

41. Mager, *Gender and the Making of a South African Bantustan*, 87.

42. Special-purpose money is a form of money that can only serve specific uses and can only be used by certain people, as opposed to general-purpose money that can serve all money uses for anyone. The economic value of cattle cannot be dissociated from its social value and thus cannot be reduced to its market value. Concretely, a wife cannot simply exchange cattle for its market-value to get access to these resources. See Polanyi, "Economy as Instituted Process"; or Bohannan and Dalton, *Markets in Africa.*

43. Moodie, *Going for Gold*, 38. Emphasis added.

44. SAB, ARB, vol. 174, file COM 1/9/1, "Meeting at the Native Commissioner's Office, Durban," March 11, 1942.

45. On masculinity and interpersonal violence on the mines, see Breckenridge, "Allure of Violence."

46. SAB, ARB, vol. 2976, file 1069/197, part 1, Zulu Phungula, "Report of Our Workers in Natal," September 20, 1948.

47. SAB, ARB, vol. 174, file COM 1/9/1, "Meeting at the Native Commissioner's Office, Durban," March 11, 1942.

48. Cf. Marks, "Patriotism, Patriarchy and Purity," 226; Singleton, "'House' and 'Home,'" 180–81; McClendon, *Genders and Generations Apart*, 21.

49. This phrase is borrowed from Colin Murray's PhD dissertation, titled "Keeping House in Lesotho."

50. Fakier and Cock, "Gendered Analysis of the Crisis of Social Reproduction," 354–55.

51. Cf. Kandiyoti, "Bargaining with Patriarchy."

52. Ferguson, "Declarations of Dependence."

53. Cf. McClendon, *Genders and Generations Apart*, 59–60, 68.

54. Ferguson, "Declarations of Dependence."

55. Murray, *Families Divided*, 150.

56. Cf. Kark, "Health Implications."

57. Cf. Epprecht, *"This Matter of Women Is Getting Very Bad,"* 59.

58. Florence Phewa and Talent Gumbi, interviews. See also Kark, "Health Implications," 210.

59. Sihle Zungu, Nelson Ndaba, Talent Gumbi, and Fikile Mlotshwa, interviews.

60. Sen, "Gender and Cooperative Conflicts."

61. Gyekye, *Essay on African Philosophical Thought*, 143–46, 159–61.

62. The quote is from Fikile Mlotshwa, interview, but almost all female interviewees expressed comparable sentiments.

63. Cf. Brandel, "Urban Lobolo Attitudes."

64. Mark Hunter, "Bond of Education."

65. Marks, "Patriotism, Patriarchy and Purity," 226; Lee, *African Women and Apartheid*, 17–19.

66. Lee, *African Women and Apartheid*, 36–37.

67. Cf. Makhulu, *Making Freedom.*

68. On transactional sex, see Mark Hunter, "Materiality of Everyday Sex."
69. Posel, *Making of Apartheid*.
70. Cf. Makhulu, *Making Freedom*, 26.
71. See also Lee, *African Women and Apartheid*, 47; Mark Hunter, "Changing Political Economy of Sex."
72. Neves and du Toit, "Rural Livelihoods in South Africa," 93–115.

Chapter Five

1. Harries, *Work, Culture, and Identity*, 222.
2. Engels, *Condition of the Working Class in England*, 224.
3. Hobsbawm, *Primitive Rebels*, especially chapter 2.
4. Ibid., 5.
5. Scott, *Weapons of the Weak*, 290. Emphasis in original.
6. Bayat, "From 'Dangerous Classes' to 'Quiet Rebels,'" 541–45. For Gillian Hart, Scott's emphasis on everyday resistance rests on "a voluntarist conceptualisation of agency. Scott's subject is a free-willed individual decision-maker, with fixed and unambiguous identity and interests." See "Engendering Everyday Resistance."
7. Hobsbawm, "Social Banditry."
8. Van Onselen, "Regiment of the Hills."
9. Austen, "Social Bandits and Other Heroic Criminals," 102–3.
10. E. P. Thompson discusses anonymous threatening letters in eighteenth-century England as reactions to the enclosure and criminalization of such common rights. See "Crime of Anonymity."
11. While this chapter focuses on the 1950s, pilferage of course occurred before that time as well. See "Thefts at the Point," *Natal Witness*, August 27, 1918, 5; PAR, NHD, vol. I/1/21, Natal Harbour Board, minutes of meetings, June 17, 1898.
12. Ditton, "Perks, Pilferage and the Fiddle," 39; Mars, *Cheats at Work*, 3.
13. Ditton, "Perks, Pilferage and the Fiddle," 49–49, 55.
14. Colquhoun, *Treatise on the Commerce and Police of the River Thames*, 58–64; Mars, "Dock Pilferage."
15. Cooke Johnson, "Criminality on the Docks," 722; Colin Davis, *Waterfront Revolts*, 40; Fingard, *Jack in Port*, 137.
16. La Hausse, "Cows of Nongoloza," 88n45.
17. Atkins, *The Moon Is Dead!*, 124.
18. Harries, *Work, Culture, and Identity*, 113.
19. Cf. Colquhoun, *Treatise on the Commerce and Police of the River Thames*, 62; Mars, "Dock Pilferage," 216. See also *On the Waterfront* (film), directed by Kazan.
20. All interviewees were informed that they could remain anonymous. Nobody chose that option, even when activities were discussed that were strictly speaking illegal. Seeing that most of the activities described happened

in a rather distant past, most of these activities were hardly serious crimes, and none of the interviewees are still working on the docks, interviewees will be identified either in the text or in references. Exceptions will be made in a few cases where bigger goods or guns were stolen.

21. South African Container Stevedores in-house museum in Durban, visited on June 11, 2009, on invitation by Yoga Thinnasagren.

22. Cooke Johnson, "Criminality on the Docks," 725.

23. Eric Ryland, interview.

24. Similarly, James Scott notes that the pilferage of rice paddies had very little impact on the output of the better-off farmers who were the usual victims, but a substantial effect on the consumption levels of poor pilferers and their households. Scott, *Weapons of the Weak*, 267–69.

25. SAB, ARB, vol. 2854, file 1069/70, "Notes of Interview," May 9, 1941. This does not necessarily mean that Zulu Phungula did not engage in pilferage, as he would likely not have admitted this when asking for a raise to make up for the increased cost of living.

26. Gcinokwakhe Sobiso, interview. Of course, this also happened elsewhere. Mars describes how stevedores in St. John's purposefully dropped a crate of whisky and were ready with their containers to recuperate the spilled liquor; see "Dock Pilferage," 218. A similar incident is depicted in the movie *On the Waterfront*, directed by Kazan.

27. Withdrawal of Water Police: DAR, 3/DBN, vol. 4/1/2/1044, file 264, part 2, Secretary of the Natal Chamber of Industries to Town Clerk, April 12, 1929. During the wartime blackout the lack of light at night would have made pilferage and theft easier: DAR, 3/DBN, vol. 1/2/11/1/6, Native Administration Committee minutes, July 24, 1942. The only complaint I found without such a specific context dates from 1898: PAR, NHD, vol. I/1/21, Natal Harbour Board, minutes of meetings, June 17, 1898.

28. Ditton, "Perks, Pilferage and the Fiddle," 52–53.

29. "Thefts at the Point," *Natal Witness*, August 27, 1918, 5.

30. This interviewee shall remain nameless because of the nature of the goods stolen. This person retired in the early 1960s.

31. Mzwakhe Sosibo, interview.

32. Bhekinkosi Zimu, Zakhele Mthembu, and Mzwakhe Sosibo, interviews.

33. Phumla Nyathikazi, interview.

34. Since this does not concern small-scale pilferage, the name of this worker is withheld.

35. "Cause of Durban Crime," *Natal Daily News*, January 22, 1943; KCAL, PNAB, KCF 21, file H2/CM, "Memorandum: re Supply of Goods to Illegal Traders," n.d.; KCF 57, file T9, vol. 3, Licensing Officer to Manager of the Municipal Native Affairs Department, August 30, 1950; handwritten notes in the same file, titled "Illegal Trading" and "Illegal trading Cato Manor," September 6, 1950.

36. The trauma of arrest and police raids is an important theme in black South African literature of the apartheid era. See Abrahams, *Mine Boy*, 24–25;

la Guma, *Stone Country*. Wulf Sachs discusses John Chavafambira's traumatic experience of being arrested and paraded in cuffs through the city, while his wife did not know what happened to him for two weeks. See Sachs, *Black Hamlet*, 142, 203–204.

37. Eileen Jensen Krige notes that many of the most respectable women in Marabastad and Bantule, Pretoria, were beer brewers and that there was no stigma attached to this illegal activity: "Some Social and Economic Facts," 96.

38. Mars, *Cheats at Work*, 4, 105.

39. Thompson discusses how a moral economy legitimated actions that were strictly speaking illegal, for example food riots: "This was rarely a mere uproar which culminated in the breaking open of barns or the looting of shops. It was legitimized by the assumption of an older moral economy, which taught the immorality of any unfair method of forcing up the price of provisions by profiteering upon the necessities of the people." *Making of the English Working Class*, 67–68. In an important 1971 article, he further develops this notion of collective legitimation of crowd action, criticizing explanations of rioting and protest that were based on a "crass economic reductionism" and did not take the cultural context of these riots into account. Food riots were seen by the population as a legitimate reaction to illegitimate hoarding: "It is possible to detect in almost every eighteenth-century crowd action some legitimizing notion. By the notion of legitimation I mean that the men and women in the crowd were informed by the belief that they were defending traditional rights or customs; and, in general, that they were supported by the wider consensus of the community. On occasion this popular consensus was endorsed by some measure of license afforded by the authorities. More commonly, the consensus was so strong that it overrode motives of fear or deference." "Moral Economy of the English Crowd," 78. See also "The Moral Economy Reviewed."

40. Scott's *Moral Economy of the Peasant* also played an important role in spreading the concept of moral economies. And although he never uses the phrase as such, it is implicitly also present in Polanyi's *Great Transformation*. On the history, different interpretations, and critiques of this concept, see Hann, "Moral Economy," 187–98.

41. Moodie, *Going for Gold*, 86.

42. However, I did not find evidence of the same sort of strictly defined, almost institutionalized, guidelines that could be found in other ports. For example, Mars notes that dock workers in St. John's had a formula to calculate how much they could pilfer from a particular ship and that personal goods (passengers' luggage, for example) were out of bounds. See Mars, "Dock Pilferage," 224–25; *Cheats at Work*, 106. While the interviewees did not express such clear guidelines, there was nothing that could be considered personal cargo among the goods that they mentioned pilfering.

43. Personal conversation with Sibongo Dlamini, Durban, October 20, 2009. In Tanga, Tanzania, workers made the distinction between *wizi hasada* (adverse theft) and *wizi halali* (legitimate theft). See Kaijage, "War of Clubs," 302.

44. Cf. Atkins, *The Moon Is Dead!*; la Hausse, "Cows of Nongoloza."

45. Bhekinkosi Zimu, interview.

46. A term used in casual dock labor in Britain and elsewhere for those men who are preferred by the foremen and get hired more regularly than others. See Taplin, *Dockers' Union*, 15–16.

47. Doda Nxele, Co Pityana, Dumile Ndlovu, and Lungani Xulu, interviews.

48. Cooke Johnson, "Criminality on the Docks," 723. Emphasis in original.

49. Atkins, *The Moon Is Dead!*, 125–26; Mbatha, "Migrant Labour and Its Effects on Tribal and Family Life," 128–33.

50. Sicelo Mbokazi, Mtukatshelwa Phewa, and Mdu Jama, interviews.

51. Isaacman et al., "Cotton Is the Mother of Poverty"; Crummey, *Banditry, Rebellion and Social Protest.*

52. Cohen, "Resistance and Hidden Forms of Consciousness."

53. Genovese, *Roll, Jordan, Roll*; Gutman, *Black Family in Slavery and Freedom.*

54. Examples of pilferage discussed as a coping mechanism can be found in Nuttall, "Class, Race and Nation," 185; and Cooke Johnson, "Criminality on the Docks," 727.

55. Glaser, *Bo-Tsotsi*, 4.

56. Cooke Johnson, "Criminality on the Docks," 726.

57. Hobsbawm, *Primitive Rebels*, chapter 2; for different contexts see also Antony, "Peasants, Heroes and Brigands"; Austen, "Social Bandits and Other Heroic Criminals."

58. Gedla Lukhozi and Doda Nxele, interviews.

59. Freund, "Theft and Social Protest"; Cohen, "Resistance and Hidden Forms of Consciousness."

60. Freund, "Theft and Social Protest," 69.

61. Ibid. Emphasis in original.

62. Ibid., 79.

63. Kaijage, "War of Clubs," 302.

64. Van Onselen, *Chibaro*, 240.

65. SAB, ARB, vol. 174, file COM 1/9/1, "Meeting Held at Native Commissioner's Office, Durban," March 11, 1942.

66. Cohen, "Resistance and Hidden Forms of Consciousness," 12.

67. Scott, *Weapons of the Weak.*

68. Isaacman et al., "Cotton Is the Mother of Poverty," 604.

69. Bheka Dlaba and Mr. Sibiya, interviews.

70. Cf. Bayat, "From 'Dangerous Classes' to 'Quiet Rebels,'" 549.

71. SAB, NTS, vol. 7665, file 46/332, Native Riots Commission, minutes of evidence, evidence by Akob Ally Mahomed, July 5, 1929, and by Mcijelo and Alfred Ngcobo, July 13, 1929; "Native Dock Workers Stop Work in Durban," *Natal Witness*, June 9, 1948, 1; "500 Natives Stop Work at Docks," *Natal Mercury*, November 2, 1956, 7; "New Labour Force Will Take Over," *Natal Mercury*, April 4, 1959, 2.

Chapter Six

1. This chapter does not attempt to offer a comprehensive or chronological overview of major strikes and other forms of industrial action. For a more comprehensive account, see Callebert, "Livelihood Strategies of Dock Workers," chapter 9; or Hemson, "Class Consciousness."

2. SAB, NTS, vol. 2222, file 416/280, part 1, "Notes of Meeting Held at Bell Street Barracks," July 29, 1942; SAB, ARB, vol. 2976, file 1069/197, part 1, Zulu Phungula, "Report of Our Workers in Natal," September 20, 1948.

3. University of the Witwatersrand, Historical Papers, AD 1722, SAIRR Oral History Project, tape 50, interview with Mr. Xulu and Mr. Mkhwanazi, November 25, 1982.

4. Kerr and Siegel, "Interindustry Propensity to Strike."

5. Cooper, "Dockworkers and Labour History," 535–36.

6. Hemson, "Class Consciousness," 712.

7. Lourenço-Lindell, *Africa's Informal Workers*; Adu-Amankwah, "Ghana." See also Meagher, *Identity Economics*, chapter 8.

8. Marks and Rathbone argue the same in their introduction to *Industrialisation and Social Change*, 26.

9. Hemson, "Class Consciousness," 28–32; Atkins, *The Moon Is Dead!*, 133–34.

10. "Native Wharf Strike," *Natal Mercury*, March 6, 1920, 9; "Native Strike at Durban," *Natal Witness*, March 6, 1920, 1.

11. In early twentieth-century Cape Town, living conditions in the harbor compounds were also causes for conflict. Bickford-Smith, *Ethnic Pride and Racial Prejudice*, 181.

12. SAB, ARB, vol. 1239, file 1042/1214, Divisional Inspector to Secretary for Labour, "Stoppage of Work," August 16, 1956; telegram dated August 14, 1956.

13. E.g., "The Strike Mania," *Natal Witness*, June 17, 1903, 6.

14. "500 Natives Stop Work at Docks," *Natal Mercury*, November 2, 1956, 7. See also SAB, ARB, vol. 1240, file 1042/989, Divisional Inspector of Labour to Secretary of Labour, November 6, 1956.

15. SAB, ARB, vol. 3315, file 1196/5/2, part 1, "Report on Conditions of Employment of Stevedoring Workers," May 2, 1957, 8.

16. "Insubordination at the Point," *Natal Mercury*, December 19, 1925, 10; SAB, ARB, vol. 3315, file 1196/5/2, part 2, Natal Employers' Association to the Chairman of the Wage Board, January 13, 1958; Native Labour Officer to Divisional Inspector of Labour, "Dispute: Jack Storm (PTY) Ltd. Stevedoring: Point," [October 1958].

17. "Native Dockers Stop Work in Durban," *Natal Witness*, June 9, 1948, 1; KCAL, Bourquin papers, news clippings book 22, "2,000 Native Dockers Meet in Protest at Point," unidentified newspaper, n.d. [June 1948].

18. Sideris, *Sifuna Imali Yethu*, 25–26.

19. The development of a racial consciousness was still relatively new, see Mahoney, *Other Zulus*, especially chapters 4–5.

20. "Durban Natives Want to Fight," *Natal Mercury*, August 28, 1935, 15.

21. "Zulu Number of Rand Paper," *Natal Mercury*, September 5, 1935, 17.

22. The diversity of consciousness has been stressed by Beinart, for example in "Worker Consciousness, Ethnic Particularism and Nationalism." Peter Alexander, however, has argued that the social history of the 1980s and 1990s has privileged culture too much over class and political economy, see "Oscillating Migrants, 'Detribalised Families' and Militancy."

23. DAR, 3/DBN, vol. 4/1/2/1146, file 323, part 1, report by Commissioner D. de Waal, "Native Beer Boycott," September 13, 1929, 20–21; SAB, NTS, vol. 7665, file 46/332, part 1, Chief Native Commissioner to Secretary of Native Affairs, August 31, 1929.

24. Hemson, "Class Consciousness," 221; Edwards, "Swing the Assegai Peacefully?," 70.

25. KCAL, A. W. G. Champion papers, KCM 99/6/25/8, John Argyle, "Labour Pool: The Development of Labour Control in the Stevedoring Trade," 130.

26. DAR, 3/DBN, vol. 4/1/2/1147, file 323A, part 1, *Togt* workers at the Bell Street Barracks to the Durban Borough Advisory Board of Europeans and Natives, November 21, 1930.

27. DAR, 3/DBN, vol. 4/1/2/1147, file 323A, part 2, Dick Mate, Amos Gumede and William G. Sibiya to the NAB, July 26, 1931.

28. DAR, 3/DBN, vol. 4/1/2/1054, file 369, part 8, Dick Mate to Town Clerk, November 3, 1931.

29. DAR, 3/DBN, vol. 4/1/2/1054, file 369, part 8, Dick Mate to Town Clerk, August 6, 1932.

30. DAR, 3/DBN, vol. 4/1/2/1139, file 315E, part 4, Dick Mate to Town Clerk, November 8, 1931; minutes of the NAB, October 23, 1931.

31. DAR, 3/DBN, vol. 4/1/2/1139, part 4, minutes of the NAB, December 9, 1931.

32. Ibid.

33. DAR, 3/DBN, vol. 4/1/2/1148, file 323A, part 3, Dick Mate to Native Welfare Officer, December 24, 1932.

34. DAR, 3/DBN, vol. 4/1/2/1148, file 323A, part 3, E. Makulumani Magwaza to Town Clerk, August 1, 1933; vol. 4/1/3/1575, file 323A, part 1, Paul B. Nxele to Town Clerk, October 8, 1935.

35. DAR, 3/DBN, vol. 1/2/12/1/2, minutes of the NAB, October 10, 1934; and June 11, 1936.

36. Edwards, "Recollections," 73.

37. Hemson, "In the Eye of the Storm," 158.

38. Ibid.

39. SAB, ARB, vol. 2854, file 1069/70, "Notes of Interview," May 9, 1941; vol. 174, file COM 1/9/1, "Meeting Held at Native Commissioner's Office, Durban," March 11, 1942.

40. SAB, ARB, vol. 251, file COM 1/49, Abel Mhlongo and Zulu Phungula to the Controller of Industrial Manpower, October 1, 1942.

41. SAB, ARB, vol. 174, file COM 1/9/1, "Meeting Held at Native Commissioner's Office, Durban," March 11, 1942.

42. SAB, NTS, vol. 2222, file 416/280, part 1, "Notes of Meeting Held at the Bell Street Barracks," July 29, 1942.

43. The Durban Stevedores' Association, representing the employers, was "of the opinion [that wage rates are] a legal matter to be dealt with by the Union Government." SAB, MVE, vol. 1200, file 538/159/1, Durban Stevedores' Association to Native Commissioner, July 1, 1941.

44. SAB, ARB, vol. 2976, file 1069/197, Zulu Phungula, "Report of Our Workers in Natal," September 20, 1948.

45. Hemson, "Class Consciousness," 350.

46. SAB, SAP, vol. 474, file 35/3/49, Divisional Inspector to the Commissioner of the SAP, May 2, 1949.

47. "Half Durban Stevedores Strike: Ships Delayed," *Natal Witness*, May 3, 1949, 1; "Natives' Strike May Spread," *Natal Mercury*, May 3, 1949, 9; SAB, SAP, vol. 35/3/49, "Dock Strike—Durban," May 2, 1949.

48. SAB, SAP, vol. 474, file 35/3/49, Divisional Inspector to the Commissioner of the SAP, May 2, 1949.

49. Hemson, "In the Eye of the Storm," 158. For example, when Phungula was arrested as one of ten organizers of a strike in July 1942, he was released from prison on the condition that he would address the strikers and tell them to return to work. He did address the workers but told the crowd that "we better fight and die for what we want until we get it." He thus remained in custody. SAB, ARB, vol. 174, file COM 1/9/1, Controller of Censorship to Controller of Manpower, August 15, 1942.

50. Chakrabarty, *Rethinking Working-Class History*, 138–40.

51. Hemson, "Class Consciousness," 359.

52. Zodwa Tenza, interview.

53. Hemson, "Class Consciousness," 351.

54. See also Gillian Hart, *Rethinking the South African Crisis*.

55. Freund, "Confrontation and Social Change," 133.

56. La Hausse, "Dispersal of the Regiments," 80–81.

57. Beinart and Bundy, *Hidden Struggles in Rural South Africa*, 281–82; la Hausse, "Message of the Warriors."

58. See Champion, "African Businesses."

59. Barchiesi, "Work in the Constitution of the Human."

60. Though mostly focused on the activities of the ICU in rural South Africa, Helen Bradford's *Taste of Freedom* discusses the union's organizational strategies well.

61. Mahoney, *Other Zulus*.

62. Nuttall, "Class, Race and Nation," 124.

63. SAB, K193, "Commission of Enquiry into Riots in Durban, Minutes of Evidence," vol. 3, evidence by Zulu Phungula, February 21, 1949.

64. Vinson, *The Americans Are Coming!*; Trapido, introduction to *My Life and the ICU*. Keletso Atkins traces this connection with the African diaspora in the Americas back even further to the early nineteenth century in "The 'Black Atlantic Communication Network.'"

65. La Hausse, "Message of the Warriors," 28–31.

66. SAB, NTS, vol. 2222, file 416/280, part 1, Native Commissioner to S.A.R. & H. Systems Manager, "Strike—Stevedoring Labourers," February 2–4, 1942.

67. DAR, 3/DBN, vol. 4/1/3/1582, file 323B, part 4, Zulu Phungula to Town Clerk, February 17, 1949.

68. Hemson, "Dock Workers," 108n64.

69. Edwards, "Mkhumbane Our Home," 51.

70. Edwards, "Swing the Assegai Peacefully?," 64.

71. Ibid., 86. Ellipsis in original.

72. Soske, "Wash Me Black Again," 138–39; Nuttall, "Class, Race and Nation," 317.

73. Edwards, "Swing the Assegai Peacefully?," 94; la Hausse, "Message of the Warriors."

74. Edwards, "Swing the Assegai Peacefully?," 63–64.

75. Edwards, "Mkhumbane Our Home," 83, 278; Mbatha, "Migrant Labour and Its Effects on Tribal and Family Life," 172.

76. "Stevedore Firms Offer Togt Dock Strikers Pay Increase," *Natal Mercury*, July 2, 1954, 2; "Strikers Agree to 'Go Back,'" *Natal Mercury*, July 8, 1954, 1.

77. Quoted in Sideris, *Sifuna Imali Yethu*, 15.

78. SAB, SAP, vol. 474, file 35/3/49, District Commandant to Deputy Commissioner SAP, July 26, 1954.

79. "Harbour Togt Men Seek Pay Increase," *Natal Mercury*, July 1, 1954, 1.

80. SAB, ARB, vol. 1212, file 1042/989, "Record of Discussions," July 1–7, 1954.

81. SAB, ARB, vol. 1212, file 1042/989, Full report by S. D. Mentz, July 30, 1954; "Record of Discussions," July 1–7, 1954.

82. SAB, ARB, vol. 1212, file 1042/989, "Record of Discussions," July 1–7, 1954.

83. SAB, ARB, vol. 1212, file 1042/989, Full report by S. D. Mentz, July 30, 1954; Chief Clerk of the C Division of the Department of Labour to the Under-Secretary of Labour, July 6, 1954.

84. SAB, ARB, vol. 1212, file 1042/989, newspaper cutting "Durban Dockers Double-Crossed—They Allege," from *Advance*, August 5, 1954.

85. SAB, ARB, vol. 1212, file 1042/989, "Record of Discussions," July 1–7, 1954.

86. SAB, ARB, vol. 3315, file 1196/5/2, part 1, "Notes from Meetings," August 15, 1956.

87. Cf. Atkins, *The Moon Is Dead!*, 56–61.

88. E.g.: SAB, ARB, vol. 1239, file 1042/1214, Divisional Inspector to Secretary for Labour, "Stoppage of Work," August 16, 1956; telegram dated August

14, 1956; vol. 1240, file 1042/989, Divisional Inspector of Labour to Secretary of Labour, November 6, 1956.

89. KCAL, Bourquin papers, KCM 55228, "Native Unrest in Durban 1958–1960," February 15, 1961. This document contains four pages of incidents of "native unrest" in the city between 1958 and 1960.

90. *Asinamali*, 39–40; Lodge, *Black Politics in South Africa*, especially chapters 2, 3, and 8.

91. "Native Stevedores Refuse to Work Overtime," *Natal Mercury*, April 19, 1958, 3.

92. "1,500 Stevedores Down Tools," *Natal Mercury*, February 25, 1959, 2; SAB, SAP, vol. 474, file 35/3/49, "Notes of Meeting with 1,200–1,400 strikers," February 25, 1959; District Commandant to Deputy Commissioner SAP, February 27, 1959.

93. "Durban Stevedores Return on New Pay Basis," *Natal Mercury*, February 27, 1959, 8; SAB, ARB, vol. 1229, file 1042/15/1959, telegram from Arbeid Pretoria to Arbeid Cape Town, February 26, 1959; "Natives' Ban Will Hold Up Shipping," March 27, 1959, 15.

94. "Overtime Ban Hits Shipping," *Natal Mercury*, March 26, 1959, 1; "Shipping Congestion Continues," *Natal Mercury*, April 2, 1959, 16; SAB, ARB, vol. 3315, file 1196/5/2, part 2, Divisional Inspector to Secretary for Labour, March 28, 1959.

95. "Docks Return to Normal Routine," *Natal Mercury*, April 7, 1959, 1.

96. Dubbeld, "Labour Management and Technological Change," 72.

97. SAB, ARB, vol. 3315, file 1196/5/2, part 2, statement by Sergeant Ngcobo, October 6, 1961.

98. Sipho Zondi, Dumile Ndlovu, Lihlo Shange, Mabhalane Dlamini, and Bheka Dlaba, interviews.

99. Cooper, *On the African Waterfront*, 79, 97; Linebaugh and Rediker, *Many-Headed Hydra.*

100. SAB, NTS, vol. 2222, file 416/280, part 1, "Notes of Meeting Held at Bell Street Barracks," July 29, 1942.

101. "Stevedore Firms Offer Togt Dock Strikers Pay Increase," *Natal Mercury*, July 2, 1954, 2; "Violence Breaks Out in Native Dockers' Strike," *Natal Mercury*, February 26, 1959, 1–2.

102. For example, in May 1941 Zulu Phungula and a number of other *togt* stevedores had a meeting with officials: SAB, ARB, vol. 2854, file 1069/70, "Notes of Interview," May 9, 1941. In late July 1956, three workers from the Consolidated Company came to "make representations through the correct channels": SAB, ARB, vol. 3315, file 1196/5/2, part 1, "Notes from Meetings," August 15, 1956.

103. Sipho Mkhize, Mzenkosi Duma, Sidumo Chiliza, Zodwa Tenza, and Bheka Dlaba, interviews.

104. Lihlo Shange, Mabhalane Dlamini, Siphesihle Dladla, and Mzwakhe Sosibo, interviews.

105. University of the Witwatersrand, Historical Papers, AD 1722, SAIRR Oral History Project, tape 50, interview with Mr. Xulu and Mr. Mkhwanazi, November 25, 1982. Reformatted for clarity by author.

106. "Drastic Labour Replacement Plan: 11 Freighters Idle in Durban," *Natal Witness*, April 4, 1959, 1; SAB, ARB, vol. 3315, file 1196/5/2, part 2, Divisional Inspector to Secretary for Labour, March 28, 1959.

107. Cf. Jensen, *Hiring of Dock Workers and Employment Practices.*

108. Dubbeld, "Breaking the Buffalo."

109. Edwards, "Cato Manor, June 1959," 111.

110. Shula Marks notes this for the 1920s in *The Ambiguities of Dependence*, 103. As the petty bourgeoisie was increasingly squeezed by government policies designed to limit the scope of independent African trading and to limit the social mobility of middle-class Africans, the distinction between these groups remained murky in subsequent decades as well. See also Bonner, "Transvaal Native Congress 1917–1920."

111. SAB, NTS, vol. 7665, file 46/332, part 1, "Native Riots Commission: Minutes of Evidence," July 3–13, 1929; la Hausse, "Struggle for the City," 171–72.

112. Nesvåg, "Street Trading from Apartheid to Post-apartheid."

Conclusion

1. Defining globalization is difficult, and it is not my intention here to enter that debate. However, for a discussion of globalization as financialization, see Sassen, "Global City."

2. Popular accounts of globalization based on increased international trade, multinational corporations, global entrepreneurialism, and the knowledge economy tend to remove labor almost entirely from the picture. See Spivak, "Globalizing Globalization," especially 20:20–26:33.

3. Where Michael Hardt and Antonio Negri see an empire of global neoliberal capitalism flattening social relations and creating a global multitude of the oppressed (*Empire*), Aihwa Ong paints a more complicated picture in *Neoliberalism as Exception.* For Ong, neoliberalism operates through a logic of exception, which compartmentalizes space and populations, involves both inclusion and exclusion, and involves both state discipline and market governance.

4. I explore this argument in more detail in "Entrepreneurs or Wage Laborers?"

5. On the cosmopolitanism of dock labor and port cities, see Shor, "Left Labor Agitators"; Cole, "No Justice, No Ships Get Loaded."

6. Mabhalane Dlamini, interview.

7. Horne, *Red Seas*, 90–91, 147.

8. For a discussion, see Sitas, "New Tribalism."

9. Lewis, "Economic Development with Unlimited Supplies of Labour"; Rostow, *Stages of Economic Growth.*

10. Mbeki, "Address."

11. Rogerson, "Unpacking National Policy towards the Urban Informal Economy."

12. See Marais, *South Africa Pushed to the Limit.* These programs are the Reconstruction and Development Programme; Growth, Employment and Redistribution; the Accelerated and Shared Growth Initiative for South Africa; New Growth Path; and the National Development Plan 2030. For a brief overview of postapartheid South Africa's succession of macroeconomic policy programs, see "South Africa's Key Economic Policies Changes."

13. Frye, "'Second Economy' as an Intellectual Sleight of Hand"; Neves and du Toit, "Money and Sociality."

14. Seekings and Nattrass, *Class, Race, and Inequality.* For an extended discussion of the implications of this approach, see Callebert, Seekings, Bolt, Guyer, "Approaching African Economies."

15. This continues to be the case today: Fay, "Keeping Land for Their Children."

16. Similarly, Émile Durkheim and his nephew Marcel Mauss both emphasize the noncontractual element of the private contract. This noncontractual element is the social glue that made these seemingly asocial market transactions possible, i.e., state, law, custom, morality, social order, etc. See Durkheim, *Division of Labor in Society,* chapter 7; Mauss, *Gift.*

17. Polanyi, *Great Transformation,* 3.

18. On the irreducibility of the social to the market, see Soni and Callebert, "Political Economy of the Humanities."

19. Stanfield, "Karl Polanyi and Contemporary Economic Thought," 267.

20. Cf. Mauss, *Gift.*

21. On the importance of a distributive political economy, see Ferguson, *Give a Man a Fish,* especially chapter 3.

22. Marcel Mauss's account of the gift is often read as constructing a moralist and nostalgic dualism between market and nonmarket societies (*Gift*). However, as Keith Hart points out, no such dualism exists for Mauss, and he was very critical in his writing of what he saw as a Bolshevik antimarket ideology. See Hart, "Marcel Mauss."

23. Smith, *Wealth of Nations,* 117.

24. Mill, "On the Definition and Method of Political Economy."

25. Persky, "Ethology of *Homo Economicus,*" 223, 228.

26. Mill, "On the Definition and Method of Political Economy," 60.

27. Persky, "Ethology of *Homo Economicus,*" 222–23; Stanfield, "Karl Polanyi and Contemporary Economic Thought," 266–67.

28. Polanyi, *Great Transformation,* 30.

29. Though the work of Polanyi is very useful to highlight the ethnocentrism in assumptions of a universal market rationality, *The Great Transformation* offered an account of global history that focused almost entirely on Europe and its offshoots. See Keith Hart, "Karl Polanyi's Legacy."

30. Polanyi, *Livelihood of Man,* 20.

31. Guyer, *Marginal Gains.*

32. Berry, *No Condition Is Permanent,* 14–15.

33. I make this argument in more detail in Callebert, "African Mobility and Labor in Global History."

34. Standing, *Precariat.*

35. Mezzadra, "How Many Histories of Labour?"

36. For example, Lucassen, *Global Labour History.*

37. Van der Linden, *Workers of the World.*

38. Van der Linden, "Promise and Challenges of Global Labor History."

39. Van der Linden, "Global Labor History," 219.

40. Bozzoli, "Marxism, Feminism and South African Studies," 144.

41. Cf. Brenner, "Origins of Capitalist Development."

42. Barchiesi, "How Far from Africa's Shore?"

43. Ferguson, *Global Shadows,* 14.

44. For an extended feminist and Marxist critique of the wage labor system, see Weeks, *Problem with Work.*

45. I am grateful to Raji Singh Soni, who came up with this formulation.

Epilogue

1. Devey, Skinner, and Valodia, "State of the Informal Economy"; Bezuidenhout and Fakier, "Maria's Burden"; Frye, "'Second Economy' as an Intellectual Sleight of Hand."

2. Tevera, "African Migrants, Xenophobia and Urban Violence"; Vahed and Desai, "May 2008 Xenophobic Violence."

3. Steinberg, *South Africa's Xenophobic Eruption.*

4. Fanon, *Wretched of the Earth,* 103.

5. Ibid., 144.

6. Gillian Hart, *Rethinking the South African Crisis.*

7. I should note that the South African trade union landscape could be redrawn after the 2014 expulsion of COSATU's largest union, the National Union of Metalworkers of South Africa (NUMSA), and the 2015 ousting of COSATU's Secretary General Zwelinzima Vavi. It is at the time of writing not yet clear where these changes will lead.

8. Hlatshwayo, "Is There Room for International Solidarity within South African Borders?"

9. Andrae and Beckman, "Alliances across the Formal-Informal Divide."

10. Barchiesi, *Precarious Liberation.*

Glossary

abakhaya	people from one's home area
amadlozi	spirits of the ancestors
amalaita	Zulu youth gangs in Durban
bakkie	pickup truck
dagga	marijuana
ilobolo	bridewealth, typically paid in cattle
induna, pl. *izinduna*	headman, either in traditional Zulu political hierarchy or African intermediary in the workplace
isifebe, pl. *izifebe*	prostitute or adulteress
mahewu	fermented porridge
pass laws	laws that required Africans to carry pass books whenever they left the Reserves
Reserve	land set aside for African residence and farming; Africans could not legally own or lease land outside these areas
samp	porridge made from coarsely ground corn
shebeen	unlicensed bar patronized by Africans
spaza shop	small informal store run from the home or shack
stokvel	rotating credit association
togt	casual labor
ubudoda	manhood, masculinity
ukulobola	marriage through the exchange of *ilobolo*
ukusisa	loaning out of livestock
umnumzane, pl. *abanumzane*	homestead head
umuzi, pl. *imizi*	homestead
utshwala	low-alcohol sorghum beer

Bibliography

Archival Sources

Official Sources

Durban Archives Repository, Durban (DAR)

2/DBN: Commissioner of Durban
  Civil Cases, Records of Proceedings
3/DBN: Archives of the Town Clerk, Durban
  Town Council minutes
  Native Affairs and Police Committee minutes, 1918
  Native Administration Committee minutes, 1942–50
  Minutes of the Native Advisory Board (NAB), 1934–53
  Correspondence files

Killie Campbell Africana Library and Campbell Collections at the University of KwaZulu-Natal, Durban (KCAL)

PNAB: Port Natal Native Administration Board

National Archives Repository, Pretoria (SAB)

ARB: Department of Labour
GG: Office of the Governor-General of South Africa
MVE: Ministry of Transport
NTS: Department of Native Affairs
SAP: South African Police
VWN: Social Welfare and Pensions
K193: Commission of Inquiry into Riots in Durban, 1949

Pietermaritzburg Archives Repository, Pietermaritzburg (PAR)

CNC: Chief Native Commissioner
NHD: Natal Harbour Department
SNA: Secretary of Native Affairs

University of the Witwatersrand, Historical Papers

AD 1438: Native Economic Commission, Minutes of Evidence and Memoranda

Unofficial Sources

Killie Campbell Africana Library and Campbell Collections at the University of KwaZulu-Natal, Durban (KCAL)

Manuscript collections
  Bourquin papers
  A. W. G. Champion papers
  Marwick papers
  Miriam Janisch papers
  Nolan-Wackernow-Ward papers
Killie Campbell Audio-Video Collection (KCAV)
  Oral History Programme of the University of Natal

University of the Witwatersrand, Historical Papers

AD 1722: South African Institute of Race Relations Oral History Project

Official Publications

Colony of Natal. *Census of the Colony of Natal, April 1904.* Pietermaritzburg: Government Printers, 1905.

———. *Report of the Native Affairs Commission, 1906–7.*

Union Government Publications are numbered "U.G. Number-Year" and ordered by year:
  "Report of the Economic and Wage Commission (1925)." U.G. 14-'26.
  "Report of the Native Economic Commission, 1930–2," U.G. 22-'32.
  "Report of the Department of Native Affairs for the Years 1945–7." U.G. 14-'48.

Newspapers

Consulted on microfilm at Killie Campbell Africana Library and Campbell Collections at the University of KwaZulu-Natal, Durban (KCAL)
  Natal Daily News (Durban)
  Natal Mercury (Durban)
  Natal Witness (Pietermaritzburg)

Interviews

Conducted by the Author

Wandile Mzamo, Durban, eThekwini, KwaZulu-Natal, April 15, 2009.
Eric Ryland, Durban, eThekwini, KwaZulu-Natal, December 18, 2009.

Conducted by Sibongo Dlamini

Lihlo Budu, Izingolweni, Ugu, KwaZulu-Natal, June 29, 2009.
Zithulele Chemane, Siphofu, Ugu, KwaZulu-Natal, July 9, 2009.
Sidumo Chiliza, Springs, eThekwini, KwaZulu-Natal, November 14, 2009.
Nkomozethu Cikane, Lusikisiki, OR Tambo, Eastern Cape, August 4, 2009.
Bheka Dlaba, Mooi River, uMgungundlovu, KwaZulu-Natal, November 17, 2009.
Siphesihle Dladla, Sweetwaters, uMgungundlovu, KwaZulu-Natal, October 24, 2009.
Mabhalane Dlamini, Hebuhebu, uMgungundlovu, KwaZulu-Natal, October 22, 2009.
Mzenkosi Duma, Mkhunya North, Sisonke, KwaZulu-Natal, November 13, 2009.
Lalani Dumakude, Impendle, uMgungundlovu, KwaZulu-Natal, June 7, 2009.
Bongeka Faku, Magusheni, Mbizana, Eastern Cape, June 27, 2009.
Sipho Gazu, iXopo, Sisonke, KwaZulu-Natal, May 27, 2009.
Velile Goba, uMzimkhulu, Sisonke, KwaZulu-Natal, June 17, 2009.
Makhehle Gxokwana, Lusikisiki, OR Tambo, Eastern Cape, August 7, 2009.
Mpho Jaca, Hlabeni, Sisonke, KwaZulu Natal, October 21, 2009.
Xolile Jaca, Mabheleni, Ugu, KwaZulu-Natal, July 10, 2009.
Mdu Jama, Izingolweni, Ugu, KwaZulu-Natal, May 30, 2009.
Takulu Kheswa, Lusikisiki, OR Tambo, Eastern Cape, August 1, 2009.
Cacile Khozana, Flagstaff, OR Tambo, Eastern Cape, August 8, 2009.
Zolile Khumalo, Newcastle, Amajuba, KwaZulu-Natal, May 16, 2009.
Gedla Lukhozi, Polela, uMgungundlovu, KwaZulu-Natal, June 6, 2009.
Sosha Masikane, Mooi River, uMgungundlovu, KwaZulu-Natal, October 23, 2009.
Lunguza Mbelu, uMbumbulu, eThekwini, KwaZulu-Natal, June 14, 2009.
Gobile Mbhele, Springs, eThekwini, KwaZulu-Natal, July 14, 2009.
Zandile Mbile, Highflats, Sisonke, KwaZulu-Natal, July 7, 2009.
Sicelo Mbokazi, Nhlakazu, eThekwini, KwaZulu-Natal, July 16, 2009.
Kotozi Memela, Deepdale, Sisonke, KwaZulu-Natal, October 20, 2009.
Thembinkosi Miya, iXopo, Sisonke, KwaZulu-Natal, May 26, 2009.
Sipho Mkhize, Jolivet, Sisonke, KwaZulu-Natal, November 5, 2009.
Thoko Mlaba, New Hanover, uMgungundlovu, KwaZulu-Natal, June 8, 2009.

Godidi Msomi, uMkomaas, eThekwini, KwaZulu-Natal, May 21, 2009.
Zakhele Mthembu, Nhlavini, Sisonke, KwaZulu-Natal, November 3, 2009.
Galo Mtolo, Izingolweni, Ugu, KwaZulu-Natal, June 30, 2009.
Vela Mtolo, Bulwer, Sisonke, KwaZulu-Natal, May 28, 2009.
Zifo Mzizi, Underberg, Sisonke, KwaZulu-Natal, June 16, 2009.
Mzo Mzongo, Izingolweni North, Ugu, KwaZulu-Natal, June 30, 2009.
Nelson Ndaba, Nkwezela, Sisonke, KwaZulu-Natal, July 17, 2009.
Doda Ndaweni, Gxuha, OR Tambo, Eastern Cape, June 28, 2009.
Dumile Ndlovu, Port Shepstone, Ugu, KwaZulu-Natal, May 20, 2009.
Gampu Ngcamu, Sinadini, uMgungundlovu, KwaZulu-Natal, October 25, 2009.
Hlolomzi Ngcwangula, Lusikisiki, OR Tambo, Eastern Cape, July 29, 2009.
Xolani Ngema, Kranskop, uMzinyathi, KwaZulu-Natal, June 9, 2009.
Sofa Nkomo, Dumisa, Sisonke, KwaZulu-Natal, July 12, 2009.
Xhegu Ntozakhe, Lusikisiki, OR Tambo, Eastern Cape, August 3, 2009.
Doda Nxele, uMzinto, Ugu, KwaZulu-Natal, July 11, 2009.
Phumla Nyathikazi, Lusikisiki, OR Tambo, Eastern Cape, August 1, 2009.
Mtukatshelwa Phewa, Izingolweni, Ugu, KwaZulu-Natal, May 29, 2009.
Co Pityana, Mt. Frere, Alfred Nzo, Eastern Cape, July 28, 2009.
Gugulethu Pityana, Mt. Frere, Alfred Nzo, Eastern Cape, July 25, 2009.
Libho Qoza, Upper Umkomaas, eThekwini, KwaZulu-Natal, June 15, 2009.
Lihlo Shange, Sizamenjane, Sisonke, KwaZulu-Natal, October 20, 2009.
Amos Sibiya, eMpangeni, uThungulu, KwaZulu-Natal, June 10, 2009.
Mr. Sibiya, Dumile Sibiya's son, eShowe, uThungulu, KwaZulu-Natal, November 18, 2009.
Zwelinjani Sithole, Nkumba, Sisonke, KwaZulu-Natal, October 20, 2009.
Gcinokwakhe Sobiso, Creighton, Sisonke, KwaZulu-Natal, June 18, 2009.
Nhlanhla Sokhela, Greytown, uMzinyathi, KwaZulu-Natal, May 17, 2009.
Mzwakhe Sosibo, Ngwagwane, Sisonke, KwaZulu-Natal, October 25, 2009.
Zodwa Tenza, Hlokozi, Sisonke, KwaZulu-Natal, November 15, 2009.
Mandla Xaba, Bulwer, Sisonke, KwaZulu-Natal, May 28, 2009.
Zitha Xaba, Lusikisiki, OR Tambo, Eastern Cape, August 2, 2009.
Lungani Xulu, Mkhunya, Ugu, KwaZulu-Natal, July 13, 2009.
Bhekinkosi Zimu, Elandskop, uMgungundlovu, KwaZulu-Natal, October 22, 2009.
Sonke Zizi, Lusikisiki, OR Tambo, Eastern Cape, July 13, 2009.
Sipho Zondi, Pietermaritzburg, uMgungundlovu, KwaZulu-Natal, May 7, 2009.
Khethekwakhe Zondo, KwaMbonambi, uThungulu, KwaZulu-Natal, May 6, 2009.
Sihle Zungu, Highflats, Sisonke, KwaZulu-Natal, July 8, 2009.

Conducted by Snegugu Lerato Mchunu

Dudu Dumakude, Bulwer, Sisonke, KwaZulu-Natal, June 25, 2014.
Mmeli Gumbi, uMlazi, eThekwini, KwaZulu-Natal, June 13, 2014.

Talent Gumbi, uMlazi, eThekwini, KwaZulu-Natal, June 13, 2014.
Thandiwe Mcanyina, uMlazi, eThekwini, KwaZulu-Natal, July 9, 2014.
Fikile Mlotshwa, Bulwer, Sisonke, KwaZulu-Natal, June 25, 2014.
Ningi Mlotshwa, Bulwer, Sisonke, KwaZulu-Natal, June 25, 2014.
Banelisiwe Phewa, Izingolweni, Ugu, KwaZulu-Natal, June 4, 2014.
Florence Phewa, Izingolweni, Ugu, KwaZulu-Natal, June 4, 2014.
Matha Phewa, Izingolweni, Ugu, KwaZulu-Natal, June 4, 2014.
Thembeni Phewa, Izingolweni, Ugu, KwaZulu-Natal, June 4, 2014.

Secondary Sources

Abrahams, Peter. *Mine Boy*. New York: Collier Books, 1970.

Adu-Amankwah, Kwasi. "Ghana." *Labour Education* 116, no. 3 (1999): 1–14.

Alexander, Peter. "Oscillating Migrants, 'Detribalised Families' and Militancy: Mozambicans on Witbank Collieries, 1918–1927." *JSAS* 27, no. 3 (2001): 505–25.

Alexander, Peter, Thapelo Lekgowa, Botsang Mmope, Luke Sinwell, and Bongazi Xezwi. *Marikana: Voices from South Africa's Mining Massacre*. Athens: Ohio University Press, 2013.

Ambler, Charles, and Jonathan Crush. "Alcohol in Southern African History." In *Liquor and Labor in Southern Africa*, edited by Jonathan Crush and Charles Ambler, 1–55. Athens: Ohio University Press, 1992.

Andrae, Gunilla, and Björn Beckman. "Alliances across the Formal-Informal Divide: South African Debates and Nigerian Experiences." In *Africa's Informal Workers: Collective Agency, Alliances and Transnational Organizing in Urban Africa*, edited by Ilda Lindell, 85–98. London: Zed Books, 2010.

Antony, Robert J. "Peasants, Heroes and Brigands: The Problems of Social Banditry in Early Nineteenth Century South China." *Modern China* 15, no. 2 (1989): 123–48.

Argyle, John. "Kalela, Beni, Asafo, Ingoma and the Rural-Urban Dichotomy." In *Tradition and Transition in Southern Africa: Festschrift for Philip and Iona Mayer*, edited by Andrew D. Spiegel and P. A. McAllister, 65–86. Johannesburg: Witwatersrand University Press, 1991.

Ashforth, Adam. *Witchcraft, Violence, and Democracy in South Africa*. Chicago: Chicago University Press, 2005.

Asinamali: Organising in the 1950s. Cape Town: Labour History Group, 1985.

Atkins, Keletso E. "The 'Black Atlantic Communication Network': African American Sailors and the Cape of Good Hope Connection." *Issue: A Journal of Opinion* 24, no. 2 (1996): 23–25.

———. *The Moon Is Dead! Give Us Our Money! The Cultural Origins of an African Work Ethic, Natal, South Africa, 1843–1900*. Portsmouth, NH: Heinemann, 1993.

Austen, Ralph A. "Social Bandits and Other Heroic Criminals: Western Models of Resistance and Their Relevance for Africa." In *Banditry, Rebellion and Social Protest in Africa,* edited by Donald Crummey, 89–108. Portsmouth, NH: Heinemann, 1986.

Ballard, Charles. "The Repercussions of Rinderpest: Cattle Plague and Peasant Discipline in Colonial Natal." *International Journal of African Historical Studies* 19, no. 3 (1986): 421–50.

Bank, Leslie. *Home Spaces, Street Styles: Contesting Power and Identity in a South African City.* Johannesburg: Wits University Press, 2011.

Barchiesi, Franco. "How Far from Africa's Shore? A Response to Marcel van der Linden's Map for Global Labor History." *ILWCH* 82 (2012): 77–84.

———. *Precarious Liberation: Workers, the State, and Contested Social Citizenship in Postapartheid South Africa.* Albany: State University of New York Press, 2011.

———. "Work in the Constitution of the Human: Twentieth-Century South African Entanglements of Welfare, Blackness, and Political Economy." *South Atlantic Quarterly* 115, no. 1 (2016): 149–74.

Barnum, Howard N., and Lyn Squire. "An Econometric Application of the Theory of the Farm-Household." *Journal of Development Economics* 6, no. 1 (1979): 79–102.

Baskin, Jeremy. "GWU and the Durban Dockworkers." *SALB* 8, no. 3 (1982): 18–33.

Bayat, Asef. "From 'Dangerous Classes' to 'Quiet Rebels': Politics of the Urban Subaltern in the Global South." *International Sociology* 15 (2000): 533–57.

Beinart, William. "Chieftaincy and the Concept of Articulation: South Africa circa 1900–50." In *Segregation and Apartheid in Twentieth-Century South Africa,* edited by William Beinart and Saul Dubow, 176–88. London: Routledge, 1995.

———. "Labour Migrancy and Rural Production: Pondoland c. 1900–1950." In *Black Villagers in an Industrial Society: Anthropological Perspectives on Labour Migration in South Africa,* edited by Philip Mayer, 81–108. Cape Town: Oxford University Press, 1980.

———. *The Political Economy of Pondoland, 1860–1930.* Cambridge: Cambridge University Press, 1982.

———. "Transkeian Migrant Workers and Youth Labour on the Natal Sugar Estates, 1918–1948." *JAH* 32, no. 1 (1991): 41–63.

———. "Worker Consciousness, Ethnic Particularism and Nationalism: The Experience of a South African Migrant, 1930–1960." In *The Politics of Race, Class and Nationalism in Twentieth-Century South Africa,* edited by Shula Marks and Stanley Trapido, 186–309. London: Longman, 1987.

Beinart, William, and Colin Bundy. *Hidden Struggles in Rural South Africa: Politics and Popular Movements in the Transkei and Eastern Cape 1890–1930.* Johannesburg: Ravan Press, 1987.

Berry, Sara S. *Fathers Work for Their Sons: Accumulation, Mobility, and Class Formation in an Extended Yorùbá Community*. Berkeley: University of California Press, 1985.

———. *No Condition Is Permanent: The Social Dynamics of Agrarian Change in Sub-Saharan Africa*. Madison: University of Wisconsin Press, 1993.

———. "Social Institutions and Access to Resources." *Africa* 59, no. 1 (1989): 42.

Bezuidenhout, Andries, and Khayaat Fakier. "Maria's Burden: Contract Cleaning and the Crisis of Social Reproduction in Post-apartheid South Africa." *Antipode* 38, no. 3 (2006): 462–85.

Bickford-Smith, Vivian. "Black Labour at the Docks at the Beginning of the Twentieth Century." *Studies in the History of Cape Town* no. 2 (1980): 75–125.

———. *Ethnic Pride and Racial Prejudice in Victorian Cape Town*. Johannesburg: Witwatersrand University Press, 1995.

Birla, Ritu. *Stages of Capital: Law, Culture, and Market Governance in Late Colonial India*. Durham, NC: Duke University Press, 2009.

Bohannan, Paul, and George Dalton, eds. *Markets in Africa*. Evanston, IL: Northwestern University Press, 1962.

Bond, Patrick. *Elite Transition: From Apartheid to Neoliberalism in South Africa*. London: Pluto Press, 2000.

Bonner, Philip. "The Decline and Fall of the ICU: A Case of Self-Destruction?" In *Essays in Southern African Labour History*, edited by Edward Webster, 114–20. Johannesburg: Ravan Press, 1978.

———. "'Desirable or Undesirable Basotho Women?' Liquor, Prostitution and the Migration of Basotho Women to the Rand, 1920–1945." In *Women and Gender in Southern Africa to 1945*, edited by Cherryl Walker, 221–50. Cape Town: David Philip, 1990.

———. "'The Great Migration' and 'The Greatest Trek': Some Reflections." *JSAS* 30, no. 1 (2004): 87–114.

———. "The Transvaal Native Congress 1917 1920: The Radicalisation of the Petty Bourgeoisie on the Rand." In *Industrialisation and Social Change in South Africa: African Class Formation, Culture, and Consciousness, 1870–1930*, edited by Shula Marks and Richard Rathbone, 270–313. London: Longman, 1982.

Bonner, Philip, and Noor Nieftagodien. *Alexandra: A History*. Johannesburg: Wits University Press, 2008.

Bonnin, Debby. "Claiming Spaces, Changing Places: Political Violence and Women's Protests in KwaZulu-Natal." *JSAS* 26, no. 2 (2000): 301–16.

"Boycott: Durban Dockworkers Block Arms to Zimbabwe." *Maritime Workers' Journal*, July/August 2008.

Bozzoli, Belinda. "Marxism, Feminism and South African Studies." *JSAS* 9, no. 2 (1983): 139–71.

Bozzoli, Belinda, with the assistance of Mmantho Nkotsoe. *Women of Phokeng: Consciousness, Life Strategy, and Migrancy in South Africa, 1900–1983.* Portsmouth, NH: Heinemann, 1991.

Bradford, Helen. "Mass Movements and the Petty Bourgeoisie: The Social Origins of ICU Leadership, 1924–1929." *JAH* 25, no. 3 (1984): 295–310.

———. *A Taste of Freedom: The ICU in Rural South Africa, 1924–1930.* New Haven, CT: Yale University Press, 1987.

———. "'We Are Now the Men': Women's Beer Protests in the Natal Countryside, 1929." In *Class, Community and Conflict: South African Perspectives,* edited by Belinda Bozzoli, 292–323. Johannesburg: Ravan Press, 1987.

Brandel, Mia. "Urban Lobolo Attitudes: A Preliminary Report." *African Studies* 17, no. 1 (1958): 34–51.

Breckenridge, Keith. "The Allure of Violence: Men, Race and Masculinity on the South African Goldmines." *JSAS* 24, no. 4 (1998): 669–93.

Brenner, Robert. "The Origins of Capitalist Development: A Critique of Neo-Smithian Marxism." *New Left Review* 1, no. 104 (1977): 25–92.

Broeze, Frank. "Militancy and Pragmatism: An International Perspective on Maritime Labour, 1870–1914." *International Review of Social History* 36, no. 2 (1991): 165–200.

Brown, Carolyn. "Race and the Construction of Working-Class Masculinity in the Nigerian Coal Industry: The Initial Phase, 1914–1930." *ILWCH* 69 (2006): 35–56.

———, ed. "Scholarly Controversy: Defining Global Labor History." *ILWCH* 82 (2012): 54–113.

Bundy, Colin. *The Rise and Fall of the South African Peasantry.* London: Heinemann, 1979.

Burawoy, Michael. "The Functions and Reproduction of Migrant Labor: Comparative Material from Southern Africa and the United States." *American Journal of Sociology* 81, no. 5 (1976): 1050–87.

Callebert, Ralph. "African Mobility and Labor in Global History." *History Compass* 14, no. 3 (2016): 116–27.

———. "Cleaning the Wharves: Pilferage, Bribery and Social Connections on the Durban Docks in the 1950s." *Canadian Journal of African Studies* 46, no. 1 (2012): 23–38.

———. "Entrepreneurs or Wage Laborers? The Elusive *Homo Economicus.*" In *Entrepreneurship in Africa,* edited by Moses Ochonu. Bloomington: Indiana University Press, forthcoming.

———. "Livelihood Strategies of Dock Workers in Durban, c. 1900–1959." PhD diss., Queen's University, 2011.

———. "Rethinking the Underclass: Future Directions in Southern African Labor History." *ILWCH* 82 (2012): 136–42.

———. "Transcending the Dual Economy: Reflections on 'Popular Economies in South Africa.'" *Africa* 84, no. 1 (2014): 119–34.

———. "Working Class Action and Informal Trade on the Durban Docks, 1930s–1950s." *JSAS* 38, no. 4 (2012): 847–61.

Callebert, Ralph, Jeremy Seekings, Maxim Bolt, Jane I. Guyer. "Approaching African Economies." Debate section, *Africa* 84, no. 1 (2014): 119–50.

Carton, Benedict. *Blood from Your Children: The Colonial Origins of Generational Conflict in South Africa.* Charlottesville: University Press of Virginia, 2000.

Chakrabarty, Dipesh. *Provincializing Europe: Postcolonial Thought and Historical Difference.* Princeton, NJ: Princeton University Press, 2000.

———. *Rethinking Working-Class History: Bengal 1890–1940.* Princeton, NJ: Princeton University Press, 1989.

Champion, A. W. G. "African Businesses." In *The Views of Mahlathi: Writings of A. W. G. Champion, a Black South African, with a Biography of A. W. G. Champion by R. R. R. Dhlomo,* edited by M. W. Swanson, translated by E. R. Dahle and A. T. Cope, 163–66. Pietermaritzburg: University of Natal Press; Durban: Killie Campbell Africana Library, 1982.

Chayanov, Alexander V. *The Theory of Peasant Economy.* Edited by Daniel Thorner, Basile Kerblay, and R. E. F. Smith. Homewood, IL: American Economic Association, 1966.

Chirwa, Wiseman Chijere. "'Theba' Is Power: Rural Labour, Migrancy and Fishing in Malawi, 1890s–1985." PhD diss., Queen's University, 1992.

Cohen, David William, Stephan F. Miescher, and Luise White. "Introduction: Voices, Words, and African History." In *African Words, African Voices: Critical Practices in Oral History,* edited by Luise White, Stephan F. Miescher, and David William Cohen, 1–27. Bloomington: Indiana University Press, 2001.

Cohen, Robin. "Resistance and Hidden Forms of Consciousness amongst African Workers." *Review of African Political Economy* 19 (1980): 8–22.

Cole, Peter. "No Justice, No Ships Get Loaded: Political Boycotts on the San Francisco Bay and Durban Waterfronts." *International Review of Social History* 58, no. 2 (2013): 185–217.

Colquhoun, Patrick. *A Treatise on the Commerce and Police of the River Thames: Containing an Historical View of the Trade of the Port of London.* London: Joseph Mawman, 1800.

Comaroff, Jean. *Body of Power, Spirit of Resistance: The Culture and History of a South African People.* Chicago: University of Chicago Press, 1985.

Comaroff, John L. Preface to *Essays on African Marriage,* edited by Eileen Jensen Krige and John L. Comaroff, xii–xvii. Cape Town: Juta, 1982.

Communist Party of South Africa (CPSA). *The People Overflow: The Story of the Johannesburg Squatters.* Johannesburg: Saraswathi Vilas Press, c.1947.

Connell, R. W. *Gender and Power: Society, the Person and Sexual Politics.* Stanford, CA: Stanford University Press, 1987.

Cooke Johnson, Linda. "Criminality on the Docks." In *Dock Workers: International Explorations in Comparative Labour History,* edited by Sam Davies, Colin J. Davis, David de Vries, Lex Heerma van Voss, Lidewij Hesselink, and Klaus Weinhauer, 721–45. Burlington VT: Ashgate, 2000.

Cooper, Frederick. *Colonialism in Question: Theory, Knowledge, History.* Berkeley: University of California Press, 2005.

———. *Decolonization and African Society: The Labor Question in French and British Africa.* Cambridge: Cambridge University Press, 1996.

———. "Dockworkers and Labour History." In *Dock Workers: International Explorations in Comparative Labour History, 1790–1970,* edited by Sam Davies, Colin J. Davis, David de Vries, Lex Heerma van Voss, Lidewij Hesselink, and Klaus Weinhauer, 523–41. Burlington VT: Ashgate, 2000.

———. *On the African Waterfront: Urban Disorder and the Transformation of Work in Colonial Mombasa.* New Haven, CT: Yale University Press, 1987.

———. "Work, Class and Empire: An African Historian's Retrospective on E. P. Thompson." *Social History* 20, no. 2 (1995): 235–41.

Cooper, Frederick, Allen F. Isaacman, Florencie E. Mallon, William Roseberry, and Steve J. Stern. *Confronting Historical Paradigms: Peasants, Labor, and the Capitalist World System in Africa and Latin America.* Madison: University of Wisconsin Press, 1993.

Cope, Nicholas. "The Zulu Petit Bourgeoisie and Zulu Nationalism in the 1920s: Origins of Inkatha." *JSAS* 16, no. 3 (1990): 431–51.

Coplan, David. "The Emergence of an African Working-Class Culture." In *Industrialisation and Social Change in South Africa: African Class Formation, Culture, and Consciousness, 1870–1930,* edited by Shula Marks and Richard Rathbone, 358–75. London: Longman, 1982.

Coquery-Vidrovitch, Catherine, and Paul Lovejoy. "The Workers of Trade in Precolonial Africa." In *The Workers of African Trade,* edited by Catherine Coquery-Vidrovitch and Paul Lovejoy, 9–24. Beverley Hills, CA: Sage, 1985.

Cowen, Michael, and Kabiru Kanyanjui. *Some Problems of Capital and Class in Kenya.* Occasional Paper No. 26. Nairobi: University of Nairobi, Institute for Development Studies, 1977.

Cowen, Michael, and Robert Shenton. *Doctrines of Development.* London: Routledge, 1996.

———. "The Origin and Course of Fabian Colonialism in Africa." *Journal of Historical Sociology* 4, no. 2 (1991): 143–74.

Crais, Clifton C. *White Supremacy and Black Resistance in Pre-industrial South Africa: The Making of the Colonial Order in the Eastern Cape, 1770–1865.* Cambridge: Cambridge University Press, 1992.

Crummey, Donald, ed. *Banditry, Rebellion and Social Protest in Africa.* Portsmouth, NH: Heinemann, 1986.

Crush, Jonathan. "Migrancy and Militance: The Case of the National Union of Mineworkers of South Africa." *African Affairs* 350 (1989): 5–23.

Crush, Jonathan, Alan Jeeves, and David Yudelman. *South Africa's Labor Empire: A History of Black Migrancy to the Gold Mines.* Boulder, CO: Westview Press, 1991.

"David Hemson." *South African History Online.* http://www.sahistory.org.za/people/david-hemson.

Davie, Grace. "Strength in Numbers: The Durban Student Wages Commission, Dockworkers and the Poverty Datum Line, 1971–1973." *JSAS* 33, no. 2 (2007): 401–20.

Davies, Rob. "Notes on the Theory of the Informal Sector with Reference to Zimbabwe." *SALB* 3, no. 5 (1977): 54–71.

Davis, Colin J. *Waterfront Revolts: New York and London Dockworkers, 1946–61.* Urbana: University of Illinois Press, 2003.

Davis, Mike. *Late Victorian Holocaust: El Niño Famines and the Making of the Third World.* London: Verso, 2001.

Delius, Peter. *The Land Belongs to Us: The Pedi Polity, the Boers and the British in the Nineteenth-Century Transvaal.* Berkeley: University of California Press, 1984.

———. *A Lion amongst the Cattle: Reconstruction and Resistance in the Northern Transvaal.* Randburg: Ravan Press, 1996.

———. "The Ndzundza Ndebele: Indenture and the Making of Ethnic Identity." In *Holding Their Ground: Class, Locality and Culture in 19th and 20th Century South Africa,* edited by Philip Bonner, Isabel Hofmeyr, Deborah James, and Tom Lodge, 227–58. Johannesburg: Witwatersrand University Press, 1989.

De Soto, Hernando. *The Mystery of Capital: Why Capitalism Triumphs in the West and Fails Everywhere Else.* New York: Basic Books, 2000.

Devey, Richard, Caroline Skinner, and Imraan Valodia. "The State of the Informal Economy." In *State of the Nation, South Africa 2006–2006,* edited by Sakhela Buhlungu, John Daniel, Roger Southall, and Jessica Lutchman, 223–47. Cape Town: HSRC Press, 2006.

Dikobe, Modikwe. *The Marabi Dance.* Portsmouth, NH: Heinemann, 1973.

Ditton, Jason. "Perks, Pilferage and the Fiddle: The Historical Structure of Invisible Wages." *Theory and Society* 4, no. 1 (1977): 39–71.

Dobler, Gregor. *Traders and Trade in Colonial Ovamboland: Elite Formation and the Politics of Consumption under Indirect Rule and Apartheid, 1925–1990.* Basel: Basler Afrika Bibliographien, 2014.

"Dock Workers to Boycott Israeli Ship." *Mail & Guardian,* February 3, 2009. http://mg.co.za/article/2009-02-03-dock-workers-to-boycott-israeli-ship.

Dubbeld, Bernard. "Breaking the Buffalo: The Transformation of Stevedoring Work in Durban between 1970 and 1990." *International Review of Social History* 48, no. 1 (2003): 97–122.

———. "Labour Management and Technological Change: A History of Stevedoring in Durban, 1959–1990." Master's thesis, University of Natal, 2002.

Dubow, Saul. "Introduction: South Africa's 1940s." In *South Africa's 1940s: Worlds of Possibilities,* edited by Saul Dubow and Alan Jeeves, 1–19. Cape Town: Double Storey Books, 2005.

Durkheim, Émile. *The Division of Labor in Society.* New York: Free Press, 1997 [1893].

Du Toit, Darcy. *Capital and Labour in South Africa: Class Struggle in the 1970s.* London: Kegan Paul International, 1981.

Edwards, Iain. "Cato Manor, June 1959: Men, Women, Crowds, Violence, Politics and History." In *The People's City: African Life in Twentieth-Century Durban,* edited by Paul Maylam and Iain Edwards, 102–42. Pietermaritzburg: University of Natal Press, 1996.

———. "Mkhumbane Our Home: African Shantytown Society in Cato Manor Farm, 1946–1960." PhD diss., University of Natal, 1989.

———. "Recollections: The Communist Party and Worker Militancy in Durban, early 1940s." *SALB* 11, no. 4 (1986): 65–84.

———. "Swing the Assegai Peacefully? 'New Africa', Mkhumbane, the Cooperative Movement and Attempts to Transform Durban Society in the Late Nineteen-Forties." In *Holding Their Ground: Class, Locality and Culture in 19th and 20th Century South Africa,* edited by Philip Bonner, Isabel Hofmeyr, Deborah James, and Tom Lodge, 95–103. Johannesburg: Witwatersrand University Press, 1989.

Eldredge, Elizabeth. *A South African Kingdom: The Pursuit of Security in Nineteenth Century Lesotho.* Cambridge: Cambridge University Press, 1993.

Engels, Friedrich. *The Condition of the Working Class in England.* London: Penguin, 1987.

———. *The Origin of the Family, Private Property and the State.* Chippendale, AUS: Resistance Books, 2004.

Epprecht, Marc. *Hungochani: The History of a Dissident Sexuality in Southern Africa.* Montreal: McGill-Queen's University Press, 2004.

———. *"This Matter of Women Is Getting Very Bad": Gender, Development and Politics in Colonial Lesotho.* Pietermaritzburg: University of Natal Press, 2000.

Etherington, Norman. *Preachers, Peasants, and Politics in Southeast Africa, 1835–1880: African Christian Communities in Natal, Pondoland and Zululand.* London: Royal Historical Society, 1978.

Fakier, Khayaat, and Jacklyn Cock. "A Gendered Analysis of the Crisis of Social Reproduction in Contemporary South Africa." *International Feminist Journal of Politics* 11, no. 3 (2009): 354–55.

Fanon, Frantz. *The Wretched of the Earth.* New York: Grove Press, 2004 [1961].

Fay, Derick. "'Keeping Land for Their Children': Generation, Migration and Land in South Africa's Transkei." *JSAS* 41, no. 5 (2015): 1083–97.

Ferguson, James. *The Anti-politics Machine: "Development," Depoliticization, and Bureaucratic Power in Lesotho.* Minneapolis: University of Minnesota Press, 1994.

———. "Declarations of Dependence: Labour, Personhood, and Welfare in Southern Africa." *Journal of the Royal Anthropological Institute* 19, no. 2 (2013): 223–42.

———. *Expectations of Modernity: Myths and Meanings of Urban Life on the Zambian Copperbelt.* Berkeley: University of California Press, 1999.

———. *Give a Man a Fish: Reflections on the New Politics of Distribution.* Durham, NC: Duke University Press, 2015.

———. *Global Shadows: Africa in the Neoliberal World Order.* Durham, NC: Duke University Press, 2006.

Fingard, Judith. *Jack in Port: Sailortowns of Eastern Canada.* Toronto: Toronto University Press, 1982.

Francis, Elizabeth. *Making a Living: Changing Livelihoods in Rural Africa.* London: Routledge, 2000.

Freund, Bill. *The African Worker.* Cambridge: Cambridge University Press, 1988.

———. "City Hall and the Direction of Development: The Changing Role of the Local State as a Factor in Economic Planning and Development in Durban." In *(D)urban Vortex: South African City in Transition,* edited by Bill Freund and Vishnu Padayachee, 11–41. Scottsville: University of Natal Press, 2002.

———. "Confrontation and Social Change: Natal and the Forging of Apartheid, 1949–72." In *Political Economy and Identities in KwaZulu-Natal: Historical and Social Perspectives,* edited by Robert Morrell, 119–40. Durban: Indicator Press, 1996.

———. *Insiders and Outsiders: The Indian Working Class of Durban 1910–1990.* Portsmouth, NH: Heinemann, 1995.

———. "Labour Studies and Labour History in South Africa: Perspectives from the Apartheid Era and After." *International Review of Social History* 58, no. 3 (2013): 493–519.

———. "Theft and Social Protest among Tin Miners of Northern Nigeria." *Radical History Review* 26 (1982): 68–86.

Frye, Isobel. "The 'Second Economy' as an Intellectual Sleight of Hand." *Africanus: Journal of Development Studies* 37, no. 2 (2007): 175–90.

Gasa, Nomboniso. "Feminism, Motherism, Patriarchies and Women's Voices in the 1950s." In *Women in South African History: Basus'iimbokodo, Bawel'imilambo / They Remove Boulders and Cross Rivers,* edited by Nomboniso Gasa, 207–27. Cape Town: HSRC Press, 2007.

———, ed. *Women in South African History: Basus'iimbokodo, Bawel'imilambo / They Remove Boulders and Cross Rivers.* Cape Town: HSRC Press, 2007.

Geertz, Clifford. "The Rotating Credit Association: A 'Middle Rung' in Development." *Economic Development and Cultural Change* 10, no. 3 (1962): 241–63.

Genovese, Eugene D. *Roll, Jordan, Roll: The World the Slaves Made.* New York: Vintage Books, 1976.

Glaser, Clive. *Bo-Tsotsi: The Youth Gangs of Soweto, 1935–1976.* Portsmouth, NH: Heinemann, 2000.

Gluckman, Max. *Malinowski's Sociological Theories.* Rhodes-Livingstone Papers no. 16. Livingstone, Northern Rhodesia: Rhodes-Livingstone Institute, 1949.

Goebel, Allison. "'Our Struggle Is for the Full Loaf': Protests, Social Welfare and Gendered Citizenship in South Africa." *JSAS* 37, no. 2 (2011): 369–88.

Green, Anna. "The Work Process." In *Dock workers: International Explorations in Comparative Labour History, 1790–1970,* edited by Sam Davies, Colin J. Davis, David de Vries, Lex Heerma van Voss, Lidewij Hesselink, and Klaus Weinhauer, 560–79. Burlington, VT: Ashgate, 2000.

Grown, Caren A., and Jennefer Sebstad. "Introduction: Toward a Wider Perspective on Women's Employment." *World Development* 17, no. 7 (1989): 937–52.

Gutman, Herbert G. *The Black Family in Slavery and Freedom, 1750–1925*. New York: Vintage Books, 1976.

Guy, Jeff. "Colonial Transformations and the Home." In *Ekhaya: The Politics of Home in KwaZulu-Natal*, edited by Meghan Healy-Clancy and Jason Hickel, 23–47. Scottsville: University of KwaZulu-Natal Press, 2014.

———. "Gender Oppression in Southern Africa's Precapitalist Societies." In *Women and Gender in Southern Africa to 1945*, edited by Cherryl Walker, 33–47. Cape Town: David Philip, 1990.

———. "Shaka's Shadow." *South African Historical Journal* 39, no. 1 (1998): 211–27.

———. "Women in Labour: The Birth of Colonial Natal." Paper presented at the History and African Studies Seminar at the University of KwaZulu-Natal, Durban, April 29, 2009.

Guy, Jeff, and Motlatsi Thabane. "Basotho Miners, Ethnicity and Workers' Strategies." In *Workers in Third-World Industrialization*, edited by Inga Brandell, 75–103. London: Macmillan, 1991.

Guyer, Jane I. "Household and Community in African Studies." *African Studies Review* 24, nos. 2/3 (1981): 87–137.

———. *Marginal Gains: Monetary Transactions in Atlantic Africa*. Chicago: University of Chicago Press, 2004.

———, ed. "Wealth in People, Wealth in Things." *JAH* 36, no. 1 (1995): 83–140.

Gyekye, Kwame. *An Essay on African Philosophical Thought: The Akan Conceptual Scheme*. Cambridge: Cambridge University Press, 1987.

Hann, Chris. "Moral Economy." In *The Human Economy: A Citizen's Guide*, edited by Keith Hart, Jean-Louis Laville, and Antonio David Cattani, 187–98. Cambridge: Polity Press, 2010.

Hardt, Michael, and Antonio Negri. *Empire*. Cambridge, MA: Harvard University Press, 2000.

Harries, Patrick. "Plantations, Passes and Proletarians: Labour and the Colonial State in Nineteenth Century Natal." *JSAS* 13, no. 3 (1987): 372–99.

———. *Work, Culture, and Identity: Migrant Laborers in Mozambique and South Africa, c. 1860–1910*. Portsmouth, NH: Heinemann, 1994.

Hart, Gillian. "Engendering Everyday Resistance: Gender, Patronage and Production Politics in Rural Malaysia." *Journal of Peasant Studies* 19, no. 1 (1991): 93–121.

———. *Rethinking the South African Crisis: Nationalism, Populism, Hegemony*. Athens: University of Georgia Press, 2014.

Hart, Jennifer. "'One Man, No Chop': Licit Wealth, Good Citizens, and the Criminalization of Drivers in Postcolonial Ghana." *International Journal of African Historical Studies* 46, no. 3 (2013): 373–96.

Hart, Keith. "Informal Economy." In *The Human Economy: A Citizen's Guide*, edited by Keith Hart, Jean-Louis Laville, and Antonio David Cattani, 142–53. Cambridge: Polity Press, 2010.

———. "Informal Income Opportunities and Urban Employment in Ghana." *Journal of Modern African Studies* 11, no. 1 (1973): 61–89.

———. "Karl Polanyi's Legacy." *Development and Change* 39, no. 6 (2008): 1135–43.
———. "Kinship, Contract, and Trust: The Economic Organization of Migrants in an African City Slum." In *Trust: Making and Breaking Cooperative Relations*, edited by Diego Gambetta, 176–93. New York: Blackwell, 1988.
———. "Marcel Mauss: In Pursuit of the Whole." *Comparative Studies in Society and History* 49, no. 2 (2007): 473–85.
———. *The Memory Bank: Money in an Unequal World.* London: Profile Books, 2000.
Hellmann, Ellen. "The Importance of Beer-Brewing in an Urban Native Yard." *Bantu Studies* 8, no. 1 (1934): 39–60.
———. *Rooiyard: A Sociological Survey of an Urban Native Slum Yard.* Rhodes-Livingston Papers no. 13. Cape Town: Oxford University Press, 1948.
———. "Social Change among Urban Africans." In *South Africa: Sociological Perspectives*, edited by Heribert Adam, 158–76. London: Oxford University Press, 1971.
Hemson, David. "Class Consciousness and Migrant Workers: Dock Workers of Durban." PhD diss., University of Warwick, 1979.
———. "Dock Workers, Labour Circulation, and Class Struggles in Durban, 1940–59." *JSAS* 4, no. 1 (1977): 88–124.
———. "In the Eye of the Storm: Dock-Workers in Durban." In *The People's City: African Life in Twentieth-Century Durban*, edited by Paul Maylam and Iain Edwards, 145–73. Pietermaritzburg: University of Natal Press, 1996.
Heydenrych, Lucille. "Port Natal Harbour, c. 1850–1897." In *Enterprise and Exploitation in a Victorian Colony: Aspects of the Economic and Social History of Colonial Natal*, edited by Bill Guest and John M. Sellers, 46–69. Pietermaritzburg: University of Natal Press, 1985.
Hickel, Jason. *Democracy as Death: The Moral Order of Anti-liberal Politics in South Africa.* Oakland: University of California Press, 2015.
———. "Engineering the Township Home: Domestic Transformations and Urban Revolutionary Consciousness." In *Ekhaya: The Politics of Home in KwaZulu-Natal*, edited by Meghan Healy-Clancy and Jason Hickel, 131–61. Scottsville: University of KwaZulu-Natal Press, 2014.
Hill, Stephen. *The Dockers: Class and Tradition in London.* London: Heinemann, 1976.
Hlatshwayo, Mondli. "Is There Room for International Solidarity within South African Borders? COSATU's Responses to the Xenophobic Attacks of May 2008." *Politikon* 31, no. 1 (2011): 169–89.
Hobsbawm, Eric J. *Primitive Rebels: Studies in the Archaic Forms of Social Movement in the 19th and 20th Centuries.* 3rd ed. Manchester: Manchester University Press, 1971 [1959].
———. "Social Banditry." In *Rural Protest: Peasant Movements and Social Change*, edited by Henry A. Landsberger, 142–57. London: MacMillan, 1974.
Hofmeyr, Isabel, and Michelle Williams, eds. *South Africa and India: Shaping the Global South.* Johannesburg: Wits University Press, 2011.

Horne, Gerald. *Red Seas: Ferdinand Smith and Radical Black Sailors in the United States and Jamaica.* New York: New York University Press, 2005.

Horwitz, Ralph. *The Political Economy of South Africa.* New York: Praeger, 1967.

Horwood, O. P. F., ed. *The Port of Durban,* Natal Regional Survey 15. Durban: University of Natal, Department of Economics, 1969.

———. "Some Aspects of Urban African Employment in the Durban Area." *Race Relations Journal* 25, nos. 3–4 (1958): 19–34.

Houghton, D. Hobart. *The South African Economy.* 4th ed. Cape Town: Oxford University Press, 1976.

Hunter, Mark. "The Bond of Education: Gender, the Value of Children, and the Making of Umlazi Township in 1960s South Africa." *JAH* 55, no. 3 (2014): 467–90.

———. "The Changing Political Economy of Sex in South Africa: The Significance of Unemployment and Inequalities to the Scale of the AIDS Pandemic." *Social Science and Medicine* 64, no. 3 (2007): 689–700.

———. *Love in the Time of AIDS: Inequality, Gender, and Rights in South Africa.* Bloomington: Indiana University Press, 2010.

———. "The Materiality of Everyday Sex: Thinking beyond 'Prostitution.'" *African Studies* 56, no. 1 (2002): 99–120.

Hunter, Monica. "The Effects of Contact with Europeans on the Status of Pondo Women." *Africa* 6, no. 3 (1933): 259–76.

———. *Reaction to Conquest: Effects of Contact with Europeans on the Pondo of South Africa.* 2nd ed. London: Oxford University Press, 1961.

Hyslop, Jonathan. "Steamship Empire: Asian, African and British Sailors in the Merchant Marine c. 1880–1945." In *South Africa and India: Shaping the Global South,* edited by Isabel Hofmeyr and Michelle Williams, 38–55. Johannesburg: Wits University Press, 2011.

Ingpen, Brian. *Horizons: The Story of Rennies, 1849–1999.* Johannesburg: Rennies Management Services, 2000.

International Labour Organization. *Incomes, Employment and Equality in Kenya: A Strategy for Increasing Productive Employment in Kenya.* Geneva: International Labour Organization, 1972.

Isaacman, Allen, Michael Stephen, Yussuf Adam, Maria João Homen, Eugenio Macamo, and Augustinho Pililão. "'Cotton Is the Mother of Poverty': Peasant Resistance to Forced Cotton Production in Mozambique, 1938–1961." *International Journal of African Historical Studies* 13, no. 4 (1980): 581–615.

James, Deborah. *Money from Nothing: Indebtedness and Aspiration in South Africa.* Stanford: Stanford University Press, 2015.

James, Deborah, and Elizabeth Hull, eds. "Popular Economies in South Africa." Special issue, *Africa* 82, no. 1 (2012).

Jeffreys, M. D. W. "Lobolo Is Child-Price." *African Studies* 10, no. 4 (1951): 145–84.

Jeffries, Richard. *Class, Power and Ideology in Ghana: The Railwaymen of Sekondi.* Cambridge: Cambridge University Press, 1978.

Jensen, Vernon H. *Hiring of Dock Workers and Employment Practices in the Ports of New York, Liverpool, London, Rotterdam, and Marseilles*. Cambridge, MA: Harvard University Press, 1964.

Jones, Trevor. "The Port of Durban: Lynchpin of the Local Economy?" In *(D)urban Vortex: South African City in Transition*, edited by Bill Freund and Vishnu Padayachee, 69–106. Scottsville: University of Natal Press, 2002.

Kaarsholm, Preben. "Zanzibaris or Amakhuwa? Sufi Networks in South Africa, Mozambique, and the Indian Ocean." *JAH* 55, no. 2 (2014): 191–210.

Kadalie, Clements. *My Life and the ICU: The Autobiography of a Black Trade Unionist in South Africa*. New York: Humanities Press, 1970.

Kaijage, Frederick J. "The War of Clubs: Life, Labour and Struggles of the Tanga Dockworkers." In *Dock Workers*, edited by Sam Davies, Colin J. Davis, David de Vries, Lex Heerma van Voss, Lidewij Hesselink, and Klaus Weinhauer, 290–318. Burlington VT: Ashgate, 2000.

Kandiyoti, Deniz. "Bargaining with Patriarchy." *Gender and Society* 2, no. 3 (1988): 274–90.

Kark, Sidney L. "The Health Implications of the Changing Rôle of Women in Rural Pholela." In *A Practice of Social Medicine: A South African Team's Experiences in Different African Communities*, edited by Sidney L. Kark and Guy W. Steuart, 210–19. Edinburgh: E. & S. Livingstone, 1962.

———. "Migrant Labour and Family Health." In *A Practice of Social Medicine: A South African Team's Experiences in Different African Communities*, edited by Sidney L. Kark and Guy W. Steuart, 194–209. Edinburgh: E. & S. Livingstone, 1962.

Kasrils, Ronnie. "How the ANC's Faustian Pact Sold Out South Africa's Poorest." *Guardian*, June 24, 2013. http://www.theguardian.com/commentisfree/2013/jun/24/anc-faustian-pact-mandela-fatal-error.

Kazan, Elia, dir. *On the Waterfront* (film). USA: Columbia Pictures, 1954.

Kearney, Brian. "Bamboo Square: A Documentary Narrative of the 'Indian and Native Cantonment' at the Point, 1873 to 1903." *Journal of Natal and Zulu History* 20 (2002): 29–64.

Kerr, Clark, and Abraham Siegel. "The Interindustry Propensity to Strike: An International Comparison." In *Industrial Conflict*, edited by Arthur W. Kornhauser, Robert Dublin, and Arthur M. Ross, 189–212. New York: McGraw-Hill, 1954.

Krige, Eileen Jensen. "Some Social and Economic Facts Revealed in Native Family Budgets." *Race Relations* 1, no. 4 (1934): 94–108.

Kuper, Adam. *Wives for Cattle: Bridewealth and Marriage in Southern Africa*. London: Routledge and Kegan Paul, 1982.

Kuper, Hilda, and Selma Kaplan. "Voluntary Associations in an Urban Township." *African Studies* 3, no. 4 (1944): 178–86.

Kynoch, Gary. *We Are Fighting the World: A History of the Marashea Gangs in South Africa, 1947–1999*. Athens: Ohio University Press, 2005.

La Guma, Alex. *The Stone Country*. London: Heinemann, 1974.

La Hausse, Paul. "'The Cows of Nongoloza': Youth, Crime and Amalaita Gangs in Durban, 1900–1936." *JSAS* 16, no. 1 (1990): 79–111.

———. "The Dispersal of the Regiments: African Popular Protest in Durban, 1930." *Journal of Natal and Zulu History* 10 (1987): 77–102.

———. "Drink and Cultural Innovation in Durban: The Origins of the Beerhall in South Africa." In *Liquor and Labor in Southern Africa*, edited by Jonathan Crush and Charles Ambler, 78–114. Athens: Ohio University Press, 1992.

———. "The Message of the Warriors: The ICU, the Labouring Poor and the Making of a Popular Political Culture in Durban, 1925–1930." In *Holding Their Ground: Class, Locality and Culture in 19th and 20th Century South Africa*, edited by Philip Bonner, Isabel Hofmeyr, Deborah James, and Tom Lodge, 19–57. Johannesburg: Witwatersrand University Press, 1989.

———. "The Struggle for the City: Alcohol, the *Emantsheni* and Popular Culture in Durban, 1902–1936." Master's thesis, University of Cape Town, 1984.

Lambert, John. "Impoverishment of the Natal Peasantry, 1893–1910." In *Enterprise and Exploitation in a Victorian Colony: Aspects of the Economic and Social History of Colonial Natal*, edited by Bill Guest and John M. Sellers, 287–307. Pietermaritzburg: University of Natal Press, 1985.

Lambert, John, and Robert Morrell. "Domination and Subordination in Natal, 1890–1920." In *Political Economy and Identities in KwaZulu-Natal: Historical and Social Perspectives*, edited by Robert Morrell, 63–95. Durban: Indicator Press, 1996.

Landes, Joan B., ed. *Feminism, the Public and the Private.* Oxford: Oxford University Press, 1998.

Lee, Rebekah. *African Women and Apartheid: Migration and Settlement in Urban South Africa.* London: I. B. Tauris, 2009.

Legassick, Martin. "Legislation, Ideology and Economy in Post-1948 South Africa." *JSAS* 1, no. 1 (1974): 5–35.

———. "South Africa: Forced Labor, Industrialization, and Racial Differentiation." In *The Political Economy of Africa*, edited by Richard Harris, 227–70. Cambridge, MA: Schenkman, 1975.

Lewis, W. Arthur. "Economic Development with Unlimited Supplies of Labour." *Manchester School* 22, no. 2 (1954): 139–91.

Linebaugh, Peter, and Marcus Rediker. *The Many-Headed Hydra: Sailors, Slaves, Commoners, and the Hidden History of the Revolutionary Atlantic.* London: Verso, 2000.

Lodge, Tom. *Black Politics in South Africa since 1945.* London: Longman, 1983.

Longmore, L. "African Poverty and Social Unrest." *African Affairs* 57, no. 229 (1958): 291–94.

Lourenço-Lindell, Ilda, ed. *Africa's Informal Workers: Collective Agency, Alliances and Transnational Organizing in Urban Africa.* London: Zed Books, 2010.

Louw, Ronald. "Mkhumbane and New Traditions of (Un)African Same-Sex Weddings." In *Changing Men in Southern Africa,* edited by Robert Morrell, 287–96. Pietermaritzburg: University of Natal Press, 2001.

Lucassen, Jan, ed. *Global Labour History: A State of the Art.* Bern: Peter Lang, 2006.

Luke, David Fashole. "Dock Workers of the Port of Freetown: A Case Study of African Working-Class Ambivalence." *Canadian Journal of African Studies* 19, no. 3 (1985): 547–67.

Lumby, Anthony, and Ian McLean. "The Economy and the Development of the Port of Durban." In *Receded Tides of Empire: Aspects of the Economic and Social History of Natal and Zululand since 1910,* edited by Bill Guest and John M. Sellers, 25–49. Pietermaritzburg: University of Natal Press, 1994.

MacKinnon, Aran Stuart. "Africans and the Myth of Rural Retirement in South Africa, ca 1900–1950." *Journal of Cross-Cultural Gerontology* 23, no. 2 (2008): 161–79.

———. "Chiefly Authority, Leapfrogging Headmen and the Political Economy of Zululand, South Africa, ca. 1930–1950." *JSAS* 27, no. 3 (2001): 567–90.

———. "Land, Labour and Cattle: The Political Economy of Zululand, c.1930–1950." PhD diss., University of London, 1995.

———. "The Persistence of the Cattle Economy in Zululand, South Africa, 1900–1950." *Canadian Journal of African Studies* 33, no. 1 (1999): 98–135.

Mafeje, Archie. "On the Articulation of Modes of Production: Review Article." *JSAS* 8, no. 1 (1981): 123–38.

Mager, Anne Kelk. *Gender and the Making of a South African Bantustan: A Social History of the Ciskei.* Portsmouth, NH: Heinemann, 1999.

Mahoney, Michael. *The Other Zulus: The Spread of Zulu Ethnicity in Colonial South Africa.* Durham, NC: Duke University Press, 2012.

Makhulu, Anne-Maria. *Making Freedom: Apartheid, Squatter Politics, and the Struggle for Home.* Durham, NC: Duke University Press, 2015.

Mamdani, Mahmood. *Citizen and Subject: Contemporary Africa and the Legacy of Late Colonialism.* Princeton, NJ: Princeton University Press, 1996.

Marais, Hein. *South Africa Pushed to the Limit: The Political Economy of Change.* London: Zed Books, 2011.

Margaretten, Emily. "Parting Homes in KwaZulu-Natal." In *Ekhaya: The Politics of Home in KwaZulu-Natal,* edited by Meghan Healy-Clancy and Jason Hickel, 190–213. Scottsville: University of KwaZulu-Natal Press, 2014.

Marks, Shula. *The Ambiguities of Dependence in South Africa: Class, Nationalism, and the State in Twentieth-Century Natal.* Johannesburg: Ravan Press, 1986.

———. "Patriotism, Patriarchy and Purity: Natal and the Politics of Zulu Ethnic Consciousness." In *The Creation of Tribalism in Southern Africa,* edited by Leroy Vail, 215–40. London: James Currey, 1989.

Marks, Shula, and Richard Rathbone. Introduction to *Industrialisation and Social Change in South Africa: African Class Formation, Culture, and Consciousness, 1870–1930,* edited by Shula Marks and Richard Rathbone, 1–43. London: Longman, 1982.

Mars, Gerald. *Cheats at Work: An Anthropology of Workplace Crime.* London: George Allen & Unwin, 1982.

———. "Dock Pilferage: A Case Study in Occupational Theft." In *Deviance and Social Control,* edited by Paul Rock and Mary McIntosh, 209–26. London: Travistock, 1974.

Marx, Karl. *Eighteenth Brumaire of Louis Bonaparte.* Charleston, SC: BiblioBazaar, 2007.

Marx, Karl, and Friedrich Engels. *The German Ideology.* Amherst, NY: Prometheus Books, 1998.

Mauss, Marcel. *The Gift: The Form and Reason for Exchange in Archaic Societies.* London: Routledge, 2001 [1925].

Mayer, Philip, and Iona Mayer. *Townsmen or Tribesmen: Conservatism and the Process of Urbanization in a South African City.* Cape Town: Oxford University Press, 1961.

Maylam, Paul. "The Changing Political Economy of the Region, 1920–1950." In *Political Economy and Identities in KwaZulu-Natal: Historical and Social Perspectives,* edited by Robert Morrell, 97–118. Durban: Indicator Press, 1996.

Maylam, Paul, and Iain Edwards, eds. *The People's City: African Life in Twentieth-Century Durban.* Pietermaritzburg: University of Natal Press, 1996.

Mbatha, Mphiwa Buxton. "Migrant Labour and Its Effects on Tribal and Family Life among the Nyuswa of Botha's Hill." Master's thesis, University of Natal, 1960.

Mbeki, Thabo. "Address by President Thabo Mbeki to the National Council of Provinces." November 11, 2003. http://www.sarpn.org/documents/d0000830/P944-SARPN_Second_Economy_Nov2004.pdf.

McClendon, Thomas V. *Genders and Generations Apart: Labor Tenants and Customary Law in Segregation-Era South Africa, 1920s–1940s.* Portsmouth, NH: Heinemann, 2002.

———. *White Chiefs, Black Lords: Shepstone and the Colonial State in Natal, South Africa, 1845–1878.* Rochester, NY: University of Rochester Press, 2010.

Meagher, Kate. *Identity Economics: Social Networks and the Informal Economy in Nigeria.* Suffolk: James Currey, 2010.

Meillassoux, Claude. "The Economic Bases of Demographic Reproduction: From the Domestic Mode of Production to Wage-Earning." *Journal of Peasant Studies* 11, no. 1 (1983): 50–61.

———. *Maidens, Meal and Money: Capitalism and the Domestic Community.* Cambridge: Cambridge University Press, 1981.

Mezzadra, Sandro. "How Many Histories of Labour? Towards a Theory of Postcolonial Capitalism." *Postcolonial Studies* 14, no. 2 (2011): 151–70.

Miers, Suzanne, and Igor Kopytoff, eds. *Slavery in Africa: Historical and Anthropological Perspectives.* Madison: University of Wisconsin Press, 1977.

Mill, John Stuart. "On the Definition and Method of Political Economy." In *The Philosophy of Economics: An Anthology,* edited by Daniel M. Hausman, 52–68. Cambridge: Cambridge University Press, 1994.

Mills, Herb. "The San Francisco Waterfront: The Social Consequences of Industrial Modernization, Part One: 'The Good Old Days.'" *Urban Life* 5, no. 2 (1976): 221–50.

Monson, Jamie. *Africa's Freedom Railway: How a Chinese Development Project Changed Lives and Livelihoods in Tanzania.* Bloomington: Indiana University Press, 2009.

Moodie, T. Dunbar. "The Moral Economy of the Black Miners' Strike of 1946." *JSAS* 13, no. 1 (1986): 1–35.

Moodie, T. Dunbar, with Vivienne Ndatshe. *Going for Gold: Men, Mines, and Migration.* Berkeley: University of California Press, 1994.

Moodley, Loshini. "Three Stokvel Clubs in the Urban Black Township of KwaNdangezi, Natal." *Development Southern Africa* 12, no. 3 (1995): 360–66.

Moroney, Sean. "The Development of the Compound as a Mechanism of Worker Control, 1900–1912." *SALB* 4, no. 3 (1978): 29–49.

Morrell, Robert, ed. *Changing Men in Southern Africa.* Pietermaritzburg: University of Natal Press, 2001.

Morris, Mike. "The Development of Capitalism in South African Agriculture: Class Struggle in the Countryside." *Economy and Society* 5, no. 3 (1976): 292–343.

———. "Stevedoring and the General Workers Union, Part I." *SALB* 11, no. 2 (1986): 90–114.

———. "Stevedoring and the General Workers Union, Part II." *SALB* 11, no. 4 (1986): 100–18.

Mosoetsa, Sarah. *Eating from One Pot: The Dynamics of Survival in Poor South African Households.* Johannesburg: Wits University Press, 2011.

Moyo, Dambisa. *Dead Aid: Why Aid Is Not Working and How There Is a Better Way for Africa.* New York: Farrar, Straus and Giroux, 2009.

Murray, Colin. *Families Divided: The Impact of Migrant Labour in Lesotho.* Cambridge: Cambridge University Press, 1981.

———. "High Bridewealth, Migrant Labour and the Position of Women in Lesotho." *Journal of African Law* 21, no. 1 (1977): 79–96.

———. "Keeping House in Lesotho: A Study of the Impact of Oscillating Migration." PhD diss., University of Cambridge, 1976.

———. "Marital Strategy in Lesotho: The Redistribution of Migrant Earnings." *African Studies* 35, no. 2 (1976): 99–122.

Nattrass, Jill. "Migrant Labour and Underdevelopment: The Case of KwaZulu." Interim Research Report No. 3, Black/White Income Gap Project, University of Natal, Durban, 1977.

Nesvåg, Stein Inge. "Street Trading from Apartheid to Post-apartheid: More Birds in the Cornfield?" *International Journal of Sociology and Social Policy* 20, no. 3/4 (2000): 34–63.

Neves, David, and Andries du Toit. "Money and Sociality in South Africa's Informal Economy." *Africa* 82, no. 1 (2012): 131–49.

———. "Rural Livelihoods in South Africa: Complexity, Vulnerability and Differentiation." *Journal of Agrarian Change* 13, no. 1 (2013): 93–115.

Ngubane, Harriet. "The Consequences for Women of Marriage Payments in a Society with Patrilineal Descent." In *Transformations of African Marriage*, edited by David Parkin and David Nyamwaya, 173–82. Manchester: Manchester University Press, 1987.

Nuttall, Timothy Andrew. "Class, Race and Nation: African Politics in Durban, 1929–1949." PhD diss., University of Oxford, 1991.

Oberst, Timothy. "Transport Workers, Strikes and the 'Imperial Response': Africa and the Post World War II Conjuncture." *African Studies Review* 31, no. 1 (1988): 117–33.

O'Laughlin, Bridget. "Proletarianisation, Agency and Changing Rural Livelihoods: Forced Labour and Resistance in Colonial Mozambique." *JSAS* 28, no. 3 (2002): 511–30.

———. "Review Essay: Livelihoods." *Development and Change* 35, no. 2 (2004): 385–92.

Ong, Aihwa. *Neoliberalism as Exception: Mutations in Citizenship and Sovereignty.* Durham, NC: Duke University Press, 2006.

Osborn, Emily Lynn. *Our New Husbands Are Here: Households, Gender, and Politics in a West African State from the Slave Trade to Colonial Rule.* Athens: Ohio University Press, 2011.

Padayachee, Kamini. "Sending Arms to Zim 'a Recipe for Conflict.'" *Mercury*, April 18, 2008.

Pauw, B. A. *Christianity and Xhosa Tradition: Belief and Ritual among Xhosa-speaking Christians.* Cape Town: Oxford University Press, 1975.

Penvenne, Jeanne Marie. *Women, Migration and the Cashew Economy in Southern Mozambique, 1945–1975.* Woodbridge, UK: James Currey, 2015.

Persky, Joseph. "The Ethology of *Homo Economicus*." *Journal of Economic Perspectives* 9, no. 2 (1995): 221–31.

Phillips, Anne. *The Enigma of Colonialism: British Policy in West Africa.* London: James Currey, 1989.

Polanyi, Karl. "The Economy as Instituted Process." In *Trade and Market in Early Empires: Economies in History and Theory*, edited by Karl Polanyi, Conrad M. Arendsberg, and Harry W. Pearson, 243–70. Glencoe IL: Free Press, 1957.

———. *The Great Transformation: The Political and Economic Origins of Our Time.* Boston: Beacon Press, 1957 [1944].

———. *The Livelihood of Man*, edited by Harry W. Pearson. New York: Academic Press, 1977.

Port Natal: The Coaling Station. Durban: Glencoe (Natal) Collieries, 1907.

Posel, Deborah. *The Making of Apartheid, 1948–1961: Conflict and Compromise.* Oxford: Clarendon Press, 1991.

Potts, Deborah. *Circular Migration in Zimbabwe and Contemporary Sub-Saharan Africa.* Woodbridge, UK: James Currey, 2010.

———. "The Urban Informal Sector in Sub-Saharan Africa: From Bad to Good (and Back Again?)." *Development Southern Africa* 25, no. 2 (2008): 151–67.

Power, Joey. "Building Relevance: The Blantyre Congress, 1953 to 1956." *JSAS* 28, no. 1 (2002): 45–65.

Preston-White, Eleanor. "Women Migrants and Marriage." In *Essays on African Marriage in Southern Africa*, edited by Eileen Jensen Krige and John L. Comaroff, 158–73. Cape Town: Juta, 1981.

Reader, Desmond Harold. *Zulu Tribe in Transition: The Makhanya of Southern Natal.* Manchester: Manchester University Press, 1966.

Rey, Pierre-Philippe. *Les alliances de classes: Sur l'articulation des modes de production, suivi de matérialisme historique et luttes de classes.* Paris: Maspero, 1973.

Roberts, Andrew. "Nyamwezi Trade." In *Pre-colonial African Trade*, edited by Richard Gray and David Birmingham, 39–74. London: Oxford University Press, 1970.

Rockel, Stephen. *Carriers of Culture: Labor on the Road in Nineteenth-Century East Africa.* Portsmouth, NH: Heinemann, 2006.

Rogerson, Christian. "Unpacking National Policy towards the Urban Informal Economy." In *Mean Streets: Migration, Xenophobia and Informality in South Africa*, edited by Jonathan Crush, Abel Chikanda, and Caroline Skinner, 229–48. Rondebosch: Southern African Migration Programme, 2015.

Ross-Watt, D. M. "Housing of Bantu Stevedores." B.Arch. thesis, University of Natal, 1970.

Rostow, W. W. *The Stages of Economic Growth: A Non-communist Manifesto.* Cambridge: Cambridge University Press, 1960.

Roux, Edward. *Time Longer Than Rope: A History of the Black Man's Struggle for Freedom in South Africa.* 2nd ed. Madison: University of Wisconsin Press, 1964.

Sachs, Wulf. *Black Hamlet.* Johannesburg: Witwatersrand University Press, 1996.

Sack, Gerald D. "Izimpohlo: The Bachelors, a Study of Black Migrant Labourers Living in Compounds in Durban." Master's thesis, University of Haifa, 1991.

Sassen, Saskia. "The Global City: Strategic Site / New Frontier." *American Studies* 41, nos. 2/3 (2000): 79–95.

Saul, John S. *Liberation Lite: The Roots of Recolonization in Southern Africa.* Trenton, NJ: Africa World Press, 2011.

Saunders, Christopher. *The Making of the South African Past: Major Historians on Race and Class.* Cape Town: David Philip, 1988.

Scott, James C. *The Moral Economy of the Peasant: Rebellion and Subsistence in Southeast Asia.* New Haven, CT: Yale University Press, 1976.

———. *Weapons of the Weak: Everyday Forms of Peasant Resistance.* New Haven, CT: Yale University Press, 1985.

Seekings, Jeremy. "The Rise and Fall of the Weberian Analysis of Class in South Africa between 1949 and the Early 1970s." *JSAS* 35, no. 4 (2009): 865–81.

Seekings, Jeremy, and Nicoli Nattrass. *Class, Race, and Inequality in South Africa.* Scottsville: University of KwaZulu-Natal Press, 2005.

Sen, Amartya K. "Gender and Cooperative Conflicts." In *Persistent Inequalities: Women and World Development*, edited by Irene Tinker, 123–49. New York: Oxford University Press, 1990.

Shor, Francis. "Left Labor Agitators in the Pacific Rim of the Early Twentieth Century." *ILWCH* 67 (2005): 148–63.

Sibisi, Harriet. "How African Women Cope with Migrant Labor in South Africa." *Signs* 3, no. 1 (1977): 167–77.

Sicard, S. v. "The 'Zanzibaris' in Durban, South Africa." *Journal of Muslim Minority Affairs* 3, no. 1 (1981): 128–37.

Sideris, Tina. *Sifuna Imali Yethu: The Life and Struggles of Durban Dockworkers, 1940–1981.* Oral History Series No. 3. Johannesburg: SAIRR, Archives Department, 1983.

Simkins, Charles. *Agricultural Production in the African Reserves of South Africa, 1918–1969.* Development Studies Research Group Working Paper No. 10. Pietermaritzburg: Department of Economics, University of Natal, 1979.

———. "Agricultural Production in the African Reserves of South Africa, 1918–1969." *JSAS* 7, no. 2 (1981): 256–83.

Singleton, Judith L. "'House' and 'Home': Changing Meanings and Practices in a Post-apartheid Township." In *Ekhaya: The Politics of Home in KwaZulu-Natal,* edited by Meghan Healy-Clancy and Jason Hickel, 162–89. Scottsville: University of KwaZulu-Natal Press, 2014.

Sitas, Ari. "The New Tribalism: Hostels and Violence." *JSAS* 22, no. 2 (1996): 235–48.

———. "Wolpe's Legacy of Articulating Political Economy." *Africanus: Journal of Development Studies* 37, no. 2 (2007): 39–45.

Sithole, Jabulani. "Zuluness in South Africa: From 'Struggle' Debate to Democratic Transformation." In *Zulu Identities: Being Zulu, Past and Present,* edited by Benedict Carton, John Laband, and Jabulani Sithole, xii–xvii. Scottsville: University of KwaZulu-Natal Press, 2008.

Smith, Adam. *The Wealth of Nations.* London: Penguin, 1986 [1776].

Smith, R. H. *Labour Resources of Natal.* Cape Town: Oxford University Press, 1950.

Smuts, Jan. Foreword to *Reaction to Conquest: Effects of Contact with Europeans on the Pondo of South Africa,* by Monica Hunter. 2nd ed. London: Oxford University Press, 1961.

Soni, Raji Singh, and Ralph Callebert. "A Political Economy of the Humanities: Turning Tables with Marx and Kant." *Australian Humanities Review* no. 59 (May 2016): 1–22.

Soske, Jon. "'Wash Me Black Again': African Nationalism, the Indian Diaspora, and Kwa-Zulu Natal, 1944–1960." PhD diss., University of Toronto, 2009.

"South Africa's Key Economic Policies Changes since 1994–2013." *South African History Online.* http://www.sahistory.org.za/article/south-africa's-key-economic-policies-changes-1994-2013.

Spear, Thomas. "Neo-traditionalism and the Limits of Invention in British Colonial Africa." *JAH* 44, no. 1 (2003): 3–17.

Spivak, Gayatri Chakravorty. "Globalizing Globalization." Plenary lecture at Rethinking Marxism Conference, University of Massachusetts at Amherst, September 21–24, 2000. YouTube video, 33:31. Posted on October 11, 2012. http://youtu.be/gSe555TYIts.

Standing, Guy. *The Precariat: The New Dangerous Class.* London: Bloomsbury, 2016.

Stanfield, J. R. "Karl Polanyi and Contemporary Economic Thought." *Review of Social Economy* 47, no. 3 (1989): 266–79.

Steinberg, Jonny. *South Africa's Xenophobic Eruption.* ISS Paper 169. Tshwane: Institute for Security Studies, 2008.

Swanson, Maynard. "'The Asiatic Menace': Creating Segregation in Durban, 1870–1900." *International Journal of African Historical Studies* 16, no. 3 (1983): 401–21.

———. "'The Durban System': Roots of Urban Apartheid in Colonial Natal." *African Studies* 35, nos. 3/4 (1976): 159–76.

———. "The Rise of Multiracial Durban: Urban History and Race Policy in South Africa, 1830–1930." PhD diss., Harvard University, 1964.

———. "The Sanitation Syndrome: Bubonic Plague and Urban Native Policy in the Cape Colony, 1900–1909." *JAH* 18, no. 3 (1977): 387–410.

Taplin, Eric. *The Dockers' Union: A Study of the National Union of Dock Labourers, 1889–1922.* Leicester: Leicester University Press, 1985.

———. "Dock Labour at Liverpool: Occupational Structure and Working Conditions in the Late Nineteenth Century." *Transactions of the Historic Society of Lancashire and Cheshire* 127 (1978): 133–54.

Tevera, Daniel. "African Migrants, Xenophobia and Urban Violence in Post-apartheid South Africa." *Alternation* 7 (2013): 9–26.

Thomas, Elmar. "Rotating Credit Associations in Cape Town." In *South Africa's Informal Economy*, edited by Eleanor Preston-Whyte and Christian Rogerson, 290–303. Cape Town: Oxford University Press, 1991.

Thompson, E. P. "The Crime of Anonymity." In *Albion's Fatal Tree: Crime and Society in Eighteenth Century England*, by Douglas Hay, Peter Linebaugh, John G. Rule, E. P. Thompson, and Cal Winslow, 255–344. New York: Pantheon Books, 1975.

———. *The Making of the English Working Class.* London: Penguin Books, 1991 [1963].

———. "The Moral Economy of the English Crowd in the Eighteenth Century." *Past and Present* 50 (1971): 76–136.

———. "The Moral Economy Reviewed." In *Customs in Common*, 259–351. New York: New Press, 1991.

Thornberry, Elizabeth. "Sex, Violence, and Family in South Africa's Eastern Cape." In *Domestic Violence and the Law in Colonial and Postcolonial Africa*, edited by Emily Burrill, Richard Roberts, and Elizabeth Thornberry, 117–37. Athens: Ohio University Press, 2010.

Trapido, Stanley. Introduction to *My Life and the ICU: The Autobiography of a Black Trade Unionist in South Africa,* by Clements Kadalie, 11–25. New York: Humanities Press, 1970.

Turner, Victor W. *Schism and Continuity in an African Society: A Study of Ndembu Village Life.* Manchester: Manchester University Press, 1957.

Turrell, Robert Vicat. *Capital and Labour on the Kimberley Diamond Fields, 1871–1890.* Cambridge: Cambridge University Press, 1987.

Union of South Africa, Department of Agricultural Economics and Marketing. *Handbook of Agricultural Statistics, 1904–1950.* Pretoria: Government Printer, 1960.

University of Natal, Department of Economics. *The African Factory Worker: A Sample Study of the Life and Labour of the Urban African Worker.* Cape Town: Oxford University Press, 1950.

Vahed, Goolam, and Ashwin Desai. "The May 2008 Xenophobic Violence in South Africa: Antecedents and Aftermath." *Alternation* 7 (2013): 145–75.

Van der Horst, Sheila T. *Native Labour in South Africa.* London: Oxford University Press, 1942.

Van der Linden, Marcel. "Global Labor History: Promising Challenges." *ILWCH* 84 (2013): 218–25.

———. "The Promise and Challenges of Global Labor History." *ILWCH* 82 (2012): 57–76.

———. *Workers of the World: Essays toward a Global Labour History.* Leiden: Brill, 2008.

Van Onselen, Charles. *Chibaro: African Mine Labour in Southern Rhodesia, 1900–1933.* London: Pluto Press, 1976.

———. "Reactions to Rinderpest in Southern Africa, 1896–97." *JAH* 13, no. 3 (1972): 473–88.

———. "'The Regiment of the Hills': South Africa's Lumpenproletariat Army, 1890–1920." *Past and Present* 80 (1978): 91–121.

———. *The Seed Is Mine: The Life of Kas Maine, a South African Sharecropper, 1894–1983.* Cape Town: David Philip, 1996.

Vansina, Jan. *Oral Tradition as History.* Madison: University of Wisconsin Press, 1985.

Vilakazi, Absolom. *Zulu Transformations: A Study of the Dynamics of Social Change.* Pietermaritzburg: University of Natal Press, 1965.

Vinson, Robert Trent. *The Americans Are Coming! Dream of African American Liberation in Segregationist South Africa.* Athens: Ohio University Press, 2012.

———. "'Sea Kaffirs': 'American Negroes' and the Gospel of Garveyism in Early Twentieth-Century Cape Town." *JAH* 47, no. 2 (2006): 281–303.

Von Holdt, Karl. *Transition from Below: Forging Trade Unionism and Workplace Change in South Africa.* Pietermaritzburg: University of Natal Press, 2003.

Walker, Cherryl. "Gender and the Development of the Migrant Labour System, c. 1850–1930: An Overview." In *Women and Gender in Southern Africa to 1945,* edited by Cherryl Walker, 168–96. Cape Town: David Philip, 1990.

———, ed. *Women and Gender in Southern Africa to 1945.* Cape Town: David Philip, 1990.

Wallerstein, Immanuel. "The Three Stages of African Involvement in the World Economy." In *Political Economy of Contemporary Africa*, edited by Peter C. W. Gutkind and Immanuel Wallerstein, 30–57. Beverley Hills, CA: Sage, 1976.

Waterman, Peter. "The Concept of the 'Semi-proletarianised Peasantry', the Lagos Dock Strike of 1968, and the Necessity for Reconceptualising the Role of the Less-Proletarianised Workers in Africa." Paper presented at the Seminar on Third World Strikes at the Institute of Social Studies, The Hague, 1977.

Webb, Maurice. "Vanishing Lands and Migrant Labour." *Race Relations* 11, nos. 3/4 (1944): 45–50.

Webster, David. "The Origins of Migrant Labour, Colonialism, and the Under-Development of Southern Mozambique." In *Working Papers in Southern African Studies: Papers Presented at the A.S.I. African Studies Seminar*, vol. 1, edited by Philip Bonner, 236–79. Johannesburg: African Studies Institute, University of the Witwatersrand, 1977.

Webster, Edward. "The 1949 Durban 'Riots': A Case-Study in Race and Class." In *Working Papers in Southern African Studies: Papers presented at the A.S.I. African Studies Seminar*, vol. 1, edited by Philip Bonner, 1–54. Johannesburg: African Studies Institute, University of the Witwatersrand, 1977.

Webster, Edward, and Karl von Holdt, eds. *Beyond the Apartheid Workplace: Studies in Transition*. Scottsville: University of KwaZulu-Natal Press, 2005.

Weeks, Kathi. *The Problem with Work: Feminism, Marxism, Antiwork Politics, and Postwork Imaginaries*. Durham, NC: Duke University Press, 2011.

Weinhauer, Klaus. "Power and Control on the Waterfront: Casual Labour and Decasualization." In *Dock Workers: International Explorations in Comparative Labour History, 1790–1970*, edited by Sam Davies, Colin J. Davis, David de Vries, Lex Heerma van Voss, Lidewij Hesselink, and Klaus Weinhauer, 580–603. Burlington, VT: Ashgate, 2000.

Wellings, Paul, and Michael Sutcliffe. "Developing the Urban Informal Sector in South Africa: The Reformist Paradigm and Its Fallacies." *Development and Change* 15, no. 4 (1984): 517–50.

Wellman, David. *The Union Makes Us Strong: Radical Unionism on the San Francisco Waterfront*. Cambridge: Cambridge University Press, 1995.

White, Luise. *The Comforts of Home: Prostitution in Colonial Nairobi*. Chicago: University of Chicago Press, 1990.

Wilson, Monica, and Leonard Thompson, eds. *The Oxford History of South Africa*. 2 vols. Oxford: Oxford University Press, 1969, 1971.

Wolpe, Harold, ed. *The Articulation of Modes of Production: Essays from Economy and Society*. London: Routledge and Kegan Paul, 1980.

———. "Capitalism and Cheap Labour-Power in South Africa: From Segregation to Apartheid." *Economy and Society* 1, no. 4 (1972): 425–56.

Worger, William. *South Africa's City of Diamonds: Mine Workers and Monopoly Capitalism in Kimberley, 1867–1895*. New Haven, CT: Yale University Press, 1987.

Index

An italicized page number indicates a figure or table.